THE COMPLETE IDIOT'S GUIDE TO

Arranging and Orchestration

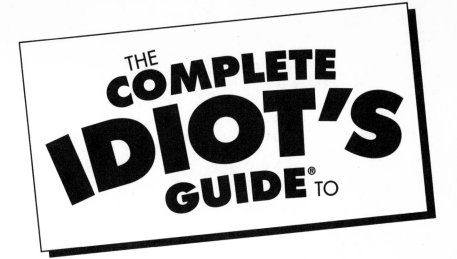

THE
COMPLETE
IDIOT'S
GUIDE® TO

Arranging and Orchestration

by Michael Miller

ALPHA

A member of Penguin Group (USA) Inc.

To Sherry: Love waits.

ALPHA BOOKS

Published by the Penguin Group

Penguin Group (USA) Inc., 375 Hudson Street, New York, New York 10014, USA

Penguin Group (Canada), 90 Eglinton Avenue East, Suite 700, Toronto, Ontario M4P 2Y3, Canada (a division of Pearson Penguin Canada Inc.)

Penguin Books Ltd., 80 Strand, London WC2R 0RL, England

Penguin Ireland, 25 St. Stephen's Green, Dublin 2, Ireland (a division of Penguin Books Ltd.)

Penguin Group (Australia), 250 Camberwell Road, Camberwell, Victoria 3124, Australia (a division of Pearson Australia Group Pty. Ltd.)

Penguin Books India Pvt. Ltd., 11 Community Centre, Panchsheel Park, New Delhi—110 017, India

Penguin Group (NZ), 67 Apollo Drive, Rosedale, North Shore, Auckland 1311, New Zealand (a division of Pearson New Zealand Ltd.)

Penguin Books (South Africa) (Pty.) Ltd., 24 Sturdee Avenue, Rosebank, Johannesburg 2196, South Africa

Penguin Books Ltd., Registered Offices: 80 Strand, London WC2R 0RL, England

International Standard Book Number: 978-1-59257-626-5
Library of Congress Catalog Card Number: 2006940219

09 08 07   8 7 6 5 4 3 2 1

Interpretation of the printing code: The rightmost number of the first series of numbers is the year of the book's printing; the rightmost number of the second series of numbers is the number of the book's printing. For example, a printing code of 07-1 shows that the first printing occurred in 2007.

Printed in the United States of America

Publisher: *Marie Butler-Knight*
Editorial Director: *Mike Sanders*
Managing Editor: *Billy Fields*
Acquisitions Editor: *Tom Stevens*
Development Editor: *Jennifer Moore*
Senior Production Editor: *Janette Lynn*
Copy Editor: *Jan Zoya*

Cartoonist: *Shannon Wheeler*
Cover Designer: *Bill Thomas*
Book Designer: *Trina Wurst*
Indexer: *Johnna Vanhoose Dinse*
Layout: *Brian Massey*
Proofreader: *Aaron Black*

Contents at a Glance

Contents

Appendixes

Introduction

I learned to arrange music before I learned to write it. I was in junior high school at the time, and wanted to put together my own version of a Blood, Sweat & Tears or Chicago-like jazz/rock band. That meant arranging music for a horn section—which then meant learning how to create those arrangements.

Unfortunately for me, there weren't any arranging or orchestration courses for me to take, and precious few books on the topic. I learned by trial and error, which isn't necessarily the best approach. Over time, I figured out what I was doing, but I sure could have used some sort of guide to help me along.

That is why I've written this book. *The Complete Idiot's Guide to Arranging and Orchestration* is the book I wished I'd had back in junior high school and beyond. It's designed to teach you, the budding arranger, everything you need to know to create your own arrangements. You'll start at step one and keep going until you're confident in arranging your own music—for whatever type of ensemble you're writing for.

Personally, I think arranging is the most fulfilling part of the entire musical process. Yes, composing is artistically challenging and performing gives one a real rush, but it's the art of arranging that makes the most use of all my musical talents. I get a real sense of accomplishment when I piece together the various parts of an arrangement, choose the instruments I want to hear, create interlocking musical lines, and then listen to what I've written. There's nothing else like it.

A composition without an arrangement is just a melody and some chords. You need to arrange that melody and those chords to create a finished musical work—whether that's a four-voice church hymn, a big-band chart, a drum corps show, a rock song on CD, or a symphony for full orchestra. Whatever the audience ends up hearing is the work of the arranger.

Of course, the role of the arranger can differ considerably, depending on the situation. Some arrangers create arrangements from existing compositions. Other arrangers arrange their own works, as part of the composition process. There are even separate orchestrators, who take basic arrangements and flesh them out with full instrumentation.

It doesn't matter what type of arranging you do, the tools required are the same. You have to visualize the structure of the finished piece, adapt the existing melody and chords into a full arrangement, and then assign specific instruments or voices to each part. To do all this, you need a thorough grounding in arranging and composing skills, so that you can create the necessary chord progressions, voicings, countermelodies, and the like. The end result is a finished chart, arranged for the ensemble of choice, which can then be dissembled into the component parts for the musicians to play or sing.

That's the process. The skills you need to perfect that process are in the pages that follow. Read and learn.

Who This Book Is For

This is the sixth music book I've written, and it's pitched at a higher level than my previous books. That's because arranging and orchestration are advanced tasks that require advanced skills. Arranging is even more involved than composing, and requires even more formal training to be successful.

To that end, *The Complete Idiot's Guide to Arranging and Orchestration* is written for anyone who desires to arrange or orchestrate music of any type—whether that be for church choir, high school marching band, or professional orchestra. If you have prior arranging or orchestration experience, you should benefit from some of the advanced techniques discussed here; if you have no prior experience, you'll be able to start at the beginning and advance from there.

What You Need to Know Before You Start

If you've read any of my previous music books, you might be surprised at the fast pace of this book. That's because *The Complete Idiot's Guide to Arranging and Orchestration* assumes you have the musical training and knowledge necessary to attack this rather advanced subject. In particular, you need a thorough grounding in music theory and an understanding of compositional techniques.

How much prior knowledge do you need? I assume that you can both read and write music competently, that you know the difference between a major ninth and a dominant seventh chord, that you can work your way through both basic and more sophisticated chord progressions, and that you can deconstruct a melody into its structural tones—and then reconstruct it using connecting and embellishing notes. If any of these topics are foreign to you, stop where you are and read (or re-read) my two previous books, *The Complete Idiot's Guide to Music Theory, Second Edition,* and *The Complete Idiot's Guide to Music Composition.* They'll get you up to speed.

In fact, when you put this book together with the other two books, you have a nice little music-education trilogy. You start by learning essential music theory, progress to composing your own melodies and chord progressions, and end up learning how to arrange and orchestrate your work for various instruments and voices. It's a neat progression, and the three books definitely build on one another. Those of you who've read my prior work will appreciate the journey; those of you new to my writing owe it to yourselves to check out the other books in the trilogy.

What You'll Find in This Book

This book takes you through the arranging and orchestration process, from the initial planning to writing the final arrangement. It also covers specific types of arrangements, from rock bands and big bands to choirs and symphonies.

The Complete Idiot's Guide to Arranging and Orchestration contains 18 chapters that lead you step by step through the process of arranging and orchestrating a piece of music. The chapters are organized into three general parts, as follows:

Part 1, "Essential Skills," guides you through the nuts and bolts of the arranging and orchestration process. You'll learn how to structure an arrangement, harmonize with chords and progressions, utilize different voicings and voice leading, work with melodies and countermelodies, and decide on the best instrumentation for a piece.

Part 2, "Instruments and Voices: Ranges and Techniques," is the orchestration section of the book. I'll walk you through each of the instrument families, from the string family through the voices of the choir, and describe each instrument's range, transposition, and characteristics—as well as offer tips and advice for writing for each section.

Part 3, "Real-World Arranging," is the hands-on part of the book—and a lot of fun. Here we'll work with a single composition and learn how to arrange it for different types of ensembles, including a basic rock band, big band, marching band, orchestra, and choir. We'll end the book by combining all these different types of arranging to create a popular recording, complete with rhythm section, backup vocals, and string section.

The Complete Idiot's Guide to Arranging and Orchestration concludes with a glossary of musical terms, a collection of the arrangements used in Part 3 of the book, and a listing of the tracks on the accompanying CD. When you get to the end of the book, you should be ready to create your own arrangements—and like what you hear.

How to Get the Most out of This Book

To get the most out of this book, you should know how it is designed. I've tried to put things together to make reading the book and learning how to arrange both rewarding and fun.

This book includes a mix of text-based information and musical examples. Most of the musical examples are also present on the CD that accompanies this book, so you can see them in the text and then hear what they sound like on the CD. The CD track number is listed beside each exercise, so they should be easy to reference.

In addition to the musical examples sprinkled throughout each chapter, you'll find a number of little text boxes (what we in publishing call *sidebars* and *margin notes*) that present additional advice and information. These elements enhance your knowledge or point out important pitfalls to avoid, and they look like this:

Note	Caution
These boxes contain additional information about the topic at hand.	These boxes warn you of common mistakes to avoid.

def•i•ni•tion

def•i•ni•tion	Tip
These boxes contain definitions of musical terms you might not be familiar with. Refer to Appendix A to find a more comprehensive glossary of musical terms.	These boxes contain tips and hints on how to improve your compositional skills.

In addition, you'll see a few icons in the margins, like this one:

Track 1

As mentioned previously, this indicates that the musical example next to the icon is available on the book's accompanying CD, for you to listen to. The track number of the example is also noted.

What's On the CD

There are three types of items on the CD that accompanies this book.

First, as previously noted, you'll find audio snippets that demonstrate some of the musical examples used throughout the book. These snippets let you listen to different techniques, voicings, and combinations of instruments that might be difficult to grasp without hearing them first.

Second, the CD contains examples of different types of musical styles or grooves, from straight-ahead rock to shuffle and swing. These short examples illustrate the style information presented in Chapter 13, "Arranging for the Rhythm Section."

Finally, the CD contains six complete arrangements of "Love Waits," an original composition by yours truly. These arrangements demonstrate the specific arranging techniques discussed in Part 3 of this book, "Real-World Arranging," and include versions of the song for rock band, big band, marching band, orchestra, and choir, as well as a fully produced version as you might find on a commercial recording. It's the same song, but presented in six very different styles—which, I hope, will help to inspire you to create your own arrangements of this song. (And make sure you listen to the bonus track at the end of the CD—it demonstrates how to build an effective backing track, instrument by instrument!)

And in case you're wondering, no, I didn't hire an expensive orchestra to play through these examples and arrangements. While that would have been nice, the publisher simply didn't have the budget for it. Instead, I used digital instrument sample libraries to provide the sounds. At their best, these sample libraries do a decent job of approximating a live performance—after all, they're sampled from live performers. Information about the software I used, as well as credit for the tracks' live performers, are listed at the end of Appendix C.

Additional Reading and Reference

As you read through this book, know that no serious arranger or orchestrator should be without a complete library of useful reference books. This book is only a start; there are many other well-known books that should be on every musician's bookshelf. My favorites include these:

◆ *Arranging Concepts Complete* (Dick Grove, Alfred Publishing, 1989)

◆ *Contemporary Choral Arranging* (Arthur E. Ostrander and Dana Wilson, Prentice Hall, 1986)

◆ *Principles of Orchestration* (Nikolay Rimsky-Korsakov, Dover Publications, 1964)

◆ *Sounds and Scores: A Practical Guide to Professional Orchestration* (Henry Mancini, Warner Brothers Publications, 1973)

◆ *The Study of Orchestration, Third Edition* (Samuel Adler, W.W. Norton & Company, 2002)

Why these books? They're all indispensable guides for their particular types of music. The Rimsky-Korsakov is a great guide to traditional classical orchestration. The Mancini book is great for arranging popular music. The Grove book is essential for jazz and big-band arrangers. The Ostrander/Wilson book is a must for choral arrangers. And the Adler book is nothing less than the Bible for instrumental orchestration. You'll get value out of all of them.

And I'd be remiss if I didn't mention again my two previous books that serve as both prologue and accompaniment to the book you're reading:

◆ *The Complete Idiot's Guide to Music Theory, Second Edition* (Michael Miller, Alpha Books, 2005), the perfect introduction to the music theory you need to arrange and orchestrate your own music

◆ *The Complete Idiot's Guide to Music Composition* (Michael Miller, Alpha Books, 2005), which teaches the compositional skills necessary to create fully formed arrangements

If you haven't read these two books yet, I suggest you get a copy of each and keep them handy when working through this text. They'll help you over any rough spots you might encounter.

Let Me Know What You Think

I always love to hear from my readers. Feel free to email me at arranging@ molehillgroup.com. I can't promise that I'll answer every e-mail, but I will promise that I'll read each one!

And, just in case a few mistakes happen to creep into the printed book, you can find a list of any corrections or clarifications on my website (www. molehillgroup.com/arranging.htm). That's also where you can find a list of my other books, so feel free to look around—and maybe do a little online shopping!

Acknowledgements

Thanks to the usual suspects at Alpha Books, including but not limited to Marie Butler-Knight, Tom Stevens, Jennifer Moore, Jan Lynn, and Jan Zoya, for helping to turn my manuscript into a printed book.

Special thanks go to the gifted musicians who contributed their talents to the book's accompanying CD. Thanks to Kevin Barnard, Joanna Jahn, Paula Lammers, and Tom Witry (all members of the Zephyr Cabaret) for lending their voices to the vocal tracks, and to Sherry Elliott for her singing, contracting the other musicians, contributing the recording space, and offering feedback on all the vocal arrangements. Thank you all!

Special Thanks to the Technical Reviewer

The Complete Idiot's Guide to Arranging and Orchestration was reviewed by an expert who double-checked the accuracy of what you'll learn here, to help us ensure that this book gives you everything you need to know about composing music. Special thanks are extended to Jim Anderson for his review and comments in this regard.

Jim is a fine arranger in his own right. Jim taught vocal music for 6 years and currently works as a freelance pianist, vocalist, music educator, and arranger in the Minneapolis/St. Paul area. He currently serves part time as a music minister for a Minneapolis-area church, and arranges music for high school show choirs.

My heartfelt thanks to Jim for his assistance and advice—and for helping to make this a better book.

Trademarks

All terms mentioned in this book that are known to be or are suspected of being trademarks or service marks have been appropriately capitalized. Alpha Books and Penguin Group (USA) Inc. cannot attest to the accuracy of this information. Use of a term in this book should not be regarded as affecting the validity of any trademark or service mark.

Part 1

Essential Skills

To create any type of arrangement, you have to master a set of basic skills—chord progressions, voicing, voice leading, countermelodies, and the like. Read on to learn and master the nuts and bolts of the arranging process.

Understanding the Arranging and Orchestration Process

In This Chapter

♦ Different approaches to arranging and orchestration

♦ Arranging the composition

♦ Orchestrating the arrangement

♦ Preparing the score and individual parts

♦ Using a music notation program

Arranging and orchestration are those parts of the music creation process where the final work comes into being. The late music educator Dick Grove described the process as "the art of being able to conceive a musical effect and then transfer it to paper so that that particular effect comes alive." To me, it's the act of taking the sounds and colors you hear in your head and expressing them in a way that other musicians can reproduce.

That means taking a piece of music, either newly composed or preexisting, arranging it so that it makes structural sense, and then orchestrating it for a particular group of instruments and voices. Arranging expands the original composition, while orchestration defines it. Combined, they're the musical equivalent of constructing a house from a set of blueprints. All the fine detail of the finished item is the work of the arranger and the orchestrator.

As such, there is a definite process involved in the arranging and orchestration of a piece of music. It starts with a basic composition and ends with individually copied instrumental and vocal parts—and involves a lot of work in between.

Composition, Arranging, and Orchestration: Which Is Which?

When it comes to creating music, the individual pieces of the puzzle are easily confused—primarily because they're not always easily distinguishable from one another. When you create a piece of music for a jazz band, church choir, or television commercial, are you a composer, an arranger, or an orchestrator? Or are you all three?

To some extent, the different parts of the process overlap. If you're composing a piece for orchestra, chances are you're also creating the arrangement and doing the orchestration, all as part of the composition process. If you're arranging an existing piece of music, you may be composing new melodies and countermelodies within the piece, and orchestrating the individual parts, as well. And even if you're just orchestrating someone else's arrangement, you'll have to employ basic composition and arranging techniques to create the final piece. Like I said, it's all interrelated.

That said, the three processes can be defined—even if the definitions necessarily overlap. Here are how I define the processes:

- **Composition**   The act of creating a new piece of music.

- **Arranging**   The act of adapting an existing composition for instruments or voices other than those for which it was originally written.

- **Orchestration**   The act of deciding which instruments or voices to use for a musical work.

Of these three processes, composition appears to be the most distinct. Arranging and orchestration, on the other hand, tend to blend—both in formal definition and in real life.

Here's how I think of the process. The *composition* is the creation of the original piece of music—typically a melody and accompanying chords. That composition is then *arranged* into a larger work, complete with multiple structural sections and the addition of any necessary new material. Finally, the arrangement is *orchestrated* for specific instruments and voices. The completed work can variably be called a composition, an arrangement, or an orchestration.

The three parts of the process can be performed by a single individual, or by two or more separate individuals. In some instances, a composer creates a rough arrangement and then hands over the orchestration to a separate orchestrator. In other instances, an arranger both arranges and orchestrates a piece based on an existing work by another composer. Any and all combinations are possible.

Note

If you're not using a computerized music notation program, there's an additional individual in the mix—the *copyist*. A copyist does what her title implies, manually copying individual parts from the master score.

The Arranging and Orchestration Process: Different Approaches

While the arranging and orchestration process is easy enough to understand, how one actually approaches the process differs from individual to individual, and from project to project. There's no one "right" way to go about it; as with most creative endeavors, the only rule is that there are no rules.

That said, let's take a look at the process in more detail, so you can determine the best way to approach your next project.

The Basic Process

The basic process of creating a fully orchestrated musical work looks something like this:

1. The composer creates the original piece of music.

2. The arranger either obtains a lead sheet of the composition, like the one shown in Figure 1.1, or transcribes the melody and chords from an existing performance. (A lead sheet typically contains chords, melody line, and lyrics.)

3. Working from the transcription or lead sheet, the arranger blocks out the harmonization and major structural sections of the arrangement, expanding upon the basic composition as necessary to create a fully structured sketch.

4. Working from the rough sketch of the arrangement, the orchestrator assigns individual instruments or voices to each note in the arrangement, essentially filling in the details to create a master score, in either concert key or in each instrument's transposed key.

5. The copyist extracts the individual parts for each instrument and voice from the master score, transposing each part as necessary.

In other words, the piece is composed, arranged, orchestrated, and copied—in that order. The individual steps may be performed by different individuals (the composer, the arranger, the orchestrator, and the copyist), by a single individual who assumes multiple roles, or by some combination of the above.

Love Waits

Michael Miller

Figure 1.1

It all starts with a melody and chords, typically in lead-sheet format.

The Rough-Sketch Approach

Many composers and arrangers like to start with broad strokes, by creating a rough sketch of the arrangement without delineating the individual parts. When employing this approach, the arranger typically sketches in major melodies and countermelodies, ensemble patterns, and basic harmonies but leaves out all inessential detail. By employing this approach, musical ideas can be written down quite quickly, without spending time working through the fiddly details of each part.

This type of rough sketch is normally written in concert key, either on a piano staff (dual treble and bass clef staves, as shown in Figure 1.2) or on four- or five-staff paper (one staff for each family of instruments, as shown in Figure 1.3). Sketches can be done by hand using pencil and paper, or on computer using notation software. You can even create your rough sketch without any formal notation, using a MIDI keyboard and home studio setup to create a demo mix using sampled instruments; this mix can then be transcribed to create the detailed score.

Sketch Score

Love Waits

Michael Miller

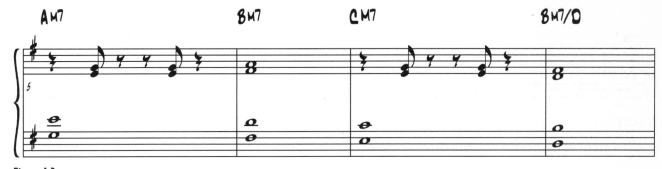

Figure 1.2

A rough sketch blocked out on piano staff paper.

Sketch Score

Love Waits

Michael Miller

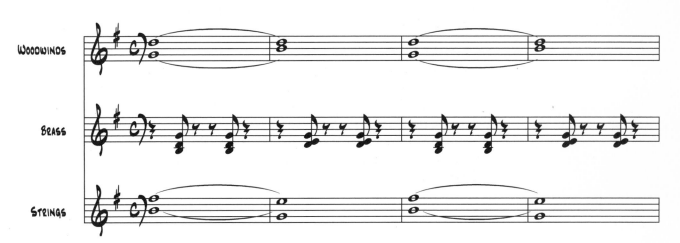

Figure 1.3

A rough sketch with separate staves for each section of the ensemble.

As you can see, the rough sketch is just that—the arrangement "roughed in," without a lot of detail. The point is to indicate the important passages and key voicings, and leave the rest of the detail (such as which individual instrument plays which specific part) for the orchestration process. You might pencil in which instruments you want playing in each section of the piece, indicate when a line is played in unison or when harmony or a countermelody needs to be created, define the broad outlines of the desired chord voicing, or even sketch in rhythmic or melodic patterns that supplement the main melody.

The point is that the sketch defines the overall vision for the final piece, and is not in itself final. It's truly like a pencil sketch that needs the details inked in and colored to reach its completed state.

Of course, once the rough sketch is completed, it still has to be developed into a full score. Someone—either the original arranger or a separate orchestrator—has to translate the rough ideas from the sketch into detailed individual parts. The details have to be worked through.

As you can imagine, there are several advantages to creating a rough sketch before a detailed score. First, it's fast; you can write down a lot of ideas very quickly when you're just sketching them out. Second, you don't have to worry about voicings, interior melodies, doublings, or transpositions; you can save those details for later. And, perhaps most important, when you create a rough sketch, you have the option of handing the sketch over to a separate orchestrator to fill in the details and create the full score.

For many professionals, this division of labor is a necessity when deadlines loom. It's also a boon if you have great musical ideas but scant musical training; this approach is used by many younger composers and producers who don't have formal training in music theory or orchestration.

In fact, it's the rough-sketch approach that many professional composers and arrangers employ, especially in the film and television industries. Given the tight schedules of most movie and TV projects, the composer/arranger simply doesn't have time to both create the composition and orchestrate it. So the composer/arranger creates a rough sketch of the arrangement and then hands it off to a separate orchestrator, who fills in the details to create all the individual parts of the finished orchestration.

The Full-Score Approach

In contrast to the rough-sketch approach, many arrangers prefer to go directly to full score, thus eliminating the need for a separate orchestrator. With this approach, the full arrangement is worked out from scratch, each part created in full, as shown in Figure 1.4. There's no rough sketch to work from; ideas flow directly from the mind of the arranger to the finished score.

Score

Love Waits

Michael Miller

Figure 1.4

A full score (in concert pitch).

Note

The score can be either in concert key or transposed to each instrument's key. If the score is in concert key, the copyist must transpose each part when extracting the parts.

There are several advantages to working directly to a full score. First, you have complete control over the final piece; as the arranger/orchestrator, you dictate every single note in the arrangement, so nothing is left to chance or the whims of an outside orchestrator. Second, by going straight to score, you eliminate the rough-sketch piece of the process, thus reducing the number of steps from start to finish—and theoretically making for a faster process, since you're not creating the same arrangement twice. Third, if you score in each instrument's transposed key, you help to speed up the creation of individual parts; no additional transposition is necessary by the copyist. (However, this benefit is somewhat negated by the use of notation software that automatically transposes and extracts parts from a concert-key score.)

The primary disadvantage to this approach is that it takes time to create a full score. While you can speed from measure to measure relatively quickly when creating a rough sketch, you'll spend a lot more time on each measure when you have to notate each individual part, one at a time. And the full-score approach locks you in as the sole creator; you can't hand off the orchestration job when you're doing double-duty as arranger and orchestrator.

That said, the full-score approach is quite common in the jazz and pop fields, and with many concert and marching band arrangers. If anything, this approach has been made easier by the use of music notation software, which automates some of the previously-manual labor involved with transposing and extracting parts.

Arranging the Composition

No matter how you approach your project, you have to arrange the music. Arranging involves the creation of a fully structured piece out of the original melody and chords; you turn whatever it is you start with into a fully realized work.

The act of arranging a piece of music typically involves one or more individual actions. Depending on what it is you're arranging, you may need to do the following:

Note

Learn more about the arranging process in Chapter 2.

- ◆ Re-envision the original piece in a different style (rock, jazz, soul, etc.)
- ◆ Re-envision the original piece for a different grouping of instruments
- ◆ Harmonize or reharmonize an existing melody
- ◆ Expand or enhance an existing melody—make it longer or more complex
- ◆ Alter or supplement an existing chord progression
- ◆ Supplement an existing melody with countermelodies and rhythmic patterns
- ◆ Repeat all or part of a melody either exactly or in an enhanced fashion

♦ Add new pieces of melody to the original, in the form of choruses or bridges

♦ Voice or revoice a piece's harmonies—that is, determine which notes of a chord you want played in which order

In other words, you take a short and simple thing and turn it into a longer and typically more complex one. When you're done, you have a completed work for jazz band, choir, orchestra, or some other defined ensemble.

Of course, arranging isn't just for formal music. The music you hear in a movie or television show, or on a CD, is also arranged—even if it's just guitar, bass, and drums. And, chances are, the arrangement on record or over the air is a lot more complex than you realize; it's not unusual for a pop performance to include multiple guitars and keyboards, synthesizers, brass, woodwinds, strings, even ethnic percussion of various sorts. When you decide that you want to hear a lead guitar solo on the bridge or a string section on the chorus, you're creating an arrangement.

Orchestrating the Arrangement

In many instances, orchestration occurs simultaneously with arranging. In other instances, the orchestration comes after. No matter when you do it, however, you still have to assign specific instruments or voices to specific parts. That's what orchestration is all about.

Should the lead melody be played by a trumpet or saxophone? Should the accompanying chords be played by the string section or by the woodwinds? Should you assign a countermelody to the first clarinets alone, or to the first and second clarinets? What would sound better, a French horn playing together with a cello, or a flute playing together with an oboe?

These are all decisions made by the orchestrator. The orchestrator decides which instruments play which notes in the score. He doesn't expand or elaborate on the score, as an arranger does; it's a simple matter of fitting specific instruments and voices to specific notes.

In essence, orchestration is concerned with sound. You use different combinations of instruments to create different sounds. Which instruments you assign to which notes dramatically affects the final sound of your piece; a skilled orchestrator plays the instruments of the orchestra much like an individual musician plays his or her own instrument.

To be an effective orchestrator, you must have a working knowledge of all modern instruments. Do you know what an oboe sounds like in its low range? Or what a high trombone and tenor saxophone sound like when played in unison? Or what the working range of a trumpet is, or how high a note you can reasonably expect an alto to sing? These are all the practical considerations necessary to orchestrate a piece of music. It even helps if you know a little about how each

> **Note**
>
> For the purposes of this book, we'll use the term *orchestration* to refer to the assigning of all types of instruments and voices, not just those that are part of the traditional symphonic orchestra.

> **Note**
>
> Learn more about the orchestration process in Chapter 6.

instrument works, so you know whether it's actually possible to play the music you write. You don't want to hand out copies of your latest work and then discover that you've asked a guitarist to play a seven-note chord on his six-string guitar.

Note

One of the most useful tools for a modern orchestrator is a music notation program and a library of sampled instruments. In the old days (pre-computers), the only way to hear the sounds in your head was to write them down and bring in individual instrumentalists to play them, which was both time-consuming and expensive. Today, however, you can notate your piece in Finale or Sibelius, assign each written part to a digitally sampled instrument, and then play back your piece on your computer. The results, especially if you're using quality samples, can be quite realistic—certainly realistic enough to give you a fairly good idea of how your piece will sound when performed live.

There's a downside of using sampled instruments, however—and I'm not talking about putting human musicians out of work. No, I'm talking about the capability of these programs to reproduce music that human musicians can't. If you write a G above high C for a trumpet, the digital sample will play it—even if a human trumpet player can't. It's possible for an orchestrator who has no experience with real live musicians to get into the habit of writing parts that are physically unplayable, just because the notation program lets him. Using a notation program, then, is no substitute for learning the ranges, capabilities, and limitations of the instruments you're writing for.

(That said, Finale includes a plug-in that can check the proper range for each instrument for beginning, intermediate, and advanced players. Use it!)

Preparing the Score

Once you've created and orchestrated your arrangement, you need to create a master score. The score is that piece of music used by the conductor; it includes each individual instrumental or vocal part so that the conductor can see at a glance who's supposed to be doing what, and when.

Identifying the Score

At the top of your score, you should write the piece's title, your name, and the composer's name (if different), as shown in Figure 1.5. The copyright notice—(c)or © symbol, followed by the year—should be added at the bottom of the first page.

Someone to Watch Over Me

Score for orchestra

George & Ira Gershwin
Arr. Michael Miller

Figure 1.5

Titling and identifying a formal score.

Beyond this initial identification, there are a few other guidelines you should keep in mind:

- The first instance of each staff for each instrument or voice must have its own clef sign, key signature, and time signature.

- Typically, the time signature is shown only in the very first measure and wherever a time change appears.

- The clef sign and key signature, however, should be displayed in the first measure of every staff for every instrument.

- Each instrument should be clearly marked at the beginning of each staff. (The first instance typically has the full instrument name, spelled out; subsequent staves can use abbreviations.)

- Like instruments should be grouped together (all the trumpets together, for example). If you want, you can combine all like instruments on a single staff—as we'll discuss shortly.

- For instruments that use the grand or piano staff (both bass and treble clef), group the two staves by using braces.

- Measure lines should be drawn through all the instruments belonging to the same section—but not through all the instruments in the score. (This is so the conductor can visually group the sections together, at a glance.)

- If an instrument or voice will be resting for an extended period of time, you don't have to include the staff for that instrument or voice during the rest period (after the first page of the full rest, that is).

Concert or Transposed Key?

A score can be in either concert key (all instruments represented by the pitch they sound), or with each instrument transposed to its own native key (all instruments represented by the notes they read). In this age of computerized notation programs, it's no big deal to convert a score from concert to transposed pitch (typically just a setting in a menu or dialog box), but if you're working with pencil and paper, you probably don't want to do both.

A concert-pitch score is easier for some composers (especially novice or non-trained composers) to read; they don't have to transpose what they see in front of them on the fly. On the other hand, if you have a concert pitch paper score, then your copyist will have to transpose each individual part as it's copied, which adds time and money to the process. (Remember—at some point in time, the individual instrumental parts will have to be transposed, whether that's at the score or the part-copying stage.)

Section or Individual Staves?

When you're creating your score, you also have the choice of putting an entire instrumental or vocal section on a single staff (like that in Figure 1.6) or of using individual staves for each instrument (as in Figure 1.7). The single-staff approach is easier for some conductors to read (one can more quickly see the section at a glance), while the individual-staff approach makes it easier to isolate individual parts. Again, it's a choice to make.

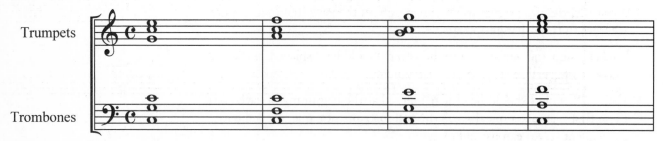

Figure 1.6

Trumpet and trombone sections, each on a single staff.

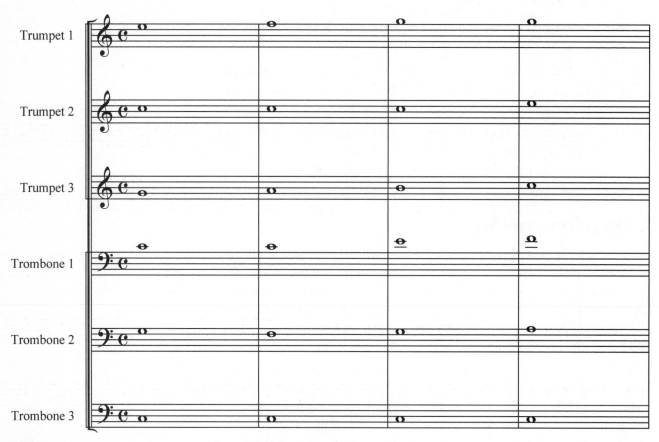

Figure 1.7

The same score, with individual trumpet and trombone parts in individual staves.

This decision also exists when you're scoring for a choir. Some vocal pieces put the soprano and alto parts on a single treble-clef staff, and the tenor and bass parts on a single bass-clef staff, as shown in Figure 1.8. This approach belies the fact that the tenor part is typically written in treble clef, which argues for the use of four separate staves—one for each part, as shown in Figure 1.9. The piano accompaniment is typically placed beneath the vocal staves.

Figure 1.8

A vocal score on two staves.

Figure 1.9

A vocal score with separate staves for each part.

Score Order

This leads to the topic of score order—the order in which you write the instruments on your score. Believe it or not, there is a consensus here, although it differs somewhat for different types of vocal and instrumental ensembles.

Symphonic Orchestra

A full symphonic orchestra can include virtually every instrument available, including a complete complement of strings, woodwinds, brass, and percussion. When you're composing an orchestral score, write for instruments listed in Table 1.1 (in top-to-bottom position).

Table 1.1   Symphonic orchestra score order

Major Section	Individual Instruments
Woodwinds	Piccolo Flute (first and second) Oboe (first and second) English horn B♭ clarinet (first and second) Bass clarinet Bassoon (first and second) Contrabassoon
Brass	French horn (first, second, third, and fourth) Trumpet (first, second, and third) Trombone (first, second, and third) Tuba
Percussion	Timpani Bells (glockenspiel) Xylophone Vibraphone Marimba Chimes Snare drum Bass drum Cymbals Other percussion
Keyboards	Harp Piano
Strings	Violin (first and second) Viola Cello Double bass

The symphonic orchestra is used for more than just symphonies. Many film and television soundtracks employ full orchestras; some rock bands even call in an orchestra to fill things out on occasion. Because of all the instruments available, the orchestra is perhaps the most versatile type of instrumental ensemble available and is worthy of your studies, of course.

Chamber Orchestra

A chamber orchestra is a stripped-down version of the full orchestra, with widely varying instrumentation. Table 1.2 details the most common chamber-orchestra lineup, in top-to-bottom order.

Table 1.2   Chamber-orchestra score order

Major Section	Individual Instruments
Woodwinds	Flute (first and second) Oboe (first and second) B♭ clarinet (first and second) Bassoon (first and second)
Brass	French horn (first and second) Trumpet (first and second)
Percussion	Timpani
Keyboards	Piano
Strings	Violin (first and second) Viola Cello Double bass

Chamber orchestras typically have fewer musicians on each part. Instead of an entire section of violins, for example, there might be only a handful of string players on each part.

String Orchestra

A string orchestra is simply the five instruments of the string section (first violin, second violin, viola, cello, and double bass), sometimes accompanied by a piano, as detailed in Table 1.3. There are no brass, woodwind, or percussion instruments in this ensemble.

Table 1.3   String-orchestra score order

Major Section	Individual Instruments
Strings	First violin Second violin Viola Cello Double bass
Keyboards	Piano

String Quartet

Another common ensemble in both classical and contemporary music is the string quartet. As the name implies, this is a grouping of four string instruments (one each—no doubling per part), as noted in Table 1.4.

Table 1.4   String-quartet score order

Major Section	Individual Instruments
Strings	First violin Second violin Viola Cello

Concert Band

A concert band includes virtually all the brass, woodwind, and percussion instruments from the larger orchestra, but without the strings. Table 1.5 details the typical score order for a concert-band arrangement.

Table 1.5   Concert-band score order

Major Section	Individual Instruments
Woodwinds	Piccolo Flute (first and second) Oboe (first and second) English horn Bassoon (first and second) B♭ clarinet (first, second, and third) Alto clarinet Bass clarinet Alto saxophone (first and second) Tenor saxophone Baritone saxophone
Brass	Cornet (first, second, and third) Trumpet (first and second) French horn (first, second, third, and fourth) Trombone (first and second) Bass trombone Baritone horn Tuba
Percussion	Timpani Bells (glockenspiel) Xylophone Vibraphone Marimba Chimes Snare drum Bass drum Cymbals Other percussion

Marching Band

A marching band has similar instrumentation to a concert band, minus a few concert instruments and with a few new percussion instruments added. Table 1.6 details the score order.

Table 1.6   Marching-band score order

Major Section	Individual Instruments
Woodwinds	Piccolo Flute B♭ Clarinet (first, second, and third) Bass clarinet Alto saxophone (first and second) Tenor saxophone Baritone saxophone
Brass	Trumpet (first, second, and third) French horn (first, second, third, and fourth) Trombone (first, second, and third) Baritone horn Tuba
Percussion	Bells (glockenspiel) Xylophone (marching or pit) Vibraphone (pit) Marimba (pit) Chimes (pit) Timpani (pit) Percussion (misc.) Snare drums Tenor drums (toms) Bass drums Cymbals

Tip

If a marching band or drum ensemble has a stationary "pit," you can score for some concert percussion instruments, such as marimba and xylophone. Otherwise, stick to those instruments that can be carried.

Drum and Bugle Corps

At first glance, drum and bugle corps (sometimes just called *drum corps*) look a lot like a marching band—but with some very major differences. First, there aren't any woodwinds. Second, there's a lot more percussion—a heavier use of tenor drums (a.k.a. toms, quads, or quints) and tonal (pitched) bass drums, as well as a reliance on the pit instruments. And third, the brass instruments are all a bit different from what you're used to.

Modern drum corps instrumentation uses three-valve bell-front instruments. (The use of the traditional bugle has actually gone by the wayside.) There are five groupings of instruments: *sopranos* (similar to trumpets), *mellophones, baritones, euphoniums,* and *contra basses* (front-firing tubas). Until recently, all these were G instruments; under revised rules, corps instruments can now be pitched in G, F, or B♭.

Note

In some corps, B♭ trumpets are used in place of sopranos.

Table 1.7 shows the score order for a modern drum and bugle corps.

Table 1.7   Drum and bugle corps score order

Major Section	Individual Instruments
Brass	Soprano (or B♭ trumpet) Mellophone Baritone Euphonium Contra bass
Percussion	Bells (glockenspiel) Xylophone (marching or pit) Vibraphone (pit) Marimba (pit) Chimes (pit) Timpani (pit) Percussion (misc.) Snare drums Tenor drums (toms) Bass drums Cymbals

Big Band (Jazz Band)

Another popular ensemble, especially in the jazz idiom, is the so-called jazz band or big band. A typical jazz band includes the instruments listed in Table 1.8.

Table 1.8   Jazz big-band score order

Major Section	Individual Instruments
Woodwinds	Flute (sometimes played by a sax player) Soprano saxophone (sometimes played by an alto or tenor-sax player) Alto saxophones (1 to 3) Tenor saxophones (1 to 3) Baritone saxophones (1 or 2)
Brass	Trumpets (3 to 5) Trombones (3 to 5)
Rhythm section	Guitar (optional) Piano Bass (electric or acoustic) Drums Other percussion (congas, tambourine, etc.)

Choir

As noted previously, choral music normally has four parts (soprano, alto, tenor, and bass), arranged with the highest voice (soprano) at the top, and the lowest voice (bass) at the bottom, as detailed in Table 1.9. The four vocal parts are grouped together with braces, and a piano accompaniment is included below the vocal parts. The top three parts use the treble clef; the bass line uses the bass clef. Lyrics are included below each staff.

Table 1.9   Choral score order

Major Section	Individual Voices
Choir	Soprano Alto Tenor Baritone (optional) Bass
Accompaniment	Piano

Lettering and Numbering

There's a final consideration to make when creating a score, and that's how you notate position and structure. You can use letters (A, B, C) to designate major sections in the arrangement, or you can number each individual measure—or you can do both. Section lettering is nice in that it helps all the musicians easily identify the major sections of a piece; measure numbering is nice in that it lets the conductor go directly to any individual measure in the score, no unnecessary counting required. Do both lettering and numbering, and you get the best of both worlds.

Copying Individual Parts

The score is read only by the conductor; individual instrumentalists and vocalists read their own individual parts. Which means, of course, that the individual parts need to be extracted and copied from the master score.

As with the score, each part should be identified with the work's title, the name of the composer and arranger, and the copyright date. Obviously, each part should also identify the instrument that it's written for, as shown in Figure 1.10.

Tip

There is typically no need to create individual vocal parts for a choral piece. All four voices read the master vocal score.

Figure 1.10

An individual trumpet part—transcribed to the instrument's native key.

Individual parts should *never* be extracted in concert pitch. Parts should always be in the transposed key for that instrument—which means you may have to transpose the part from a concert-key score.

This transposition, along with part creation in general, is easier if you use a music notation program—which we'll discuss next.

Pencil or Keyboard?

Whether you start with a rough sketch or go directly to a full score, you have a choice in how you work. You can take the old-fashioned approach and write with pencil and paper, or go high-tech and do your writing on computer, using notation software. Both approaches have their pros and cons.

Using Pencil and Paper

The obvious benefit of composing with pencil and paper is that you can do it anywhere. You don't need an electrical outlet, or desk space for your computer keyboard. Assuming that you're able to accurately transcribe the notes you hear in your head, you can pencil them in while you're sitting in your easy chair, in your local coffeehouse, or even outside sitting under a tree. When inspiration strikes, all you have to do is write it down.

There are downsides to using pencil and paper, however. First, if your handwriting is as bad as mine, you may not be able to read the notes you write. (And if you can't, then no one else can either—which becomes a problem when copying individual parts.) Second, you'll need to transfer your rough sketches to a more final score, and then transpose and copy each individual part by hand. This might not be a big deal if you have the cash to employ a copyist (and if you've taken and passed a music calligraphy course), but otherwise it's a lot of work.

Using a Music Notation Program

The other approach is to use technology to do a lot of the grunt work for you. Music notation programs such as Finale (shown in Figure 1.11), Notion, and Sibelius do a lot of the manual labor for you. You can create a piece of music by clicking onscreen buttons with your mouse, pressing keys on your computer keyboard, or inputting a musical performance from a MIDI keyboard. You can create your full score in concert pitch, and then let the notation program transpose each instrument as necessary and automatically extract individual parts. These programs also make it easy to copy parts from one instrument or section to another, and to edit individual notes on the fly. A click of the mouse is all it takes.

In addition, you can use these notation programs to help create a great-sounding demo of the piece you're working on. All of these programs come with their own sound libraries of sampled instruments; assign the right sampled instrument to each part, and you'll get a reasonable facsimile of what the finished piece will sound like. That's something you can't get out of a piece of paper.

Figure 1.11

Composing, arranging, and orchestrating with Finale— a popular music notation program.

In fact, many professional composers and orchestrators use computers to create their final works. Listen to a lot of today's prime-time television shows (and more than a few big-screen movies), and you'll hear the sound of orchestras that exist only on disk. It's a lot cheaper to produce a fully-scored work on computer, in a home studio, than it is to hire an 80-piece orchestra and rent a professional recording studio. The results—especially when using pro-level sample libraries— are often indistinguishable from the real thing.

There are three primary notation programs used by professionals today:

- ◆ Finale (www.finalemusic.com)

- ◆ Notion (www.notionmusic.com)

- ◆ Sibelius (www.sibelius.com)

Of these three programs, Finale is probably the most fully featured, but also the most difficult to use; a lot of its powerful features are hidden under multiple menus or in obscure toolbars. Sibelius offers similar features but a slightly easier-to-use interface. And Notion is more of a score composition program, complete with instrument samples from the London Symphony Orchestra, recorded at Abbey Road Studios.

Personally, I like the power of Finale, and it's easy enough to use once you figure out what's where. Both Finale and Sibelius are widely used by professional composers and arrangers, as well as in the music programs of major music schools around the globe. Notion is the newcomer to the party, carving a niche for itself as an easier-to-use program that composers can use to create ready-to-play compositions and arrangements. Any of these three programs are worth your consideration.

Note
The recordings on the CD that accompany this book were all created using music notation software and instrument samples. Here's how I created each track. I used the Finale 2007 notation program to create the basic arrangements, and then exported the arrangements as MIDI files. The MIDI files were then imported into the Cubase 4 recording program, where instrument sounds were assigned from various sample libraries, including Garritan's Personal Orchestra and Jazz & Big Band libraries, the Tapspace Virtual Drumline 2 library, and Steinberg's Virtual Guitarist 2 and HALionOne sample players. These instrumental tracks were then augmented with "live" vocals, drums, and keyboards, and then properly mixed in Cubase. Mastering was accomplished with Sony's Sound Forge software, and the master CD was burned with Sony's CD Architect program. The results, while admittedly not commercial-CD quality, are more than satisfactory for demo use.

The Least You Need to Know

◆ Composition, arranging, and orchestration are three distinct pieces of the music creation process, and can be performed by one or multiple individuals.

◆ Arranging is the act of creating a new musical structure from an existing composition—which often means adding new material to the original work.

◆ Orchestration is the act of assigning instruments and voices to perform specific notes in the arrangement.

◆ Some arrangers prefer to first create a rough sketch of the arrangement, while others prefer to go directly to detailed musical score.

◆ A master score can be created in either concert key or in each instrument's transposed key.

◆ The process of arranging and orchestrating—and extracting individual parts—can be simplified by using a music notation program, such as Finale, Notion, or Sibelius.

Chapter 2

Structuring the Arrangement

In This Chapter

- Writing for different types of performers
- Choosing musical style and form
- Utilizing key musical elements
- Controlling the flow—and building toward the musical climax

The first step in creating an arrangement is to plan out what you intend to do. You need to know where you're going before you can figure out how to get there.

An arrangement, after all, is more than just a melody orchestrated. It's an expansion of that melody that creates a fully formed piece, something with a formal beginning and ending and interesting progress from one to the other. It is a musical piece with a defined structure—which is what this chapter is all about.

Considering the Intended Performers

One of the first things to consider when you're planning an arrangement is who you're arranging for. The audience, yes, but also the performers. Who will be playing your arrangement should, in some fashion, influence the arrangement you create.

Writing for a particular ensemble can determine the precise instrumentation you use. For example, if you contract to arrange for a particular high school marching band, you can write for that band's exact instrumentation. There's no guesswork involved.

And if your arrangement is to be written for a specific group of performers, you can write for those performers' individual strengths and weaknesses. For example, if you're writing for a big band with a strong lead trumpet player capable of playing very high notes, you can incorporate some nice high trumpet parts into your arrangement. Conversely, if you're writing for a vocal group with a weak soprano section, you know to keep the soprano part within a narrow, singable range.

The age of the performers you're writing for should also be taken into account. Writing for a junior high band is much different from writing for a high school band, which is different from writing for a college or professional band. Younger musicians typically have narrower ranges, and are less capable of playing faster and more rhythmically complex passages.

The age factor is even more important when writing for voices. Junior-high-level material is particularly tricky, especially for those male voices that may or may not have yet matured. If you choose to arrange for this level of choir, I recommend you spend some time talking to school choir directors to get their input as to acceptable ranges and levels of difficulty.

Caution

Arranging is one area where the use of a music-notation program can be problematic. Your notation program can play back just about anything you write, while the intended performers will have specific musical limitations.

Choosing a Musical Style

Next up is the decision about the musical style in which to write. This may be an easy decision, especially if you're arranging an existing piece of music; you're probably not going to turn an arrangement of the latest Beyoncé single into a Dixieland piece. But beyond faithful adaptations of popular music, you have a lot of leeway as to how you approach any given arrangement.

Style is important because different styles have different conventions. Arranging in a Latin style, for example, implies the use of certain rhythms and certain Latin percussion instruments. Arranging in a blues style, as another example, requires adherence to the traditional 12-bar blues form, as well as use of blues chords and blues scales. The same goes with most other musical forms, from Broadway show tunes to jazz ballads to R&B-flavored dance tunes. Whichever style you choose, make sure you know how that style is supposed to sound—and that you can faithfully recreate that sound with the ensemble for which you're writing.

Choosing a Musical Form

Once you decide the type of piece you're creating, you need to work out the piece, section by section. Now, there are no hard and fast rules about how many and what type of sections an arrangement should include; this varies not just by musical style or type of ensemble, but literally from piece to piece and from arranger to arranger. Put bluntly, you can structure your arrangement however you like.

That said, there are some common structural forms that are used over and over again in many different types of music. Most jazz and popular music follows some sort of verse-chorus structure, comprised of one or more verses or A-sections, a repeating chorus or B-section, and sometimes a single bridge or interlude (C-section) somewhere in the middle. Using the letter designations, you get forms like A-B-A (verse, chorus, verse), A-A-B-A (verse 1, verse 2, chorus, verse 3), A-B-C-A-B (verse, chorus, bridge, verse, chorus) and so on.

The form you use for your arrangement may not be the same form as the original composition. That's because your arrangement may need to be longer than the original composition. For example, let's say the original composition has a simple verse-chorus-verse (A-B-A), but you want to create a somewhat longer arrangement. You have several options to choose from. For example, you can …

Tip

Each section in an arrangement can be any length you like, although in popular music it's common to build each section in multiples of two. Eight-measure sections are common, but so are four- and twelve-measure sections. Typically, the longer the overall piece, the longer the individual sections.

- ◆ Add a second instance of the chorus (A-B-A-B)

- ◆ Repeat the last verse and chorus (A-B-A-B-A)

- ◆ Add a bridge after the chorus (A-B-C-A)

- ◆ Add a bridge after the last verse and then repeat the chorus again (A-B-A-C-B)

- ◆ Add a bridge after the last verse and then repeat the final verse and chorus (A-B-A-C-A-B)

- ◆ Add a bridge before the last verse and then repeat the chorus (A-B-C-A-B)

- ◆ Add a distinct introduction and ending to the basic structure (Intro-A-B-A-Ending)

Of course, these are just some of the almost limitless number of variations. The structure you choose is one of the first and most important decisions you must make as an arranger.

Introduction

If you're working from a basic lead sheet or a simple melody, you may need to add some material before the main melody begins. This introduction serves as a lead-in to the main melody, literally introducing the theme or mood of the piece.

While an introduction isn't always necessary, adding an intro can serve to engage the listeners (so they want to hear the rest of the piece) and set up all of what follows throughout the entire piece of music. The goal is to provoke interest, pure and simple.

Tip

Since the introduction often utilizes musical ideas from other sections of the arrangement, it's common for the introduction to be written *after* the rest of the arrangement.

One way to provoke interest—and to set up the piece that follows—is to base the introduction on thematic material that appears later in the main work. For example, you may derive a short introduction from a segment of the main melody, the initial musical phrase, the chorus of a song, or any subsequent section of the piece.

One common approach is to extract the final cadence from either the verse (main melody) or chorus, and to use that chord progression as the basis for the introduction. Another approach is to simply reprise a bit of the main melody—not the whole melody, but perhaps a key phrase, or the opening or ending notes.

You may also want to base the introduction on a subsidiary or accompaniment part, rather than the main melody. For example, if you have a repeating theme in the accompaniment, you can repeat that theme (actually, introduce it) in the introduction. This provides a smooth transition if the first section of the piece also utilizes that same accompaniment figure.

In most instances the introduction is shorter than the other musical phrases in the piece. For example, if the main piece is composed of eight-bar phrases, you might create a two- or four-bar introduction.

In all instances, you want the introduction to lead into the first chord and note of the main melody. That might mean ending the introduction on a leading tone or leading chord. For example, if the main section of the piece starts with a C-major chord (in the key of C major), you might end the introduction with a G7 (V7) or F (IV) chord, both of which create natural cadences leading to the C chord.

Verse (A-Section)

Once you're past the introduction, it's time to move into the first main section of the piece—which, in jazz and popular music, is called the *verse* or A-section. The verse is the first melody of the piece; it's an important melody, and often is repeated several times throughout the course of the song—either identically or with some variation.

In most instances, the verse will be repeated at least once in the arrangement. Most musical forms feature some repetition of the A-section—as in A-B-A, A-A-B-A, A-B-C-A, and similar forms. As such, you'll need to arrange the melody so that the repetition is warranted (that is, you have to orchestrate the melody in an interesting fashion) and so that the repetition isn't boring.

The ability to subtly alter a melody from verse to verse is important when you're taking an existing song with lyrics and arranging it for an instrumental ensemble. That's because you don't have the lyrics to differentiate one verse from another. You have to create the differentiation with your instrumentation and by the way you phrase or expand the melody. Simply repeating the same instrumental passage two or three times in a piece will not achieve the affect of different verses; you have to vary something.

Chorus (B-Section)

The *chorus* (or B-section) is the second main melody of the piece, and is often the emotional high point of the piece. In most instances, the chorus is the same length or shorter than the verse, and is typically repeated several times

---

Note

If you have only a single melody to work with, that melody will typically become the arrangement's verse.

Learn more about expanding and embellishing a melody in Chapter 5.

throughout an arrangement—sometimes after each verse. More often than not, the chorus is also used as the final section of the piece.

You probably want to arrange the chorus so that it's different in texture from the preceding verse. That might mean a different volume level (dynamic), instrumentation, or harmonic or rhythmic approach. You need to make the chorus stand out from the verse, using all the tools at your disposal.

That said, all the melodic techniques we discussed for verses are also applicable when arranging choruses.

Bridge (C-Section)

Some arrangements include a *bridge* or *interlude*, also known as the C-section, which is kind of a break in the middle of the piece. Most bridges sound completely different from the verse and chorus and are often based on a different harmonic structure. (For example, a bridge might be based around the IV chord, instead of the I chord.) Bridges can be as short as four or eight measures, or sometimes can be longer.

Sometimes the bridge is present in the original composition, and sometimes it's a section you add when creating the arrangement. The bridge can be related to the surrounding material, perhaps blending musical motifs used in the A and B sections, although many bridges have no harmonic relation at all to the rest of the piece. All the bridge has to do is serve as a brief interlude from other sections, as well as provide a connection between what came before and what comes after. However you approach it, recognize that the bridge is of minor importance, and should not musically overwhelm the other sections in the piece.

Ending

When you're creating a longer or more formal arrangement, it's common to include an extended ending for the piece. The ending is there to prevent an abrupt halt to the piece after the end of the major thematic material; you don't want the piece to just stop—you want it to reach a logical and emotional conclusion.

Many endings simply repeat the last musical phrase, either fully or in an abbreviated fashion. For example, the ending might repeat the final cadence of the last verse or chorus, rather than repeating the entire verse or chorus.

Another approach is to rhythmically extend the final phrase, in a process formally called *augmentation*. For example, you might take the final two bars of the melody and stretch it out so that it lasts four bars, instead. You do this by doubling the length of each note and chord. The effect is that of broadening or even retarding the tempo, and it adds a bit of grandeur to the piece.

Finally, some forms of jazz and popular music feature a *tag* ending. With a tag ending, there's typically a short rhythmic motif, followed by a sudden and often accentuated final note. This type of ending is best used in up-tempo or major-key arrangements; you seldom hear tag endings in ballads.

Tip

Like the introduction, the ending is most often written after the rest of the arrangement, as it utilizes musical ideas present elsewhere in the piece.

Deciding on Essential Musical Elements

The flavor of an arrangement depends on how you use these six key musical elements:

- Instrumentation
- Texture
- Time signature
- Tempo
- Key
- Dynamics

Each section of your arrangement can—and perhaps should—include a different combination of elements. For example, the verse might employ a relatively simple instrumentation with a highly rhythmic texture, while the chorus might use more sophisticated instrumentation but with smoother rhythms. The goal is to create some contrast between sections, in the aim of retaining listener interest and propelling the piece forward.

Instrumentation

The instrumentation you choose is one of the most important decisions you make as an arranger/orchestrator. In most instances, the overall instrumentation you employ is dictated by the type of ensemble for which you're arranging. You know, for example, that a typical big band has five sax players, five trumpets, five trombones, and a rhythm section. However, you don't have to (and probably shouldn't) have all instruments playing together in all sections of a piece.

The instruments you choose to play together create the different colors in your musical palette. A full orchestra playing together is a much different color than just the oboes and flutes playing. You employ different instrumentation to achieve different effects and moods.

> **Note**
>
> The concept of instrumentation (which is just another word for orchestration) is so important that an entire section of this book is devoted to the subject. Learn more in Part 2.

Texture

Texture refers to the rhythmic and harmonic styles employed. Generally speaking, adjacent sections in an arrangement should vary somewhat in texture—although the change in texture from section to section shouldn't be overly jarring. (A challenge, that!)

Rhythmic texture is simple to describe. A smooth texture is one where simpler rhythms and longer notes are employed. A complex or rough texture is one with lots of syncopation, repeated notes, and notes of shorter duration.

Harmonic texture refers more to whether instruments play in unison or in harmony—and in how much harmony. A *homophonic* texture is one of unison playing; a *rich harmonic* texture is one where different instruments play different notes of the accompanying chord; and a *contrapuntal* texture is one where contrasting countermelodies are employed.

Obviously, you can combine different rhythmic and harmonic textures in your arrangement. You can use smooth rhythms with rich harmonies, or complex rhythms with unison harmonies, or vice versa. They're all tools for you to use.

Time Signature

Let's face it: most arrangements you create will be in simple 4/4 time. But common time isn't for everything, and it's up to you to decide when to employ 3/4 or 6/8 or some other time signature. And you're not limited to using the same time signature throughout a piece; it's perfectly acceptable to change time for effect.

Tempo

The same goes for tempo. You can dictate a constant tempo throughout a piece, or you can vary the tempo from section to section. (Just don't go overboard; nobody likes a piece that lurches around.)

More important is what tempo you set for the piece. Obviously, some tempos are dictated by style (jazz ballads are slow, be-bop tunes are fast, and so on). You can indicate tempo by traditional Italian tempo markings, or (even better) by noting the desired beats per minute at the top of the piece.

Key

You might think that picking a key signature is a no-brainer; you use the key that the original composition was written in.

Well, maybe you do, maybe you don't.

While it's noble to respect the original key of a piece, it might not be practical. For example, if a piece was written for a particular type of instrument, arranging the piece for a different instrumental ensemble might require changing the key to make the piece playable. The same goes for vocal works; a key that works for one singer might be totally unsingable for another. Put simply, you have to adjust the key to best match the instruments/voices you're writing for.

So if nothing else, choose a key based on the ranges of the instruments and voices for which you're writing. Make sure that the highest note of the melody is no higher than the highest note in the lead vocalist's or instrumentalist's range; also make sure that the lowest note is likewise reachable. That determines the range of the piece, and thus the usable keys you can write for.

In addition, different keys have different personalities. There's no hard science behind this, but the same piece played in the key of A sounds just a tad different when played in the key of C. Experiment with transposing the chords and melodies to different keys to get the precise feel you're aiming for.

Also know that certain keys are easier or harder for certain instruments to read and play. A general rule of thumb is that the more sharps and flats in a key, the more difficult it is to play or sing—especially for younger or less-experienced musicians. And the issue gets more complicated when you consider the transposition necessary for certain instruments.

For example, the concert key of A has three sharps, which is relatively easy for nontransposing instruments to read. But for B♭ instruments, such as trumpets, the transposed key is B, which has five sharps and is a bear to read. For that reason, you probably want to avoid arranging in the concert key of A—unless you want to give your trumpet section a real workout!

In general, you want to arrange things so no instrument is reading more than three sharps or flats. Taking this challenge into account, Table 2.1 shows the best—and the worst—keys for your arrangements:

Table 2.1   Good and bad concert keys

Good Keys	Acceptable Keys	Bad Keys
E♭	C	D♭
F	G	D
B♭	A♭	E
	G♭	A
		B

This particular consideration is less of an issue when you're arranging for professional musicians—but is still something to keep in mind.

Dynamics

Finally, we come to dynamics—the volume level of a piece. Should the arrangement be played loudly or softly? It definitely matters to the ultimate perception of a work by your listeners.

And here's where you can really distinguish yourself from less-skilled arrangers. Too many arrangements these days, especially in the popular music field, are dynamically challenged. That is, they start at one dynamic level (typically loud) and stay there.

That's fine for some types of music, but not for most. Music needs to breath, to ebb and flow, and one key way to accomplish this is by varying the volume level. Start soft and end loud. Start loud, get soft, then get louder again. Bring the volume up and down and up and down to emphasize different musical moods. Don't limit yourself to a single dynamic—play the volume level to make your arrangement come alive.

(And if the musicians performing your arrangement don't have the chops to pull off the dynamic changes, that's their problem!)

Planning the Musical Structure

Okay, now you've thought about the skill level of your arrangement, the musical style you want, the structure of the piece, and the different musical elements to employ. Now it's time to put everything together to create the working outline of your piece.

One way to create this musical outline is to literally chart it out. Create a blank table with the major sections of the piece down the left side, and the different musical elements (instrumentation, structure, etc.) along the top, as shown in Table 2.2. (Adjust the sections for your specific arrangement, of course.) When you fill in the intersecting grid, you create an at-a-glance guide to how you want your arrangement to proceed.

Table 2.2   Musical structure grid

	Instrumentation	Texture	Time Signature	Tempo	Key	Dynamics
Intro-duction						
Verse 1						
Chorus						
Bridge						
Verse 3						
Chorus						
Ending						

Flow and Contour

This structured approach to an arrangement's structure can provide useful guidance, but it overlooks one important item—the overall flow and emotional contour of a piece. After all, a completed arrangement is more than the sum of its parts. It's not just three verses, a chorus, and a bridge; it's how all those parts relate to and build upon each other.

As such, you also want to plan your arrangement in terms of how it flows from section to section, and how you build the emotional level throughout the piece. Ultimately, you want the arrangement to reach an emotional climax—not too soon, but toward the end of the piece. The whole arrangement should build to this climax, and then have a short release and relaxation afterward.

The climax of a composition is quite often its highest point, pitch-wise. The climax is also often the loudest point, and orchestration-wise, the busiest point. It's the part of the arrangement that you work toward, and that you then recover from.

If the high point of your arrangement comes too soon, the balance of the piece will appear long and drawn-out, an unwanted afterthought. You want your arrangement to peak toward the end, not at the beginning or in the middle. There should be some space after the climax where you let the piece gently wind down, but not so much as to bore the now-satisfied audience. Ask yourself what your arrangement is building toward; the answer to that question should be the musical climax, and it should sound every bit as important as it should be.

By the way, longer pieces may have more than one climax. That is, a longer arrangement might ebb and flow throughout, building and releasing small amounts of tension before the final larger climax is attained. It's this process of tension and release that holds the listener's interest throughout. If the emotional level were constant, the piece would be boring.

You create this emotional ebb and flow by using all the musical techniques at your disposal—instrumentation, texture, dynamics, and the like. In general, you build tension by increasing the complexity of the instrumentation and by increasing the dynamics; you release tension by simplifying the texture and bringing down the volume.

When you're successful, you'll carry your listeners through a satisfying musical experience. It's a journey from introduction to ending—a journey that you, as the arranger, control.

The Least You Need to Know

- The type of ensemble you're writing for may dictate the type and complexity of arrangement you create.

- It's important to structure the pieces of your arrangement beforehand—verses, choruses, bridges, and the like.

- You employ six key musical elements to build your arrangement—instrumentation, texture, time signature, tempo, key, and dynamics.

- All arrangements should have an emotional ebb and flow, and build toward a musical climax.

Harmonizing with Chords, Progressions, and Substitutions

In This Chapter

- ◆ Determining which chords to use to accompany a melody

- ◆ Understanding and applying chord leading rules

- ◆ Adding sophistication with extended and altered bass chords

- ◆ Changing the sound of an arrangement with chord substitutions

All things considered, you don't want to inordinately meddle with a piece's melody. While you *can* extend or embellish a melody (as you'll learn in Chapter 5), you don't want to change the melody too much, or it will become unrecognizable to the listener. A better choice, when you're looking to add some variety to your arrangement, is to make changes to the underlying harmonic structure—to reharmonize the piece with different chords and chord progressions.

You might be surprised at the difference a few new chords can make. Even a fairly simple melody can sound much more sophisticated when the accompanying chords are switched around. Changing a major chord to a major seventh, replacing a IV chord with a ii chord, or applying a completely different chord progression can alter the color and mood of a piece—while still maintaining the familiarity of the basic melody. For this reason, it's important for an arranger to understand how chords work—and to learn how to work with them.

Harmonizing a Melody with Chords

In almost all forms of popular music (and most forms of so-called classical music) the basic composition is a combination of melody and harmony—the harmony coming in the form of the chords that accompany the melody. The underlying chord progression propels the composition forward and, in many cases, guides the movement of the melody.

> **Note**
>
> Learn more about melodies and structural tones in my companion book, *The Complete Idiot's Guide to Music Composition* (Michael Miller, Alpha Books, 2005).

In fact, most melodies are composed of notes that exist in the underlying chords. If you examine a melody, you'll find that its main notes—what are called the *structural tones*—are often one of the three notes in the chord's basic triad. (Or, in some instances, an extended note from a seventh, ninth, or eleventh chord.) For example, the melody in Figure 3.1 is formed from structural tones from the accompanying chords.

Figure 3.1

A melody derived from the accompanying chords.

The relationship between melody and chords works the other way, too. You can, with a little practice, use the notes of a melody to construct the accompanying chord progression. This skill is quite useful to an arranger, as it helps you to create new chord progressions for existing melodies.

Deriving Chords from Structural Tones

Probably the easiest way to fit new chords to a melody is to deconstruct the melody into its most important notes—its structural tones. A typical melody will have no more than one or two structural tones per measure. (The other notes are connecting or embellishing notes.) The chord you apply to a structural tone should include the structural tone as one of the three notes of the basic triad.

For example, let's start with the melody displayed in Figure 3.2:

Figure 3.2

A typical melody, no chords applied.

When you simplify the melody to its structural tones, you get the notes displayed in Figure 3.3:

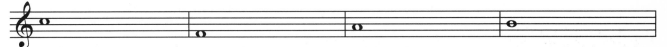

Figure 3.3

The same melody reduced to a series of structural tones.

Now comes the work of fitting chords to these structural tones. The first tone is a C, which means (in the key of C) we could apply one of three chords that include a C in the triad—F, Am, or C. We'll pick the C chord.

For the second structural tone (F), we could choose from either the F, D minor, or B diminished chords. Shying away from a parallel root-structure melody, we'll pick D minor.

As we continue on in this fashion, we can come up with any number of interesting chord progressions. Once you've assigned the chords to the structural tones, return the melody to its expanded state, and you get something like the combination displayed in Figure 3.4.

Figure 3.4

The original melody, with new chords applied.

Note that when using the structural tone method, there is no right or wrong way to decide which chords to apply. For example, I could have chosen to make the first chord an Am instead of a C, which might have led to different choices for the subsequent chords. Use your ears, and your imagination, to harmonize your melodies.

Other Tips for Harmonizing a Melody

There are other points you need to consider when fitting chords to a melody. Here are some helpful tips:

- Try some common chord changes first. You'd be surprised how many melodies fit with the I-IV-V progression!

- Generally, the slower the tempo, the more frequent the chord changes. (So if you have a long whole note, or a note held over several measures, expect to find several different chords played behind that single note.)

◆ Work backward from the end of a melodic phrase, remembering that most major-key melodies end on the I chord. You then can figure out the cadence leading to the I, and have half the melody arranged fairly quickly.

◆ Chord changes generally fit within the measure structure, which means you're likely to see new chords introduced on either the first or third beat of a measure.

And here's another important tip: most chords naturally lead to just one or two other chords. That's called chord leading, and we'll learn all about it next.

Understanding Chord Leading

Although you can create a composition using any combination of chords that sounds good to your ears—even chromatic chords or chords from other keys—most chord progressions are based on a few simple rules. These rules come from a concept called *chord leading*, which says that certain chords naturally lead to other chords.

You hear chord leading all the time, typically in the cadences that signal the end of a chord progression. One of the best examples of chord leading is the perfect cadence, where the dominant chord leads back to the tonic. That move from V to I is basic chord leading.

Table 3.1 details the inner workings of chord leading—that is, which chords lead where.

Table 3.1   Chord leading reference

These Chords ...	Lead to These chords ...
I	Any chord
ii	IV, V, vii°
iii	ii, IV, vi
IV	I, iii, V, vii°
V	I
vi	ii, IV, V, I
vii°	I, iii

So, for example, if you have a iii chord in your arrangement, you can follow it with either a ii, IV, or vi chord. Or if you have a vi chord, you can follow it with either a ii, IV, V, or I chord. And so on.

Although you don't have to follow these chord-leading rules, doing so is a relatively safe and easy way to create a pleasant-sounding chord progression. And when you break the chord-leading rules—moving from a V to a iii chord, for example—you create harmonic tension, which can be quite interesting.

Adding Sophistication with Extended Chords

Of course, chords can include more than three notes. When you get above the basic triad, the other notes you add to a chord are called *extensions*. And one of the easiest ways to make your arrangement more interesting is to embrace the use of these extended chords.

Different Types of Extensions

How do you extend a chord? Well, chord extensions are typically added in thirds. The first type of extended chord is called a *seventh chord* because the seventh is a third above the fifth; next up is the *ninth chord* (which is a third above the seventh), then the *eleventh chord* (a third above the ninth), and so on. (Figure 3.5 shows diatonic extended versions of the C-major chord, in the key of C.)

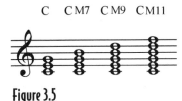

Figure 3.5

C-major 7, 9, and 11 chords.

Extended chords can be major, minor, or dominant, depending on the triads on which they're based. A *major seventh* chord takes a standard major chord and adds a major seventh on top of the existing three notes. A *minor seventh* chord takes a standard minor chord and adds a minor seventh on top of the existing three notes. A *dominant seventh* chord—sometimes just called the "seventh" chord, with no other designation—takes a major triad and adds a minor seventh on top. In other words, it's a major chord with a lowered seventh. The less-used diminished seventh chord takes a diminished triad and adds a diminished seventh (same as a major sixth) on top. (Figure 3.6 shows all the different seventh chords.)

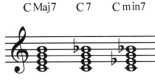

Figure 3.6

The different types of seventh chords, built from a root of C.

Extending a Progression

Once you get the hang of extending chords, you can create a very sophisticated-sounding arrangement by taking the basic triads in your chord progression and replacing them with extended chords. As an example, let's start with this very simple I-IV-I-V-I chord progression:

Track 13

C   F   C   G   C

Now we'll make each of these chords a diatonic seventh chord—that is, the form of the seventh chord that's natural within the underlying scale. So what you get is this:

CM7   FM7   CM7   G7   CM7

Sounds more sophisticated already, doesn't it? Now take the next step and change the chords into diatonic ninth chords:

CM9   FM9   CM9   G9   CM9

Very full and lush-sounding, isn't it? And it's still basically a I-IV-I-V-I progression. There's nothing fancy harmonically, save for the extended chords.

And you're not limited to using the same type of extended chord throughout a progression. You can mix and match extended chords to your heart's content—start with a simple triad, follow it with a ninth chord, then a seventh, then an eleventh, and then another triad if you want. The goal is to create harmonic interest, however you go about it.

> **Note**
>
> Another way to alter the sound of a chord is to change its inversion, or voicing—the order of notes, from bottom to top. Learn more about chord voicings in Chapter 4.

Changing the Harmonic Structure with Altered Bass Chords

Another way to add more sophisticated harmonies to your arrangement is to use *altered bass* chords. An altered bass chord is a chord that features a note in the bass different from the root of the chord. The bass note can either be another note from the chord, or a nonchord tone.

The altered bass note is notated following a slash after the chord name. For example, the notation Am7/D signifies an A minor seventh chord, but with a D added in the bass. As you can see in Figure 3.7, the D is a nonchord tone, in that it isn't part of the normal A-C-E-G notes of the chord.

> **Note**
>
> Some musicians call altered chords *slash chords* because the altered bass note is indicated after a diagonal slash mark, like this: A/B. You read the chord as "A over B," and you play it as an A chord with a B in the bass.

A m7/D

Figure 3.7

Notating an Am7/D altered bass chord.

When the altered bass note is one of the normal chord tones, then all you're doing is notating an inversion of the chord. For example, Am7/C is just the first inversion of an Am7 chord, because the C is the third of the chord. But when you use a nonchord note in the bass, you create a new chord with a much different harmonic structure.

> **Tip**
>
> You can, in theory, use altered bass notes to stick any note in the bass. In practice, however, you'll find that not all bass notes sound good when played against a given chord. You should let your ear be your guide, of course, but know that seconds and fourths of the chord typically sound better than do sixths and sevenths.

One of my favorite uses of altered bass chords is in place of a traditional V or V7 chord at the end of a phrase. Replace the V7 chord with a iim7/V altered bass chord, and you get a very sophisticated transition back to the tonic. For example, you can replace this relatively common chord progression:

C   F   C   G7   C

With this altered-bass version:

C   F   C   Am7/G   C

Track 14

A much cooler sound, don't you think?

> **Tip**
>
> You can create even more complex harmonies with *compound chords*, which stack one complete chord on top of another. You indicate compound chords by using a horizontal line between the two chord symbols, like this: $\frac{A}{D}$. (Compound chords are also sometimes notated with a hyphen between the two chords, like this: A-D.)

Adding Tension with a Pedal Point

Another way to make any chord progression more interesting is to place it over a constantly repeating bass note—what we call a *pedal point*. The pedal point creates a steady harmonic anchor, while the chord progression creates color over this tonal center. You can end up with some interesting harmonic structures just by playing a chord over a bass note that isn't included as part of the chord.

For example, let's look at a standard I-IV-V7 progression over a tonic pedal point:

Track 15

C   F/C   G7/C   C

Play this progression, and you'll hear that the repeating bass note anchors the composition to the tonic and adds tension to a somewhat-clichéd progression.

Track 16

Let's take another example, with a circular IM7-iim7-iiim7-iim7 progression played over a tonic pedal point. In the key of C, it looks like this:

CM7   Dm7/C   Em7/C   Dm7/C   CM7

This is a chord progression that sounds somewhat airy while still remaining grounded. There's a constant root to it because of the pedal point, even as it circles around and around. Some of the individual chords within the progression are quite interesting—in particular, the iim7/I (with the seventh of the chord in the bass) and iiim7/I (with the bass note existing totally outside the chord construction).

Reharmonizing a Piece with Chord Substitutions

Another widely used technique for making an arrangement sound more sophisticated is to swap out one or more chords in a progression for different chords. This is called *chord substitution*, and is a real boon when you're working with a composition that has a simple or otherwise-uninteresting chord progression.

Chord substitution is quite easy. All you have to do is take a chord, any chord, from an existing chord progression and replace it with a related chord. That's it.

The key here is the word "related." The substitute chord should have a few things in common with the chord it replaces—not the least of which is its place in the song's underlying harmonic structure. So, for example, if you replace a dominant (V) chord, then you want to use a substitute chord that also leads back to the tonic (I). Or if you replace a major chord, then you want to replace it with another major chord, or at least a chord that uses some of the same notes as in the original chord.

Diatonic Substitutions

The easiest form of chord substitution replaces a chord with a related chord either a diatonic third above or a diatonic third below the original. This type of substitution is called *diatonic substitution* because you're not altering any of the notes of the underlying scale; you're just using different notes from within the scale for the new chord. With diatonic substitution, the replacement chord has a clear relationship to the original chord—it sounds different but not wrong. That's because you keep two of the three notes of the original chord, which provides a strong harmonic basis for the new chord.

For example, the I chord in any scale can be replaced by the vi chord (the chord a diatonic third below) or the iii chord (the chord a diatonic third above). In the key of C, this means replacing the C♯ major chord (C-E-G) with either Am (A-C-E) or Em (E-G-B). Both chords share two notes in common with the C chord, so the replacement isn't too jarring.

Tip

You're not limited to substituting triads with triads. When you're substituting with a chord a third above or below, the substitute chord can be an extended chord. For example, you can replace a C-major chord with an Am7 or an Em7.

You can replace extended chords in the same manner. And because you have more notes to work with, substitute chords have more notes in common with the original chord. For example, you can replace C-major 7 with either Am7 or Em7, both of which have three notes in common with the original chord.

Caution

The further away the replacement chord is from the original, the less likely it is to fulfill the same harmonic role in the composition.

You can also replace extended chords with chords a full fifth above or below the original chord—again, because you have more notes to work with. So that C-major 7 chord can also be replaced by the F major 7 or G7 chords.

Let's work through an example. Let's say you have a fairly common I-vi-ii-V7-I progression in the key of C:

C   Am   Dm   G7   C

Using diatonic substitutions, we can turn that somewhat trite progression into something a lot more interesting:

Am   CM7   F   Em7   Am

Track 17

Dominant Seventh Substitutions

Diatonic substitutions work quite well for simple major and minor chords, but when you're dealing with dominant seventh chords—the old V7—then there are even more choices available. While you *can* do a diatonic substitution (using the diminished chords a third above or below the dominant seventh), there are more interesting possibilities, as you can see in Table 3.2:

Table 3.2   Dominant seventh chord substitutions

Substitution	Example (for the C7 Chord)
Major chord a second below	B♭ major
Diminished chord a third below	A dim
Diminished chord a third above	E dim
Major chord a second below, over the same root	B♭/C
Minor 7 chord a fourth below, over the same root	Gm7/C
Minor 7 chord a second above, over the same root	Dm7/C

To me, the most interesting substitutions here are the first one and the last two. The first substitution replaces the V7 chord with a IVM7 chord; the use of the IV chord results in a softer lead back to the I chord. The second-to-last substitution is the iim7/V altered bass substitution we examined previously, while the last substitution is a similarly tensioned vim7/V altered bass construction. Both of these altered bass substitutions provide a very sophisticated-sounding alternative to a standard dominant seventh chord.

Functional Substitutions

The dominant seventh substitutions we've just discussed are *functional substitutions*. That is, they are chords that serve the same function as the chords they replace.

The theory is simple. Within the harmonic context of a piece, different chords serve different functions. The three basic harmonic functions are those of the tonic, subdominant, and dominant—typically served by the I, IV, and V chords, respectively. But other chords in the scale can serve these same functions, even if not as strongly as the I, IV, and V.

For example, the subdominant function can be served by either the ii, IV, or vi chords. The dominant function can be served by either the V or vii° chords. And the tonic function can be served by either the I, iii, or vi chords. All these functions are shown in Table 3.3:

Table 3.3   Functional chord substitutions

Chord Function	Chords
Tonic	I, iii, vi
Subdominant	ii, IV, vi
Dominant	V, vii°

> **Note**
>
> Just in case you think you found a mistake in the preceding table, the vi chord can serve both the tonic and subdominant functions. It's a very versatile chord!

When you have a chord serving a specific function in a composition, you can replace it with another chord of the same type. So if you have a IV chord, serving a subdominant function, you can substitute any of the other subdominant-functioning chords—the ii or the vi. Along the same lines, if you have a ii chord, you can replace it with either the IV or the vi.

The same thing goes with the other functions. If you have a V chord, serving a dominant function, you can replace it with a vii° chord—or vice versa. And a I chord, serving a tonic function, can be replaced by either a iii or a vi chord—and also vice versa. It's actually a fairly easy way to make some simple chord substitutions.

The Least You Need to Know

- One of the most effective ways of changing the sound or mood of an original composition is to change the accompanying chord structure.

- New chords can be derived from a melody's structural tones.

- Chord-leading rules help guide the movement from one chord to another.

- You can make a simple chord progression sound more sophisticated by replacing simple triads with extended chords.

- Chord substitution helps you spice up a boring chord progression by replacing one or more chords with harmonically or functionally related chords.

Chapter 4

Utilizing Voicing and Voice Leading

In This Chapter

- ♦ Exploring different chord voicings
- ♦ Using open and closed voicings
- ♦ Orchestrating voicings
- ♦ Applying voice leading techniques
- ♦ Adding rhythmic interest

The simplest way to approach an arrangement is to think in terms of melody and harmony—a lead line and chords. Assign the melody to one voice or instrument, and then use the other voices or instruments to fill in the accompanying chords.

Of course, a sophisticated arrangement will end up incorporating a lot more than this, but the melody-plus-chords approach is a good place to start. It's also a good place to introduce the concept of chord voicing and voice leading—both of which are essential in the creation of any type of arrangement.

Exploring Different Chord Voicings

When you're accompanying a melody (either on a single instrument or with a group of instruments), you could just play the chords in root order—1-3-5, root on the bottom, the same from one chord to the next. But that's a bit lazy and boring-sounding, and also violates some tenets of acceptable music theory. (You don't want that many parallel intervals in a row.)

So, as any good pianist knows, you need to change up the order of the chord notes by employing different *inversions*. An inversion is just a way of playing a chord with the notes in a different order; root inversion puts the root on the bottom (1-3-5), first inversion puts the third on the bottom (3-5-1), and second inversion puts the fifth on the bottom (5-1-3). And as you've probably noticed, when you play the notes of a chord in different inversions, that chord takes on slightly different qualities.

When you employ inversions of orchestrated chords—chords assigned to different instruments in an ensemble—then you're using a technique called chord *voicing*. The order in which the chord notes are played is quite important in an arrangement. If nothing else, the note that's placed on top of the chord (the one played by the highest instrument or voice) is probably going to be heard more clearly than the other notes. In addition, the order of the notes and to which instruments they're assigned affects the color and emotional tone of a piece. So it's key that you learn the ins and outs of voicing.

As an example, let's look at a standard C-major chord played by three trombones. As you can see in Figure 4.1, you can voice the chord in its root inversion (C-E-G), which puts the root of the chord in the bottom voice; in the first inversion (E-G-C), which puts the root of the chord in the top voice; and in the second inversion (G-C-E), which sort of buries the root of the chord in the middle voice. The differences are subtle, but they're there.

Track 18

Figure 4.1

A C-major chord voiced three different ways.

Tip

All other things being equal, the outer notes in a voicing will be most prominent. In other words, the top and bottom notes in a block chord will stand out from the rest.

Voicing becomes even more interesting when you're working with extended chords. That's because you have more types of inversions to deal with. For example, a seventh chord can have a root inversion (1-3-5-7), first inversion (3-5-7-1), second inversion (5-7-1-3), and third inversion (7-1-3-5). Ninth chords have an additional fourth inversion (9-1-3-5-7), and eleventh chords have an added fifth inversion (11-1-3-5-7-9).

As you can see, the inversions of extended chords introduce a bit of dissonance, because you end up with the seventh and the root being played right together. For example, Figure 4.2 shows different voicings for a C-major 7 chord, as orchestrated for four trumpets. Listen for the seventh and the root clashing in the middle of the chord.

Track 19

Figure 4.2

A C-major 7 chord voiced four different ways.

These voicings create interesting colors—if that's what you're going for—which leads us to the topic of open and closed voicings.

Using Open and Closed Voicings

Of course, the notes of a chord don't have to be confined to standard inversions within a single octave interval. To avoid the clash of the seventh and root notes of a seventh chord, you can always spread out the notes, moving one or the other an octave higher or lower. This creates what is called an *open voicing*, where similar instruments are spaced a fourth or more apart.

Figure 4.3 shows an example of a C-major 7 chord in open voicing. When you listen to this chord, the dissonance between the root and the seventh are deemphasized, due to the relative distance between the two notes.

Tip

Closed voicings also work better at fast and medium tempos; wider voicing tends to produce a somewhat leaden effect when played rapidly.

Figure 4.3

A C-major 7 chord in open voicing.

Track 20

The opposite of open voicing is *closed voicing*. With closed voicing, similar instruments are spaced a second or third apart. As you can imagine, closed voicings impart a tighter and more dissonant sound, and serve to create a bit of tension within an arrangement.

As an example, Figure 4.4 shows the same C-major 7 chord as before, but with closed voicing. And to emphasize the effect, Figure 4.5 shows how closed voicing accentuates the tone cluster of the seventh, root, and ninth of a C-major 9 chord. (The fifth is dropped in this four-note voicing.)

Note

Closed voicing is also called *close voicing* or *tight voicing*.

Figure 4.4

A C-major 7 chord in closed voicing.

Track 21

Figure 4.5

A C-major 9 chord in closed voicing—listen to the cluster of notes in the middle of the chord.

Track 22

Closed voicings are more palatable in higher registers. In general, you want to voice your chords with wider intervals at the bottom, and tighter intervals at the top.

Voice Removal and Doubling

If you have three instruments or voices playing three-note triads, it's easy enough to assign one instrument per note of the chord. But what if these same three instruments or voices have to reproduce a four- or five-note extended chord?

Quite obviously, sometimes you have—or want—to leave some notes of a chord unplayed. It's not necessary to always voice every note of a chord. It's okay to simply imply the full harmony by sketching in some subset of the total notes available.

For example, if you want to express a four-note dominant seventh chord with just three voices, you might want to write just the root, third, and seventh, leaving out the fifth, as shown in Figure 4.6. This works because the third and the seventh express the chord's nature (major or minor in either case), and the root defines the scale tone. The fifth is the least necessary tone to express.

Track 23

Figure 4.6

A C7 chord voiced for three trumpets; the fifth is removed.

Along the same lines, it's also okay to place a single tone from the underlying chord in more than one voice. This is called voice *doubling*, and is necessary when you have more instruments playing than you have notes to play. Let's face it: if you're writing a simple three-note C-major chord for an entire orchestra to play, you're going to have to write some of the same notes twice—or three or four or five times!

For example, Figure 4.7 shows a C-major chord written for four voices. The root of the chord is doubled in the top and bottom lines.

Track 24

Figure 4.7

A C-major chord for four voices; the root is doubled.

Although it's typically the root that's doubled, you can double any of the tones in a chord. Be careful when voice-doubling, however, because the more instruments playing a given note, the weightier that tone becomes. You probably don't want more instruments playing the seventh than the root, for example, because the seventh is almost never the loudest tone. Take the chord tone that's most important at that point in your arrangement, and double that note in multiple voices.

Orchestrating Voicings

We'll get more into writing for different instruments in Chapter 6, but it's worth noting here that the instruments you assign to different voicings affect the sound of a chord. Whether you spread the notes of a chord between similar instruments in a section or between dissimilar instruments in different sections can make the difference between whether an arrangement sounds full or sparse.

Sparse Voicings

Let's take the example of a C-major chord played by a big-band horn section—saxes, trumpets, and trombones. We're going to go with a simple first-inversion voicing, where the root is on top and the third of the chord is on the bottom. But some choices remain.

For our first attempt, let's have each section play in unison, and assign one note of the chord to each section. So the trumpets (on top) play the root (C), the trombones (on the bottom) play the third (E), and the saxes (in the middle) play the fifth (G). Figure 4.7 shows what this looks like.

Track 25

Figure 4.8

A C-major chord with each section playing a single note.

As you can tell, this is a very open, kind of sparse sound. If we want it to sound slightly different, we can simply change the inversion—that is, alter which notes are played by which section. Figure 4.9 shows the same chord played in the root inversion, with the trombones taking the root (C), the saxes taking the third (E), and the trumpets now taking the fifth (G). It's subtly different; the different instrument assignments emphasize different notes in the chord.

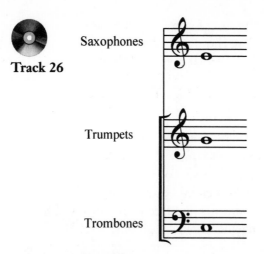

Figure 4.9

The same chord with different note assignments.

Dense Voicings

If we want a more complex sound without altering the chord at all, we can voice all the notes of the chord within each section. That is, the saxes will play E-G-C in top-to-bottom order, as will the trumpets and trombones. Figure 4.10 shows what this looks like.

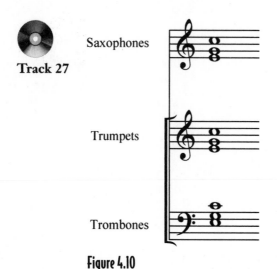

Figure 4.10

A C-major chord with each section playing the complete chord.

Sounds quite a bit different, doesn't it? It's a much fuller sound—very dense, in fact, without having to add any extended notes. That's because you have each note of the chord represented by instruments with three different tonal characteristics. This type of approach also, in effect, creates multiple voicings. The high C played by the trombone is placed below the low E of the trumpet, thus creating a multiple-note chord with lots of doubling.

Voicing Note Clusters

Now let's examine how one might deal with the challenge of note clusters, which result from closed voicings of extended chords. For our example, we'll work with a C-major 9 chord, with the note cluster of B-C-D-E—the seventh, root, ninth, and third of the chord.

If we want to emphasize the dissonance of this note cluster, we simply orchestrate all four notes in the same instrumental section in a close voicing. As you can see in Figure 4.11, it's a very jarring sound.

Track 28

Figure 4.11

A tight voicing of a note cluster for four trumpets.

If we want to deemphasize the dissonance and, instead, emphasize the rich harmony of the ninth chord, we can spread out the notes to different instruments in a more open voicing. Figure 4.12 shows one approach to this, with the notes spread between trombones, trumpets, and saxes, wide enough so that they're less jarring—in fact, the sound is quite pleasing.

Saxophones

Trumpets

Trombones

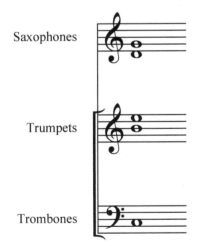

Track 29

Figure 4.12

A less-jarring open voicing, with the note cluster spread among multiple instruments.

The point here is that everything you do as an arranger and orchestrator—the notes you choose, which order you stack those notes, and which instruments you assign to which notes—has significant impact on the resulting sound. It's not nearly as simple as writing a chord in root position and assigning the instruments from lowest to highest; those same notes can sound extremely different when played in a different order, and by different instruments. Experiment and you'll hear all the different colors available.

Voicing a Chord Progression

As much fun as it can be working with different voicings, so far we've only examined voicings for a single chord at a time. But when you create an arrangement, you'll be working with lots of chords, all in a row. How do you deal with voicings when you also have to worry about creating self-contained parts for each instrument?

Remember, musicians play their parts—and listeners hear those parts—one note after another, in a linear fashion. While you might be creating your voicings "vertically," the individual parts are played "horizontally." Which means, of course, that *you* have to think horizontally as well, to create parts that have their own internal logic and melodic lines.

The challenge is not only to create individual parts that have their own interior consistency and melodic flow, but to make sure that multiple parts stack up to create the harmony and voicing you want. It's like completing a crossword puzzle; all the notes or words going one direction have to fit together with all the notes or words going the other direction.

What you have to do is think of the individual parts within the voicings you create. For example, instead of just hearing the chord accompaniment, like the one in Figure 4.13, you need to pull the individual notes out of the chords to hear each line individually, as in Figure 4.14. Then you have to ask yourself, does this part stand on its own? Is it internally consistent? Is it melodic? Can it be easily played or sung?

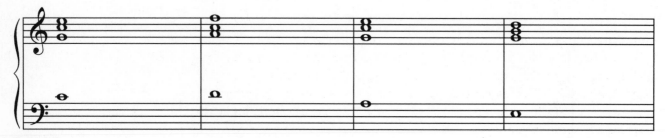

Figure 4.13

The consecutive voicings of a chord progression, expressed as a series of chord stacks.

Not only do you have to address the playability or singability of each individual line, but you also have to make sure that the lines fit together in a way that is aurally pleasing. And the more voices you write for, the more challenging it is to fit all the pieces and parts together.

Figure 4.14

The same chord accompaniment, broken out into its individual musical lines.

Then there's the issue of variety and uniqueness. The fact is, the more voices you have to write for, the more challenging it is to create distinct parts without doubling or duplicating other parts. (Not that there's anything wrong with voice doubling; it's an important technique to use when writing harmony parts.)

When you're piecing together individual parts, you have to employ a variety of different voicings to avoid parallel motion between parts and to create different harmonic textures. If each instrument always plays the same voice in a chord, all the harmony notes will move in parallel to each other as you change chords. Too much parallel movement is frowned upon because it's boring. A better approach is to vary the voicings from chord to chord so that the harmony parts don't have to move in parallel.

For example, the passage presented in Figure 4.15 uses static voicings across the entire chord progression, complete with the accompanying parallel movement—lazy writing that produces a somewhat boring sound.

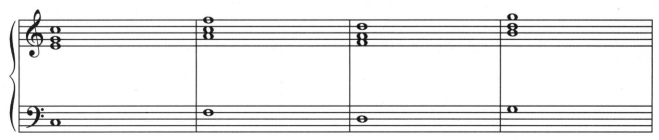

Figure 4.15

A chord progression with static voicing—lazy writing that creates a boring sound.

Track 30

A better approach is to change the voicings from chord to chord so that the same instrument isn't always playing the fifth of the chord, as an example. As you can see in Figure 4.16, it helps to create more interesting lines for each instrument or voice.

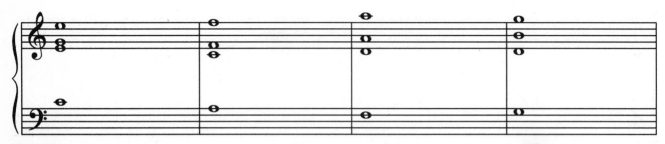

Figure 4.16

The same chord progression with varied voicing.

Track 31

Applying Voice Leading Techniques

Back to the issue of the individual lines within a harmonic accompaniment. While you're no doubt thinking of the way the notes stack "vertically," the line itself is still played "horizontally." To that end, it's important to examine the melodic lines you create for each individual instrument or voice.

Tip

A good tip when you're creating either vocal or instrumental lines is to physically sing each part yourself. If the part is boring or hard to sing, consider different inversions or swapping notes between parts. It's a fact: the best accompanying parts sound great on their own.

The lowest voice in a voicing can accept larger leaps, as long as they move along with the root notes of the underlying chord progression.

While the individual instrumental or vocal parts have to function within the voicings you create, you also need to make each line as melodic as possible, given the circumstances. If a line is particularly unmelodic or difficult to play (especially the case if you use awkward skips within the line), that line will tend to stick out—or, if it's a vocal line, it might even prove to be unsingable. If listeners can follow each instrumental line separately and have each line hold together melodically, your piece will sound much more cohesive.

One way to create a more melodic harmony line is to follow general voice-leading principles. Voice leading is what you get when you follow one harmony part from start to finish; the different intervals between the notes follow a set of conventions and act to create a pseudomelody out of the harmony line. You have to make sure that one note properly leads to the next, to avoid having the harmony line sound like a bunch of totally unconnected tones.

Let's examine some of the popular voice leading conventions.

Move Smoothly

Most often, voices should move the shortest distance possible; small movements are easier to play and sing than are big leaps. How big of a leap is too much? In traditional harmonic writing, you rarely see inner voices leaping more than an octave. Mostly they move in step-wise motion, or by leaps of a third or fourth.

For example, Figure 4.17 shows voice leading with too much skip-wise motion. Figure 4.18 shows the same chords, rewritten for smoother step-wise motion.

Figure 4.17

Voice leading with too much skip-wise motion—to be avoided.

Track 32

Figure 4.18

The same harmony, rewritten for smoother step-wise motion—a lot easier to sing or play.

Track 33

Move in Different Directions

When you're writing individual parts, you should avoid moving all the voices in
the same direction all the time. This sort of excessive parallel movement is lazy
and can sound a little boring; if some of the voices move up over the course of

a line, at least one voice should move down. Using this sort of contrary movement adds interest to the inner voices in an arrangement.

For example, Figure 4.19 shows a passage with extended parallel movement. Figure 4.20 shows the same passage, rewritten so that some of the voices move in opposite directions—which is a lot more interesting.

Figure 4.19

An excerpt with all the voices moving in the same direction—to be avoided.

Track 34

Figure 4.20

Better voice leading, with some of the voices moving in opposite directions.

Track 35

Avoid Crossing Lines

As much as you want to use contrary movement, you also want to avoid crossing lines in certain parts. Voice crossing, shown in Figure 4.21, is where one line moves up above another part, which moves down below the other part. In essence, the two lines cross.

Figure 4.21

Voice crossing—the top two parts pass each other, going in different directions.

Now, a certain amount of voice crossing is unavoidable, especially when one part is serving a primary melodic function. There's nothing wrong with that—especially if the lines are in two distinct instruments or voices. But when lines cross between similar instruments or voices, then the implied harmony gets a little muddy.

In particular, you want to avoid voice crossing within a section—by two trumpets, for example. And, when writing choral music, you also want to avoid crossing the bass and tenor lines, and the soprano and alto lines. (It's okay to have the tenor and alto lines cross, however, since the timbre of these two voices is noticeably different.)

Emphasize Common Tones

Another popular technique is to identify those notes that are the same from one chord to another—what we call *common tones*. By emphasizing the common tones between chords, you can better connect one chord to the next within a given part. When a given voice holds the same note across two (or more) chords, it creates a powerful bridge between the two chords.

For example, if you're moving from a C-major chord to an A minor to an F major and then back to the C major, the C note is common between all four chords. It's okay to have a single voice hold that note across all the chords, as the top voice does in Figure 4.22.

Figure 4.22

The common tone (C) repeated across all four chords in the top voice.

Track 36

Let Leading Tones Lead

This next voice leading guideline is right out of the melody-writing playbook. Whenever possible, you should let voices that sit on the leading tone within a scale move to the natural resolving tone—the tonic of the scale.

If you recall your music theory, the leading tone is the seventh tone of a major scale. It naturally resolves up to the tonic of the scale. So for example, if you're in the key of C major, then the leading tone is B, and it resolves up to C.

When you have a vocal or instrumental line that's holding on a leading tone, the next natural movement for that line is up to the tonic note of the scale. (Figure 4.23 shows such leading tone-to-tonic voice leading in the top voice.) While you don't have to move this line up to the tonic, it sounds good when you do.

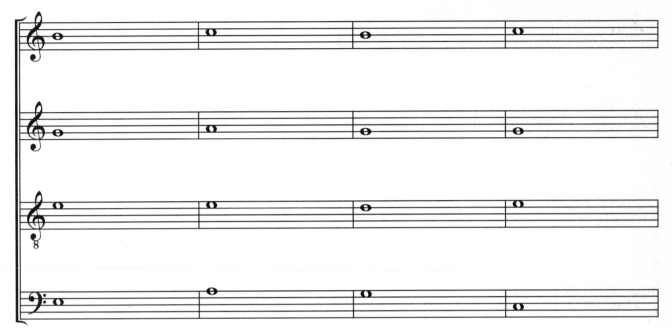

Figure 4.23

Voice leading from the seventh of the scale up to the tonic, in the top line.

Track 37

Focus on the Bass Line

It's only natural to pay attention to the parts at the top of the pile—and to place the melody on top of all the other parts. But the parts on the bottom are equally important and can often provide an interesting counterpoint to the top lines. To this end, pay particular attention to your piece's bass line; it doesn't have to simply follow your chord progression. A rhythmically and melodically interesting bass line can be the difference between an average and an exceptional composition.

For example, Figure 4.24 shows a chord progression where the bass line (in the double-bass part) strictly follows the root of the chords. Figure 4.25 offers a better approach; by giving the double bass a few notes that aren't roots, it creates a much more melodic line. (All the other parts play the same.)

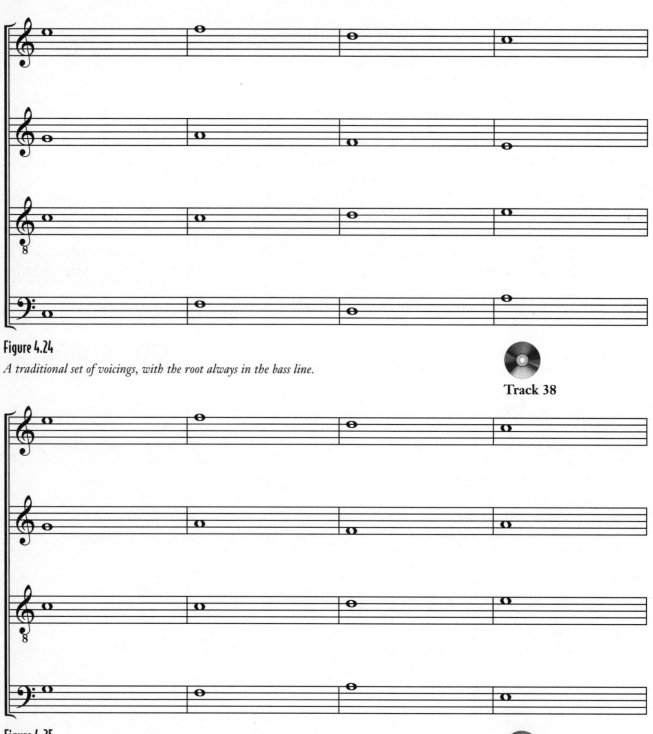

Figure 4.24

A traditional set of voicings, with the root always in the bass line.

Track 38

Figure 4.25

More interesting voice writing, with the bass line playing notes other than the roots.

Track 39

Adding Rhythmic Accompaniment

Up to this point, we've addressed the voicing of chordal accompaniment as it follows the chord progression—one voicing per chord. If you proceed in this manner, you'll have a pleasing, but ultimately static, accompaniment. Let's face it—each instrument playing a whole note every measure or so is a little boring.

There are many ways to get away from the one-voicing-per-chord trap. One approach is to simply write in a different rhythm. Instead of writing whole notes, write half notes or quarter notes or eighth notes. You don't have to get fancy. As you can see in Figure 4.26, even a series of straight quarter notes can prove interesting because this rhythm will help to propel the piece forward.

Figure 4.26

Accompanying harmonies with a quarter-note pulse.

Track 40

If you do decide to get fancy, you can use any manner of syncopation to add rhythmic interest to your arrangement. As you can see in Figure 4.27, a syncopated accompaniment is particularly effective against a smooth and slow-moving melody; the busyness in the accompaniment balances the long notes in the melody.

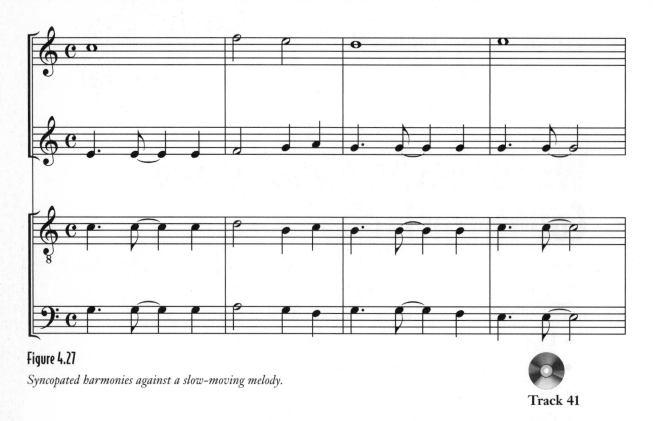

Figure 4.27

Syncopated harmonies against a slow-moving melody.

Track 41

When you have a busy melody, however, you generally don't want to clutter things up by having a busy accompaniment, too. In general, you want to play one element against the other. When the melody is static, add notes to the accompaniment; when the melody is busy, keep the accompaniment simple.

This goes not just for rhythm, of course, but also for countermelodies. When the melody is holding a whole note, that's a cue to insert a subsidiary melody in one or more of the accompanying parts. How do you add a countermelody? That's the topic for Chapter 5, so turn the page and get ready to add even more interest to your arrangements.

The Least You Need to Know

- Open voicings spread out the notes of a chord, with similar instruments voiced a fourth or more apart.

- Closed voicings emphasize more dissonant notes, with similar instruments placed a second or third apart.

- The density of a voicing can be altered by orchestrating different combinations of instruments or voices on different chord notes.

- When creating individual lines, voice-leading guidelines should be followed; avoid excessive parallel movement.

- Don't fall into the trap of writing a single voicing chord change; use accompanying parts to add rhythmic interest to your arrangements.

Chapter 5

Working with Melodies and Countermelodies

In This Chapter

- ◆ Extending an existing melody
- ◆ Embellishing and altering a melody
- ◆ Adding harmony lines
- ◆ Creating countermelodies

In the previous chapter we discussed using different voicings and voice-leading techniques to create chordal accompaniment in an arrangement. But as you learned at the end of the chapter, using nothing but block chords makes for a boring arrangement. You want to employ a variety of techniques to create a more interesting accompaniment to your main melody, from the use of rhythmic chord patterns to the construction of new and separate countermelodies—which is the focus of this chapter.

Extending a Melody

Before we get to countermelodies, however, let's take a moment to consider the main melody in your arrangement. When you're working with an existing melody, you may need to alter it somewhat—to provide some contrast when the melody is repeated in multiple sections throughout the piece, or to extend or expand it to better fit the needs of a more sophisticated arrangement.

Lengthening a melody is a nice way to fill out an arrangement, and can be achieved using a number of different techniques. In this fashion you can extend an eight-bar melody into twelve or even sixteen measures, for example. And if you do it right, the listener still hears the original melody—plus a little bit more.

One way to extend a melody is by lengthening (augmenting) the ending cadence. With this technique, you take the final measures of the melody and double the note values within those measures. A quarter note is extended into a half note, an eighth note is extended into a quarter note, and so forth. As you can see in Figures 5.1 and 5.2, this has the effect of slowing down the melody, which adds a bit of dramatic impact.

Figure 5.1

The original eight-bar melody.

Track 42

Figure 5.2

The same melody, with the final two bars extended into four, by doubling the note values.

Track 43

A similar approach is to take the existing melody and graft an additional cadence onto the end. This may be a repetition of the existing cadence, or a totally new cadence. Figure 5.3 shows an example of this technique.

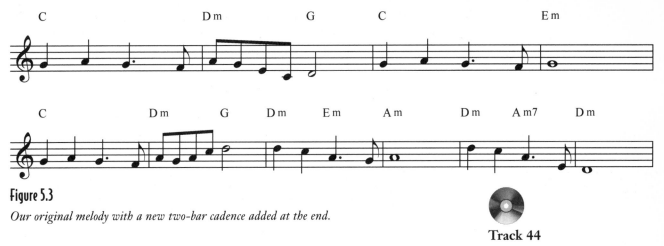

Figure 5.3

Our original melody with a new two-bar cadence added at the end.

Track 44

A different approach is to expand the melody by adding some breathing space between the main melodic phrases. As you can see in Figure 5.4, you do this by inserting rests (in this instance, with some different chords) after each internal phrase.

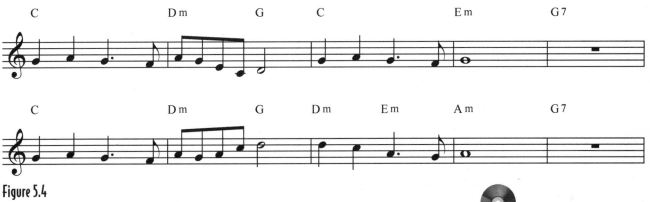

Figure 5.4

Our original melody with a new two-bar cadence added at the end.

Track 45

Finally, you can expand a melody by repeating parts of the melody—that is, repeating the inner motifs or melodic phrases. Figure 5.5 shows how this works.

continues

continued

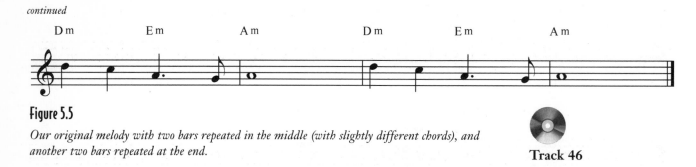

Figure 5.5

Our original melody with two bars repeated in the middle (with slightly different chords), and another two bars repeated at the end.

Track 46

Embellishing and Altering a Melody

In addition to extending a melody, you can take an existing melody and embellish it—in essence, make a simple melody more complex. The goal here is to use your arranging skills to make a simple melody more interesting, which can be accomplished in several different ways.

For example, you can take a melody that consists of a small number of long notes and embellish it by inserting additional notes between the existing structural tones. These can be connecting tones (notes that logically connect one note with the next) or leading tones (notes that lead directly up or down to a structural tone). Figure 5.6 shows our example melody embellished in this fashion.

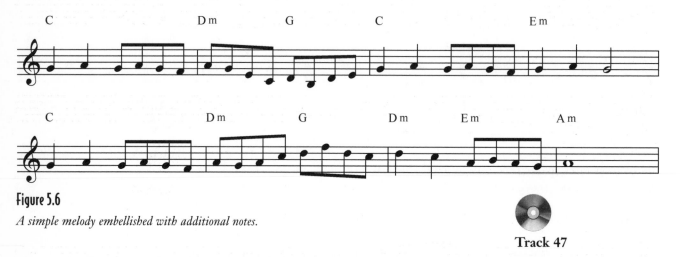

Figure 5.6

A simple melody embellished with additional notes.

Track 47

Another approach is to insert new motifs into the middle of an existing melody. You typically add these new bits at the end of existing melodic phrases, as shown in Figure 5.7.

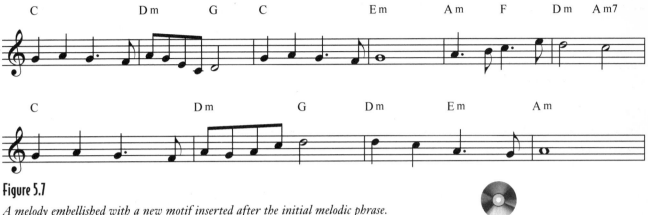

Figure 5.7

A melody embellished with a new motif inserted after the initial melodic phrase.

Track 48

Then there's the concept of melodic alteration. That is, you take an existing melody and you change it in some fashion. Maybe you remove some notes (as shown in Figure 5.8), maybe you move some notes up instead of down (Figure 5.9), maybe you syncopate the notes (Figure 5.10), or rhythmically simplify them. The goal is to subtly alter the melody to add some interest to your arrangement, while still retaining the flavor of the original melody.

Figure 5.8

An existing melody, simplified by the removal of notes.

Track 49

Figure 5.9

A melody with pitch changes.

Track 50

Figure 5.10

A rhythmically simple melody made more sophisticated via syncopation.

Track 51

Adding a Harmony Line to a Melody

Another way to add interest to a basic melody-plus-chords arrangement is to add a harmony line alongside the basic melodic line. You hear this a lot in vocal music, with a second voice singing harmony with the lead vocal, but it's also a proven technique in most types of instrumental music.

There are four main approaches to constructing a harmony line. The first approach is for the harmony line to move in parallel with the main melody, typically a constant diatonic third above or below the main line. Figure 5.11 details this approach.

Figure 5.11

Diatonic third parallel harmony.

Track 52

Tip

You can depart from the parallel third approach when that harmony is dissonant with the underlying chord. In that instance, change the harmony note to the closest chord tone.

The second approach also writes the second voice in parallel movement to the main line, but instead of keeping a constant third interval, it uses the available notes in the accompanying chord. So, for example, if the accompanying chord is a C major, the harmony voice can be either a C, E, or G—but no other note. Typically, you want to move the harmony parallel to the main melody to the next nearest chord tone. Figure 5.12 shows this approach.

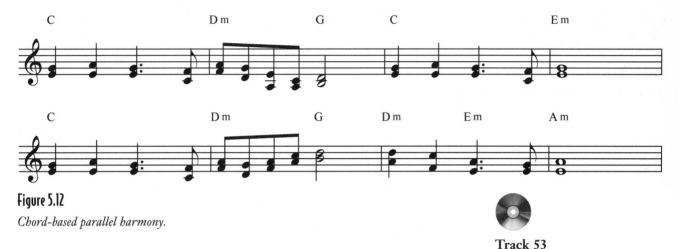

Figure 5.12

Chord-based parallel harmony.

Track 53

The third approach is similar, but instead of limiting the parallel harmony to the accompanying chord notes, it uses the notes of the relative pentatonic scale. For example, if the piece is in C major, you use the notes of the C pentatonic scale (C-D-E-G-A) as the basis for the harmony line. Again, you move the harmony line in parallel to the main melody to the nearest pentatonic tone, as shown in Figure 5.13—although some nonparallel movement is permitted, as necessary to avoid clashes with the underlying chord.

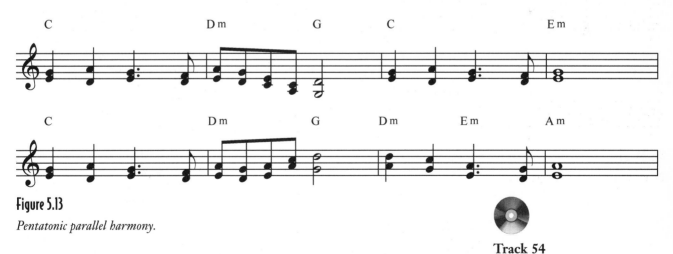

Figure 5.13

Pentatonic parallel harmony.

Track 54

Finally, you can throw parallel movement out the window and create a true countermelody in the harmony line—which we'll discuss in detail next.

Creating a Countermelody

A countermelody is a subordinate melodic line, played simultaneously with the main melody. You can write a countermelody in note-for-note rhythmic sync with the main melody, as an "answering" melody in a sort of call-and-response approach, or as an independent melody that supplements but doesn't interfere with the main melody.

Countermelody as a Harmony Line

To employ countermelody as a harmony line, you essentially write a new melody that follows the same rhythm of the main melody. You're not limited to specific intervals or tones—you can break free of the parallel third or chord tone-based harmony constrictions. All you need to do is compose a new melody, using the same rhythm as the original melody, and making sure it doesn't interfere with or overwhelm the main melody. (Figure 5.14 shows just such a countermelody harmony.)

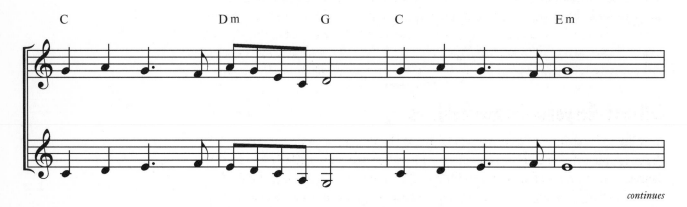

continues

continued

Figure 5.14

Countermelody as harmony.

Track 55

That isn't as easy as it sounds. First of all, you don't want the notes of the countermelody to clash with the notes of the main melody. If the main melody holds on a C, you don't want the counter melody holding on the adjacent B natural—the dissonance doesn't serve either melody well. For this reason, it's best to keep the countermelody at least a third distant from the main melody, except for the occasional passing tone.

You also want to avoid crossing melodies. If you have crossing melodies, it's difficult for listeners to retain the first melody in prominence. So if the main melody is traveling down and the countermelody is traveling up, reverse the upward movement at the point where the two lines would intersect.

And while you should strive to make the countermelody a strong independent melody—one that could stand on its own as the main melody in another piece—remember that in this piece it exists solely in service to the main melody. As such, it can't be *too* strong. The listener still has to hear the main melody as prominent, and not have his or her ears diverted to what remains a subsidiary melodic line.

Call-and-Response Countermelodies

Another approach to countermelody is to use the countermelody to "answer" the main melodic line. This is most effective when the main melody has a lot of pauses, with a series of short notes followed by a longer or held note. With this type of melody, you can use the countermelody to fill in the gaps provided by the pauses in the main melody, as shown in Figure 5.15.

Figure 5.15

Countermelody in a call-and-response function.

Track 56

When you embrace this approach, it helps if the countermelody has some melodic commonality with the main melody. For example, if the main melody ends on the dominant, use the countermelody to resolve from that dominant to the tonic. Or you can simply repeat some or all of the main melody in the answering countermelody. Let your ears be the judge. Think of the main melodic phrase as asking a question or making a statement, and the countermelodic phrase as providing the answer or balancing statement.

> **Note**
>
> In classical compositions, countermelody can also be approached in a strict contrapuntal fashion. Learn more about counterpoint in my companion book, *The Complete Idiot's Guide to Music Composition* (Michael Miller, Alpha Books, 2005).

Independent Countermelodies

Finally, we come to the most interesting type of countermelody—the truly independent melodic line. With an independent countermelody, you don't have to worry about keeping rhythmic pace or answering the main melody; the countermelody is free to weave its way in and around the main melody, as you see in Figure 5.16.

Figure 5.16

An independent countermelody.

Track 57

As with other types of countermelody, it's important that an independent countermelody doesn't significantly interfere with the main melody. Such interference can come in the form of close notes creating harmonic dissonance, or in rhythms that confuse or conflict with the rhythms in the main melody. It's a good rule of thumb to use long notes in the countermelody when there are short notes in the main melody, and vice versa.

Otherwise, you can use the voice-leading techniques discussed in Chapter 4 to help guide the construction of independent countermelodies. That means avoiding extended parallel movement, moving up when the main melody moves down (and vice versa), and so forth. You should also follow basic compositional technique, such as working from a series of structural tones and then building on those notes with connecting and embellishing tones. The goal is to create a great-sounding independent melody that enhances the main melody of the piece.

Combining Countermelodies and Other Accompaniment

Of course, you're not limited to using just one type of countermelody—or to using countermelodies exclusively. You can combine all the different types of accompaniment in your arrangements, from simple chord voicings to parallel harmony to sophisticated countermelodies. These are all just tools in the toolbox you use to create your arrangements.

For example, Figure 5.17 shows a piece with the main melody and its parallel harmony line, an independent countermelody and its own parallel harmony line, and block chord voicings behind it all. It sounds complex (and it is a bit tricky to arrange so that none of the separate parts run into one another), but it's part and parcel of modern arranging.

Figure 5.17

An arrangement with all the elements—melody, harmony line, countermelody, and block chord voicings.

Track 58

Orchestrating a Countermelody

Arranging all the melodic and harmonic elements is one thing; assigning each individual line to an instrument or voice is something else altogether.

There are many ways to orchestrate a countermelody. You can opt for using a similar instrument or voice, which works especially well for call-and-response writing. Or you can opt for a totally different tonal character, which is a good way to either emphasize the countermelody (brassy counter vs. smoother main) or subordinate the second line (soft violin counter vs. vocal main). Of course, you also have to decide just how much emphasis to give to the countermelody, which drives both the choice of instrumentation and the number of instruments you assign.

> **Tip** _____
>
> This line-splitting technique works with more than just countermelodies. You can use it to split a main melodic line between two voices, or to create very intricate rhythmic chordal accompaniment. It's like working with a jigsaw puzzle!

And here's a neat trick that I like to use in the occasional big-band arrangement. You can make a countermelody more interesting by breaking it up between two different melodic lines. That is, you assign some notes from the countermelody to one instrument or section, and other notes from the countermelody to another instrument or section. The result works especially well with highly rhythmic lines, and creates the impression of multiple counter-rhythms and countermelodies. It's actually quite fun to write—and fun for musicians to play. (Figures 5.18 and 5.19 show the original countermelody, and then how it's split between two different lines.)

Figure 5.18

The original countermelody …

Track 59

Figure 5.19

… broken into two separate-but-connected lines.

Track 60

Of course, choosing which instruments to play which parts is a crucial part of the arranging and orchestration process. To learn more, continue on to Chapter 6.

The Least You Need to Know

◆ To make a short melody fit within a longer piece, you can extend that melody, either by lengthening the final cadence or inserting extra notes or rests into the middle of the melodic line.

◆ Simple melodies can be embellished by inserting additional notes or new motifs between existing notes or phrases.

◆ Harmony lines typically move in parallel to the main melody line, either in diatonic thirds or using the underlying chord tones or pentatonic scale.

◆ Three types of countermelodies can enhance the main melody—countermelodic harmony lines, call-and-response countermelodies, and fully independent countermelodies.

Chapter 6

Deciding on the Right Instrumentation

In This Chapter

♦ Learning the essentials of orchestration

♦ Discovering general orchestration guidelines

♦ Combining instruments for different colors

Up to this point, we've covered the arranging part of the arranging/orchestration process. Now it's time to focus on the orchestration—which instruments you assign to which notes.

Orchestration is important because the instruments you choose determine how a piece will actually sound. Different instruments—and different combinations of instruments—produce different colors; it's your job as the orchestrator to choose those instruments that will best reproduce the sound colors you're trying to achieve. And when you're dealing with all the instruments of the orchestra and beyond, there are a lot of different instruments and combinations to choose from!

The Essentials of Orchestration

Before you can orchestrate a piece, you have to know as much as you can about all the available instruments and voices. The more you know about an instrument, the better you can write a part for that instrument. And the more instruments you know about, the more instruments you can choose from for your arrangements.

In particular, you need to know the following about each instrument or voice:

♦ The top-to-bottom range of that instrument or voice

♦ The comfortable range of that instrument or voice—that is, that part of the overall range that the average player can comfortably achieve

♦ How the instrument or voice sounds in each register of its range

♦ The comfortable dynamic range of the instrument or voice in each of its registers

♦ Whether the instrument sounds in concert key or is a transposing instrument

♦ Strengths and weaknesses of the instrument or voice—in particular, things that the instrument can and cannot do

♦ Specific techniques that apply to the instrument—for example, the pizzicato technique applicable to string instruments

♦ Variations possible on the instrument—for example, the various mutes one can use with brass instruments

Sound like a lot to learn? Then consider that many orchestrators spend years actually learning to play each instrument, with at least a minimal proficiency. After all, how can you expect to write a difficult part for a violin, let's say, without having personal knowledge of what is and is not possible when playing that instrument? While I don't necessarily think you need to go out tomorrow and arrange bassoon and French horn lessons, there is merit in at least laying your hands on the most popular instruments, just to get a better feel for how they tick.

Once you know how to write for each instrument, then it's a matter of choosing the right instruments for the job—which is at the heart of the orchestration process.

Understanding the Instrument Families

When choosing which instruments to use for an arrangement, it helps to know the general characteristics of each instrument family. We'll go into a lot more detail about individual instruments in the next section of this book, but for now take a look at Table 6.1, which compares and contrasts the sounds of each instrument family, by use of a numerical ranking.

Table 6.1   Comparison of instrument families

	Strength	Homogeneity	Uniformity of Register
Strings	3	1	1
Brass	1	2	2
Woodwinds	2	3	3

For comparison purposes, know that the strongest (i.e., loudest, most powerful) instruments are the brass; woodwinds and strings are less powerful. (Although, within the woodwind family, saxophones pack a particular wallop.) Strings, on the

Note

For extremely detailed and learned guidance on how to orchestrate all the instruments in the orchestra, read Samuel Adler's renowned resource, *The Study of Orchestration, Third Edition* (W.W. Norton & Company, 2002). It is, pure and simple, the definitive text on the subject—and must reading for any serious orchestrator.

other hand, are the most homogenous (they blend best together), while brass and woodwinds less so. And strings have particular uniformity of register, meaning that they retain their core sound throughout much of their range; again, brass and woodwinds produce a more varied sound from top note to bottom.

So if you need a powerful passage, enlist the brass family. For a nice blend in an ensemble passage, however, you can't go wrong with the strings. And woodwinds provide good support in both types of passages.

Note

I've left percussion and keyboards out of this comparison, as they have unique tonal characteristics—and are typically used in a much different fashion than the other instruments.

General Orchestration Guidelines

I can't cover all the intricacies of orchestration in this book; entire college degrees are dedicated to orchestration, and the pros spend a lifetime developing their skills. That said, there are some general guidelines you should keep in mind when orchestrating your arrangements:

♦ Make sure that you're writing all instruments and voices within their comfortable range. Avoid writing notes at the fringes of an instrument's range, unless specifically for effect—and unless you're writing for a mature and talented player who you know can hit the notes.

♦ When you're writing high notes for an instrument, it's best to lead up to those notes. Only the most talented musicians can hit high notes cold!

♦ The same pitch tends to sound higher on a lower-pitched instrument than on a higher-pitched one. For example, middle C played on a trombone sounds higher than middle C played on a trumpet.

Track 61

♦ Write to an instrument's strengths. Know that most instruments sound different in different registers, so choose the instrument and range appropriate to the sound you want to achieve.

♦ The larger the instrument, the less agile the instrument is. In other words, it's easier to play a faster passage on a flute than it is a tuba.

♦ When you're writing for wind players (of all types), remember that they need to rest occasionally. You should not write wind parts that are active from start to finish over the length of an extended arrangement.

♦ The need for a break is especially true when playing successive high notes on brass instruments. If, for example, you write several measures of lead trumpet at a very high pitch, give the players a few measures rest immediately afterward.

♦ Know all the different effects that can be achieved by a given instrument, and use them appropriately. For example, you need to know the sound of the different mutes that can be used with a trumpet, so you can know when to use each type of mute.

♦ Pay attention to foreground and background elements within your arrangement. Most typically, instruments playing the main melody are in the foreground, with accompaniment in the background—although, in sections where the main melody is tacit, countermelodies or other phrases may shift to the foreground. You can achieve a foreground/background balance by varying dynamics (louder in the foreground, softer in the background), rhythms, instrumentation, and instrument ranges.

♦ If all else fails, orchestrate the melody in the highest-pitched instrument or voice. To many ears, it sounds natural for the lead trumpet to carry the melody in a big band, or the first violin to carry the melody in a string orchestra, or for the soprano to carry the melody in a choir.

♦ When orchestrating a slow-moving melody against block chords or parallel harmony, work hard to make the melody more prominent than the harmony notes. This might mean placing the melody at the top of all voicings, or placing the melody in a louder or brighter instrument.

Track 62

♦ To increase the prominence of a melody, double the melody at pitch with compatible instruments, or use octave doublings with similar but different-ranged instruments, as shown in Figure 6.1. Either approach will help to fill out the sound and increase the dynamic level.

Trumpet in B♭

Trombone

Figure 6.1

Double the melody between compatible instruments—such as trumpets and trombones, at the octave—to increase its prominence.

Track 63

♦ To further emphasize the melody, orchestrate the accompaniment in contrasting instruments. For example, if the melody is played by legato strings in the lower register, orchestrate the accompaniment with short notes from higher-register brass instruments, as shown in Figure 6.2; the sharpness of the brass accompaniment emphasizes the warmth of the strings.

Track 64

♦ The melody doesn't have to be carried by the same instruments throughout its entire length. You can use a kind of tag-team approach to pass the melody between different instruments, as shown in Figure 6.3. When you swap the melody in this fashion, you should aim to achieve a seamless change by using similar-sounding instruments. You would not, for example, want to swap a melody between low flutes and high trumpets—the change would be anything but seamless!

Figure 6.2

Legato strings against a staccato brass accompaniment emphasizes the warmth of the strings.

Figure 6.3

Swapping the melody between similar instruments—clarinets and cellos.

♦ Dissonance tends to be more acute between like instruments, such as alto sax and trumpet. Conversely, if you want to deemphasize the dissonance in a note cluster, assign the different pitches to dissimilar instruments—such as alto sax and trombone.

Track 65

♦ In general, you want to voice larger intervals when writing for lower-pitched instruments.

♦ When doubling notes within a voicing, assign the doubled part to instruments that sound compatible when played together. This is especially important when the doubled part is in unison, rather than an octave apart.

♦ Don't overuse unison voice doubling. Sustained doubling can grow tiresome for the listener. It may sound better to double the part in octaves, which often provides a more brilliant—and slightly louder—sound.

♦ While you might be tempted to write certain passages in full unison, due to the powerful effect resulting from a mass of instruments playing the same line, know that not all instruments have the necessary range to play all unison passages. You may, instead, write the passage in octaves (different instruments playing the same notes an octave apart), or simply drop narrow-ranged instruments from the unison or octave (or multi-octave) passage.

- Unless you're writing for a specific ensemble, where each musician needs to get in his or her share of playing time, you don't have to use every instrument at your disposal. You should only use an instrument when it benefits the arrangement, not because it's there. Which leads to our last guideline ….

- Less is more. While you can throw the orchestral equivalent of the kitchen sink at an arrangement, you probably shouldn't. There are lots of different colors you can use, but you shouldn't use too many of them at once. Don't overload the listener; too many things going on at once can overwhelm the most important part of the piece—the main melody.

Combining Instruments for Different Colors

When you write two or more instruments in unison, the individual characteristics of each instrument begin to fade. That is, the listener hears a combined sound, rather than the sound of the individual instruments. And different instruments combine to create some very unique sound colors.

There are three different types of instrument combinations you can create—multiple instances of the same instrument, similar instruments from the same instrument family, and dissimilar instruments.

Multiple Instruments of the Same Type

Track 66

The first type of combination isn't really a combination—it's simply more than one of the same instrument, played together. For example, you could have three trumpet players playing the same note in unison. While this might not appear to be a true instrument combination, the sound of multiple players in unison is subtly different from the sound of a single player playing the same line. That's because it's virtually impossible for two or more like instruments to play perfectly in tune with each other—unless the instruments are computer samples, that is. The slight variation in pitch reduces the clarity of the line to a small degree, spreading out the resulting tone in a way that sounds slightly fuller and just a bit warmer.

Similar Instruments

Next, we have the combination of similar instruments from within the same family. For example, you could orchestrate a unison passage for clarinets and saxophones, or trumpets and trombones, or trombones and French horn, or violins and violas.

Track 67

When you combine similar instruments, what you get is a lot more of the same. It makes for a much stronger sound, while creating a kind of blended family instrument. For example, the blend of trumpet and trombone, where the trombone is in its high register and the trumpet in its low, creates a very powerful blended generic brass instrument. It's neither a trumpet nor a trombone, but is something in between—and it's quite distinctive.

Dissimilar Instruments

Track 68

Here is where the fun begins. You can create new and unique sounds by combining instruments that, at first glance, shouldn't fit well together. When you combine two dissimilar instruments, you create the sound of a new instrument that is neither the first nor the second—it's something totally unique.

Some dissimilar instruments produce a similar sound. For example, the following instrument combinations serve to emphasize a similar sound quality:

♦ Oboe and flute

♦ Trumpet and alto sax

♦ Trumpet and clarinet

♦ Trombone and tenor sax

♦ Trombone and baritone sax

♦ Trombone and bass clarinet

♦ Vibraphone and piano

♦ Xylophone and piccolo

Tip _____

When you're blending dissimilar instruments on record, the best effect comes from having two live instruments play at the same time into the same microphone. You don't get quite the same blend when the two instruments are recorded on separate tracks and then mixed together.

Other dissimilar instruments combine to create new colors. For example, you might try combining the following:

♦ Trumpet (in a higher register) and flute

♦ Flugelhorn and low-register flute

♦ Piccolo trumpet and oboe

♦ Low-register clarinet and high-register trombone

♦ Cello and low-register clarinet

♦ Viola and French horn

♦ Electric guitar and Hammond organ

Track 69

Or simply use your own imagination. Every instrument of the orchestra can be combined with any other instrument, in various registers. Some of these combinations will sound horrible; some will sound terrific. The more you experiment, the more interesting colors you can create.

Tip _____

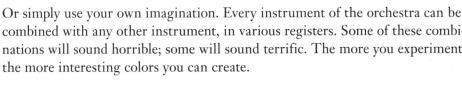

While the results are far from perfect, you can get a sense of how certain instruments sound together by using sampled instruments on your computer. The higher quality the samples, the more realistic the resulting sound will be— and it's a lot cheaper than hiring musicians to play a few notes for you.

Which leads us naturally to the issue of learning more about the sounds of individual instruments. That's what the next section of this book is about. So turn the page and get ready to digest Part II, "Instruments and Voices: Ranges and Techniques."

The Least You Need to Know

♦ Different instruments—and different combinations of instruments—produce different colors.

♦ An orchestrator must know the ranges, transpositions, sounds, techniques, and strengths and weaknesses of all instruments and voices.

♦ All instruments and voices should be written in their comfortable ranges—unless to specific effect, and for appropriately skilled players.

♦ Two or more instruments played in unison combine to create a unique sound, different from the two individual instruments.

♦ There are three distinct types of instrument combinations—multiple instances of the same instrument, similar instruments from the same family, and totally dissimilar instruments.

Part 2

Instruments and Voices: Ranges and Techniques

How high can you write a trumpet part? How does a tenor sax transpose? What instruments are available in the percussion section? Read on to learn more about all the instruments and voices you can use in your arrangements—their ranges, transpositions, and characteristics.

Chapter 7

String Instruments

In This Chapter

◆ Discover the bowed string instruments—the violin, viola, cello, and string bass

◆ Learn about the unbowed string instruments—the guitar, electric bass, mandolin, and banjo

◆ Find out how to write for the most unique instrument in the string family—the harp

When it comes time to orchestrate an arrangement, you not only need to choose the right instruments for each part, you also need to know how to write each of the instruments you choose. That means understanding how each instrument works, its range and transposition, and how it sounds in its various registers.

This section of the book provides all this information, and more, for each family of instruments. We'll start with the string family.

There are actually two different types of string instruments—bowed and unbowed. Bowed string instruments are the traditional classical instruments—violin, viola, cello, and double bass. Unbowed string instruments are those you pluck or strum—guitar (acoustic and electric), electric bass, mandolin, banjo, and the like. And then there's the harp, which is an unbowed instrument unlike any of the others. All of these string instruments are highly versatile and very popular in all types of arrangements, as you'll soon see.

Understanding Bowed String Instruments

For centuries, composers and orchestrators have written for bowed string instruments. As time has proven, these are quite adaptable instruments, equally capable of both solo and ensemble work; especially useful is the fact that their tone color stays constant over the entire range of the instrument.

Note

Violins, violas, and the like are referred to as bowed instruments because they're typically played with a bow—although they can also be plucked, for staccato notes.

Strings aren't just for classical music, of course; they can be used in just about any ensemble or genre. The top three instruments—violins, violas, and cellos—are particularly versatile, able to go from pianissimo to double forte in the blink of an eye. They're equally flexible in the sound they produce; the string section (and individual strings) can be soft and airy or broad and brawny, and everything in between.

Ranges and Transpositions

The highest voice in the string section is the violin, followed (in descending order) by the viola, cello, and double bass. The violin is written with the treble clef, while cello and double bass use the bass clef, and the viola—the oddball of the group, clef-wise—uses the alto clef. All instruments except the double bass sound as written; the double bass sounds one octave lower than written.

Table 7.1 details the ranges and transpositions of these traditional stringed instruments.

Table 7.1 Bowed string instrument ranges and transpositions

Instrument	Range (as sounds)	Range (as written)	Open strings	Transposition
Violin				Sounds as written
Viola				Sounds as written
Cello				Sounds as written
Double bass (string bass)				Write one octave above concert pitch

Common Techniques

If you plan to write a lot for strings, it behooves you to learn as much as you can about how the instruments work, in particular the various types of performance techniques. There are a lot of tricks that a string player can employ, and you want to be able to take advantage of them.

All bowed string instruments have four individual strings. While solo notes are most common—that is, these instruments typically play solo lines, not chords—two or more simultaneous notes can also be sounded, by drawing the bow across more than one string at a time. These multiple simultaneous notes are called double, triple, or quadruple stops, depending on how many strings are sounded. Use these multiple stops judiciously; they're difficult to play, and more suited to solo than ensemble playing.

On all bowed instruments, notes played on open strings sound particularly resonant, and are noticeably louder than other notes. This typically isn't a big problem, as an accomplished player will know to finger these notes so they are not open, allowing for better blending and vibrato.

A rudimentary knowledge of bowing techniques is useful if you write a lot for strings. Table 7.2 details the different types of bowing, used for all string instruments.

> **Note**
>
> While any string instrument can play multiple notes on multiple strings, it can't play more than one note at a time on a single string.

Table 7.2 Bowing techniques and notation

Technique	Notation
Traditional bowing across the strings	Arco (or no notation)
Plucking the strings	Pizzicato (pizz.)
Up-bow	V
Down-bow	⊓

Let's look at some common bowing effects:

- When you write a series of notes with no rests between, as in Figure 7.1, a string player will automatically give one bow to each note, alternating up and down for a type of legato effect.

- If you want multiple notes played on the same down-bow or up-bow, tie the notes together, as shown in Figure 7.2.

- To create a staccato effect, as notated in Figure 7.3, the player alternates short up- and down-bows.

- For an effect that is neither staccato nor legato, but rather a combination of the two, put legato marks over each note, as shown in Figure 7.4. This is called *détaché*; the player will play these notes without the bow ever leaving the string, which is a highly dramatic effect.

- For a heavily accented sound, notate consecutive down-bows, as shown in Figure 7.5.

- Bowed tremolo, which is different from a trill, is indicated as shown in Figure 7.6. With bowed tremolo, the bow is moved rapidly back and forth across the string; the pitch is constant.

> **Tip**
>
> There is normally no need to mark individual up-bows and down-bows, unless you want a specific bowing or effect.

Figure 7.1

This passage is played with alternating up- and down-bows.

Figure 7.2

The notes in this passage are played on the same up- or down-bow.

Figure 7.3

This passage is played with short alternating up- and down-bows.

Figure 7.4

The notes in this détaché passage are played with the bow never leaving the string.

Figure 7.5

Consecutive down-bows create a heavily accented sound.

Figure 7.6

A passage with bowed tremolo.

Note that short tones played with separate bow strokes sound louder than long tones on a single bow.

Finally, just as brass instruments have mutes, so do string instruments. A string mute produces a somewhat hollow, almost haunting sound. You indicate the use of a mute by inserting the word "mute" or "*sordini*" into the part.

Examining Individual Bowed String Instruments

While all the bowed string instruments share common bowing techniques, there are some important differences between the instruments. Read on to learn about each of the bowed instruments, individually.

Violin

The violin is the soprano voice of the string section. It is often used as the lead voice in ensemble passages but is also extremely versatile as a solo instrument.

It's difficult to imagine a piece for strings that doesn't use the violin. A typical string quartet uses two violins (along with a single viola and cello), and is a common way to add strings to popular music, without going overboard on a whole orchestra. And the concept of two violin parts carries over to orchestral music; a typical orchestra has both first and second violin sections, for a massed sound.

Solo violins are also widely used for melodic accompaniment in country, bluegrass, folk, and some popular music. This type of "fiddle" accompaniment is often improvised.

As with all bowed string instruments, the highest range on any violin string is difficult to control. Beyond the seventh position, the spaces between the fingers on the left hand become progressively smaller, making positioning and control more problematic. As such, be careful about writing for the violin in its very highest register; such playing can be accomplished well only by skilled professionals.

> **Note**
>
> The violin has had some popularity as a solo instrument in jazz, notably in the so-called "gypsy jazz" genre popularized by Stéphane Grappelli.

Viola

The viola is the alto voice of the string section. While only a little larger than a violin, it sounds considerably darker than its sibling, more full-bodied, and slightly lower in pitch.

The viola is equally versatile in terms of range and effects. The pairing of one or two violins with a viola creates a richer, fuller sound than just the violins alone. The viola is also useful when doubling the cello, using its lower register. In most instances, the viola is used as the inner voice in chord voicings.

And remember—unlike the other string instruments, the viola reads in alto clef.

Cello

The cello is the tenor voice of the string section. It produces a very warm and lyrical sound, especially in the middle and higher registers. This makes the solo cello a wonderful instrument to use for melodic accompaniment and counter-melodies, in addition to its traditional role as the middle or lower voice in chord-based accompaniment.

Each string on the cello has its own unique tonal quality. Notes played on the lowest, or C, string produce a very rich and sonorous bass. Notes on the G string are the least strong, and carry less well than the other strings. Notes on the D string are perhaps the most lyrical, with a quite beautiful and melodious sound. Notes on the top, or A, string are brilliant and piercing. Write accordingly.

Double Bass

The double bass is, not surprisingly, the bass voice of the string section. It can be bowed or plucked—in fact, it's more often plucked than are other string instruments. Its tone is more similar to that of the cello than to its cousin, the electric bass guitar.

The double bass typically plays the bass notes of a chord, and sometimes doubles the cello part in ensemble passages. It's not a very nimble instrument, as you can imagine, so don't write a lot of rhythmicly complex or fast notes.

> **Note**
>
> The double bass is also called the string bass, contrabass, or bass viol.

In jazz and popular music, the bass is seldom bowed; instead, it's plucked with the sides of the fingers in a form of pizzicato. Some players like to "slap" the bass, by pulling the strings away from the fingerboard and then releasing them so that they bounce off the fingerboard, which produces a metallic click.

Despite the bass's impressive size, it's actually a fairly soft instrument, primarily because its range is so low. To overcome this dynamic limitation, the typical orchestral bass section includes between four and eight bassists; in jazz and popular music, the instrument is typically amplified. If you're writing solo passages for the instrument, keep the other instrumentation relatively light so as not to cover up the sound.

When writing in the upper range of the instrument, it's best to move in single steps or small skips, rather than larger leaps. That's because the bassist has to reorient his left hand when approaching the upper register, which is somewhat difficult due to the length of the strings.

Some double basses come with a *C extension*, which extends the lowest string down to a low C. This extension is actually an extra section of fingerboard mounted over the head of the bass, which requires the bassist to reach back over the pegs to play. It's probably best not to assume the C extension in your arrangements, unless you're writing for a particular player.

Understanding Unbowed String Instruments

Violins and violas aren't the only stringed instruments out there. The guitar, mandolin, ukulele, and banjo are all technically part of the string family, as is the harp. Unlike the bowed instruments, all these instruments produce a sound when plucked or strummed.

Ranges and Transpositions

Table 7.3 describes the ranges and characteristics of the guitar and its fellow unbowed string instruments.

Table 7.3 Unbowed string instrument ranges and transpositions

Instrument	Range (as sounds)	Range (as written)	Open strings	Transposition
Guitar (acoustic and electric)				Write one octave above concert pitch
Mandolin				Sounds as written
Banjo				Write one octave above concert pitch
Electric bass				Write one octave above concert pitch
Harp			N/A	Sounds as written

Common Techniques

The guitar and similar instruments can be either plucked or strummed, using either the fingers or a pick. Most of these instruments, unlike the bowed instruments, are fretted, which makes it easier to find particular notes on the neck of the instrument. (Frets are positioned a half step apart.) It also makes it less easy to perform slides and glissandos with the left hand, although notes can be "bent" up a half step or more simply by pulling or pushing the string with the left-hand finger.

When playing in difficult keys, some players will use a *capo* to essentially transpose the guitar upward in half steps. The capo is placed on the fretboard, and enables the player to play in a higher key without changing her fingering.

A rounded piece of glass or metal, called a *slide*, is used in some blues, country, and rock music to produce a glissando effect between notes. There exists a dedicated *slide guitar* or *pedal steel guitar*, which is an electric instrument used exclusively for slide effects.

Examining Individual Unbowed String Instruments

Not all guitars or guitar-like instruments are the same. Some have four strings, some have six, and some have twelve. Read on to learn more about the individual instruments.

Guitar

There are many types of guitars, both acoustic and electric, six- and twelve-string. The basic guitar (acoustic or electric) has six strings; a twelve-string guitar doubles each of these strings at the octave, for a fuller, more ringing sound.

> **Note**
>
> Learn more about guitar notation in popular music in Chapter 13.

All guitars can play single lines or full six-note chords. Guitar parts can be written with notes on staves or, if you just want a strummed rhythm, by using the type of chord notation with slash notes shown in Figure 7.7.

Figure 7.7

Typical chord notation for a guitarist; the chord symbols can either be simple or accompanied by fingering charts.

Guitar parts can also be written in a special type of notation called *tablature*, shown in Figure 7.8, in which each string has its own line on the clef. When writing tablature, you indicate specific left-hand fingerings for each string.

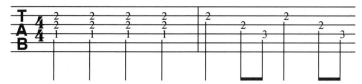

Figure 7.8

Guitar tablature; each line represents a specific string.

Acoustic guitars are used in all types of popular music, from folk and country to rock and blues. While typically used for chord accompaniment, it can also be written as a solo instrument—although it may need to be mic'd, due to it's relatively soft sound.

The electric guitar is even more versatile than the acoustic guitar, due to the almost-limitless number of sounds possible from all the various combinations of guitar bodies, strings, amplifiers, and effects boxes and pedals. An electric guitar can sound funky, chunky, buzzy, or twangy—or any other type of sound you can imagine. An electric guitar used primarily for chord accompaniment is called a *rhythm guitar; lead guitars* are used to play solo lines.

There are all manner of effects available by applying different playing techniques. The most popular of these guitar techniques are detailed in Table 7.4.

Table 7.4   Popular guitar techniques

Technique	Description	Tablature notation
Bend	The string is bent with the left-hand finger, sliding the pitch upward	
Hammer-on	The first note is plucked; then a second note is hammered at a higher fret	
Natural harmonic	The string is touched lightly at the written fret; then the string is plucked	
Palm mute	The string is touched slightly with the palm of the right hand, thus dampening the note	

continues

Table 7.4   Popular guitar techniques   (continued)

Technique	Description	Tablature notation
Pinch harmonic	The string is picked; then the edge of the thumb touches the edge of the string	P.H.- - - -¦
Pull-off	The first note is plucked; then a second note is pulled at a lower fret	P
Slide	The left-hand finger slides to another fret without moving off the fretboard	
Vibrato	The string is bent upward and pulled back to its original position, rapidly and repeatedly	

Electric Bass

The electric bass is, as the name implies, a mashup of an electric guitar and an acoustic double bass; it looks like an electric guitar, but it sounds like a double bass.

The sound of the electric bass is similar to that of the traditional double bass, but more full-bodied and obviously louder. The electric bass is typically used in place of the acoustic bass in modern jazz and popular music. Unlike the upright bass, the instrument is almost exclusively plucked.

Bass lines can be written out, or the bassist can be allowed to create his own lines from chord notation. Improvised bass lines are most common in jazz, but also common in other forms of popular music.

Mandolin

The mandolin is a smaller instrument with eight strings, tuned in pairs. The strings are pitched like the strings of a violin.

The mandolin is best used for solo lines rather than chords, either doubling the melody or as a single-line accompaniment. Sustained notes are typically played with a tremolo effect, either by playing the same note or playing two unlike notes on two adjacent strings.

Banjo

The banjo is an instrument with an interesting round body. The body itself is hollow, with a plastic or calfskin drumhead stretched across it. The traditional banjo has five strings and produces a distinctive percussive sound; it's typically used in bluegrass, folk, and other traditional types of music.

The high G string, called the thumb string, is a short string connected to an outside peg on the instrument. It is typically used for drones and similar effects.

Note
The tenor banjo is similar to the regular banjo, except it has just four strings and it's written one octave above concert pitch.

Harp

And now we come to the most unique of all string instruments, the harp. The harp is kind of like a piano, but more vertical, although its strings are plucked (like a guitar) rather than struck.

The sound of the harp is darkly colored in its lower two octaves, lightening progressively up the range. The middle two octaves are very rich and warm; the upper octaves are light and clear, but without much of a dynamic range or sustaining power.

Music for harp is notated on a grand staff, just like music for piano, with both bass and treble-clef staves. Chords may be arpeggiated or played in block fashion. Since the harpist never uses her little fingers, chords can have a maximum of eight notes.

Tuning on the harp is accomplished by means of foot pedals. With all open strings (all pedals up), the harp is tuned to C♭ major. All strings for a given note are controlled by a single pedal; when the C♭ pedal is depressed one notch, for example, the entire series of C♭ strings becomes a C-natural series. Therefore, you can't play natural notes in one octave and chromatics in another.

Different dynamics are accomplished solely by how hard the strings are plucked. Different tones are produced by different finger positions; plucking with the middle of the finger produces a warm tone, while plucking with the end of the finger produces a bright (and slightly louder) tone.

The harp is ideal for playing single lines, octaves, arpeggios, and glissandos. By default, all chords are rolled unless a bracket ([) precedes the chord; this indicates that the chord is to be played unbroken, or "flat." To indicate a slow arpeggio, place a wavy line before the chord, as shown in Figure 7.9.

Perhaps the most-used effect on the harp is the glissando. You notate the glissando in traditional fashion, as shown in Figure 7.10, giving both the starting and ending pitches.

Figure 7.9

Rolled chord notation for harp.

Figure 7.10

Notating a glissando for the harp.

The Least You Need to Know

◆ Bowed string instruments include the violin, viola, cello, and string bass, and can be both bowed or plucked.

◆ Bowed string instruments can be used for both ensemble and solo passages; the most versatile of these instruments are the violin and cello.

◆ Unbowed string instruments, such as the guitar and mandolin, are plucked or strum, rather than bowed.

◆ Guitars can be used for strummed chordal accompaniment, or to play solo lines.

◆ The harp is typically used to play arpeggios and glissandos.

Chapter 8

Brass Instruments

In This Chapter

◆ Discover the brass instruments used in the orchestra, concert band, marching band, and jazz band

◆ Learn how to notate specific articulations and effects

◆ Discover how drum corps brass instruments differ from other brass instruments

Brass instruments are wind instruments, typically made of brass, that utilize a mouthpiece (instead of a reed) and three or four valves or a slide to create different tones. The trumpet is the brash and annoying younger brother of the brass family, the trombone is the more stable older brother, and the tuba is the not-always-serious uncle. Also hanging around is the weird foreign relation, the French horn, and a few other unusual relatives, such as the baritone horn.

You can arrange for brass instruments in all types of music, from traditional orchestras to concert bands, marching bands, and jazz bands. They're also widely used in popular music, particularly in old-school soul and rhythm & blues music. And then there's the drum and bugle corps, in which brass instruments are half the ensemble.

In other words, you can't be a professional arranger and *not* use the brass family.

Understanding Concert and Orchestral Brass Instruments

Brass instruments commonly found in the orchestra include the trumpet, French horn, trombone, and tuba. Concert bands and marching bands add the baritone horn to the mix. Jazz bands and smaller ensembles tend to stick to trumpets and trombones only. Read on to learn more about the members of the brass family used in these types of ensembles.

> **Note**
>
> Drum and bugle corps use a completely different brass instrumentation, consisting of all front-firing instruments in a single key—which we'll address in the "Understanding Drum and Bugle Corps Instruments" section, later in this chapter.

Ranges and Transpositions

Concert and orchestral brass instruments run the gamut from concert pitch to various nonconcert transpositions. There's no general rule to apply; you have to learn each instrument separately.

Table 8.1 details brass instrument ranges and transpositions.

Table 8.1   Brass instrument ranges and transpositions

Instrument	Range (as sounds)	Range (as written)	Transposition
Piccolo trumpet (B♭)			Write a minor seventh below concert pitch
Trumpet (B♭)			Write a major second above concert pitch
Cornet			Write a major second above concert pitch
Flugelhorn			Write a major second above concert pitch
French horn			Write a perfect fifth above concert pitch (on treble clef)
Baritone (concert)			Sounds as written on bass clef; on treble clef, write a major ninth higher than concert pitch

Instrument	Range (as sounds)	Range (as written)	Transposition
Trombone			Sounds as written
Bass trombone			Sounds as written
Tuba			Sounds as written

Common Techniques

Smaller brass instruments, such as the trumpet, are quite nimble. Larger instruments, such as the tuba, are less so. It has to do with the amount of air required to sound a tone; the larger the instrument, the more air necessary, and the less resulting facility and speed.

Across the brass family, know that long tones tend to sound louder than short tones. Higher tones, of course, are the most prominent. Trumpets and trombones are the loudest members of this family, nearly equal in power, while French horn, tuba, and other brass instruments are considerably less powerful.

Brass instruments are capable of the same special effects found on other instruments, although a few effects are particularly used in the brass section. These include the shake, fall, glissando (or slide) up and down, growl, and upward "doit" (gliss upward after hitting a note, to a nonspecific pitch), all notated in Figure 8.1.

Figure 8.1

Brass articulations—shake, fall, glissando down, glissando up, growl, and "doit."

The sound of most brass instruments can be altered in interesting ways by inserting different types of mutes in the instruments' bells. The following are the three primary types of mutes.

Note

The Harmon mute is available for trumpets and trombones only, not for French horns and other brass instruments.

♦ **Cup mute.** This mute, which looks like a small cup or hat, is the softest of the mutes. It produces a soft and mellow sound, and helps any brass instrument blend better with other instruments, especially woodwinds.

♦ **Straight mute.** This is a longish mute that creates a piercing or biting sound.

♦ **Harmon mute.** This specialty mute produces a kind of thin, hollow, slightly chilling effect that, while distant-sounding, pierces through the other instruments. It is built with a nozzle that can be pulled in or out as desired.

In addition, trumpets and trombones can use both rubber plungers and plastic cups to further alter their sound. You indicate the use of a mute by a + sign above the note, as shown in Figure 8.2; an open (nonmuted) sound in a muted passage is noted with a circle above the note.

Figure 8.2

Muted (+) and open (○) notation.

Brass mutes work best when the instrument is played in a medium or high register. You should allow a few bars before and after the use of a mute, to give the players enough time to insert or remove the mutes from their instruments.

Examining Individual Brass Instruments

Most brass instruments are valved—but not all. Read on to learn more about the individual instruments of the brass family.

Piccolo Trumpet

The piccolo trumpet has the highest register of any brass instrument, producing a clear and piercing sound. It's a very agile instrument, but best used sparingly. Good examples of the piccolo trumpet include use in Bach's Brandenburg Concerto and the Beatles' "Penny Lane."

Trumpet

The trumpet is the soprano instrument of the brass family, and as such is often used to perform higher passages, as well as passages that demonstrate its entire range. The instrument's comfortable range extends to the concert B♭ above the staff, but skilled players can extend that range to the next F, or higher.

As the most flexible voice in the brass family, the trumpet is equally effective at both loud and soft dynamic levels. Its sound is extremely loud and powerful, and the instrument itself is very agile, capable of playing very fast passages. All types of attack and articulation are possible, with great definition. In addition, some interesting colors can be produced with various types of mutes.

Trills are executed by manipulating the valves, except in higher registers, where trills can be played by moving the lips. Try to avoid trills that involve two valves, which are awkward to play.

Writing three or more trumpets together in unison provides a very powerful sound. Also powerful is splitting the section to write in parallel octaves; this provides a bit more body to the line.

When you write multiple trumpets in unison, playing in their lower register with cup mutes, you get a sound similar to that of a French-horn section. This is a nice sound for accompaniment in ballads and softer passages.

In jazz band writing, it's common to use trumpets and trombones together, typically in the middle register, for short rhythmic accents. Write these notes staccato and, for added punch, accented.

> **Caution**
>
> More than with other brass instruments, always consider endurance when constructing a trumpet part. Trumpet players must rest their lips, especially following high-note passages.

Cornet

The cornet is similar to the trumpet, but with a slightly mellower tone. Not widely used, you can find cornets written in some older European music (especially in theater orchestras) and in some military bands.

Flugelhorn

The flugelhorn is a trumpet-like instrument that produces a mellow, lush sound. It's a darker, rounder tone than its brother the trumpet—more similar to that of the French horn, but with a trumpet's agility. It blends well with woodwinds, strings, trombones, and other low brass.

You typically find the flugelhorn in concert bands, some orchestral music, and jazz bands. It's particularly effective when used to carry the melody in ballads.

French Horn

The French horn is a distinguished member of the orchestra, and of most concert and marching bands. It produces a naturally cool sound, good for long, sustained passages. Note, however, that it's an instrument that requires talented performers; put simply, the French horn is a difficult instrument to play well. And as it's a relatively slow-speaking instrument, the French horn is not well-suited for fast passages.

When writing for French horn, know that it can serve as the bridge between sections, as it is louder than most woodwinds but softer than other brass instruments. It's also good in combination with other brass instruments; one particularly pleasing instrument combination is that of French horns and trombones, especially on sustained passages.

Tip

Also available is the half-stop, where the player puts his hand only part-way into the bell of the instrument.

Note

There's a related but quite different instrument found in drum and bugle corps that is also called the baritone. Don't confuse the two.

The French horn is also useful as a doubling instrument. The horn can double just about any line in unison, both loud and soft; it can easily double trombone, woodwind, and string passages. The result injects a particular color to the overall sound.

One interesting special effect is achieved by the player putting his hand into the bell of the horn. This is called a *stop*, and is indicated by + sign above the note. (This is the same notation as used for muted notes.) The effect is somewhat dramatic, both strained and muffled.

Baritone Horn

The baritone horn is a band, not an orchestral instrument. That means you'll find it in concert and marching bands, where it's often written along with the trombone or French-horn parts. It can be written in either treble or bass clef.

The baritone is a mellow yet agile instrument that blends well with other brass and woodwind instruments. In sound, the baritone is somewhere between the bright tones of the trombone and the mellower tone of the French horn.

Trombone

The trombone is a solid and versatile member of the brass family, found in both orchestral and band settings. Surprisingly lyrical in the upper registers, it can also play "bleating" bass notes in the lower octaves. It serves as the backbone of the brass section, and blends well with French horns, saxophones, and other woodwinds.

Unlike other brass instruments, the trombone doesn't have any valves; instead, notes are produced by moving the slide to different positions. When writing for the trombone, it's important to learn these slide positions, to avoid difficult notes and transitions.

There are seven positions of the trombone's slide; each position changes the pitch one half step from the previous position. The seventh, or furthest-out position, is obviously the most difficult to play. You need to avoid rapid note combinations that shift from the seventh to the first (full-in) position, as it's almost impossible to quickly make that change. Additionally, seventh-position notes are difficult to sustain and control. In particular, avoid the low E and the B a fifth above that, both of which are difficult seventh-position notes.

Trombones can provide a surprisingly pretty accompaniment to a vocal or instrumental solo. You can even use close voicings in the upper part of the trombone's range, which can be quite effective. Use a more open voicing to create a rich, organ-type backing.

For big, fat special effects, write to one of the trombone's four pedal tones, illustrated in Figure 8.3. A pedal tone is the fundamental of a slide position, and they're seldom used in orchestral music. These aren't soft notes; to be effective, the player must really belt them out.

Figure 8.3

Trombone pedal notes.

Bass Trombone

The bass trombone is an infrequently used variation on the traditional tenor trombone. It's used almost exclusively for very low bass passages, as it has a warmer sound in its lower register than the normal trombone.

As with the tenor trombone, beware of the physical difficulty of playing notes in specific positions, particularly low E and B. Moving from seventh-position B to first-position B♭ is also particularly problematic.

Tuba

The tuba is the bass voice of the brass family. It's a surprisingly versatile instrument, not just for the lowest of the low notes. For example, the tuba can be used as a solo voice in the upper registers, where it can be quite agile with a smooth tone.

The tuba is more typically used as an ensemble instrument. It blends well with other low-register instruments, such as cellos, double basses, bassoons, and other low woodwinds. It's also common to write the tuba in octaves with trombones, or as a bass voice in a French-horn ensemble. To create a very thick texture, write multiple tubas in octaves.

Understanding Drum and Bugle Corps Instruments

The modern American drum and bugle corps uses a different family of brass instruments, similar to the concert/orchestral brass but unique in their own ways. Not surprisingly, all drum and bugle corps instruments are derived, wholly or in part, from the traditional brass bugle.

All drum corps brass instruments have front-facing bells and three valves. Until recently, all drum corps instruments were pitched in G; recent rule changes allow for the introduction of instruments in F and B♭, as well.

Writing for drum corps brass is similar to writing for marching band brass. There are five core instruments in the corps, filling the soprano, alto, tenor, baritone, and bass voice slots—in order, the soprano bugle, mellophone, baritone, euphonium, and contra bass.

When writing for drum corps, traditional voicing is to split these instruments into nine separate parts.

- Soprano 1 (lead)
- Soprano 2
- Soprano 3
- Mellophone 1
- Mellophone 2

- Baritone 1
- Baritone 2
- Euphonium 1
- Euphonium 2
- Contra bass

Bigger horn lines can have a split lead soprano part, a third baritone part, and a second contra bass part.

Soprano Bugle

A soprano bugle, sometimes just called the soprano, is a drum and bugle corps instrument that closely resembles the B♭ trumpet, but with a narrower bell flare and larger bore. As its name implies, it serves as the soprano voice in multi-voice arrangements.

The soprano is evolved from the traditional military bugle. Unlike the bugle, however, today's sopranos have three valves and are typically pitched in G—although B♭ and F transpositions are becoming more common. Its range is similar to that of the B♭ trumpet, raised a minor third.

In a modern drum and bugle corps, the soprano line will consist of 20 to 24 instruments, typically broken into three parts.

Mellophone

The mellophone is the bell-front French-horn equivalent in drum and bugle corps music. It's the alto voice in the ensemble, typically pitched in G for drum corps use. (It can also be pitched in F, like the French horn.) The fingerings are those of the trumpet, however, not the French horn.

A typical drum corps line has 10 to 12 mellophones, in two parts.

Baritone

The drum corps baritone should not be confused with the concert-band baritone. This baritone is a three-valve, front-firing instrument that looks more like an overgrown trumpet than it does its concert-band brother. It shares a similar range to the concert baritone, however.

Despite its name, the baritone is actually the tenor voice of the corps. It can be pitched in either G or B♭, and has a mellower sound than the other drum corps brass. A typical drum corps line has 12 to 16 of these instruments, in one to three parts.

> **Note**
>
> Some drum corps have recently started using B♭ trumpets instead of sopranos.

Euphonium

The euphonium is kind of a tenor tuba or an overgrown baritone horn, and it fills the baritone (high bass) role in the ensemble. Like all drum corps brass instruments, it's a three-valved front-firing instrument; its tone is mellower than the soprano and mellophone, although not as mellow as the baritone.

Euphoniums can be pitched in either G or B♭. The instrument's range is similar to the trombone, and it can be written in either the treble or bass clef. A typical drum corps line has four to eight euphoniums, in one or two parts.

Contra Bass

The contra bass is essentially the drum and bugle corps version of the tuba, configured so that it can be carried over the shoulder with the bell firing forward. It fills the bass role in the ensemble, shares the same range as the concert tuba, and can be pitched in concert pitch, B♭, or (most typical for drum corps use) G. A full-size drum corps line will have 10 to 12 contras.

The Least You Need to Know

- Brass instruments used in the orchestra include the trumpet, French horn, trombone, and tuba.

- Brass instruments used in concert and marching bands include the trumpet, French horn, baritone horn, trombone, and tuba.

- Only the trumpet and trombone—and the occasional flugelhorn—are used in jazz bands.

- Drum and bugle corps use special front-firing three-valved instruments, typically pitched in G—the soprano, mellophone, baritone, euphonium, and contra bass.

Chapter 9

Woodwind Instruments

In This Chapter

♦ Discover the three different types of woodwinds—flutes, single reeds, and double reeds

♦ Learn about the different types of clarinets and saxophones

♦ Find out which woodwind instruments are most often used in specific types of ensembles

The woodwind family is one of the most versatile families in instrumental music. The types of instruments range from the mellow flute to the reedy oboe to the biting saxophone to the jolly bassoon.

If you want soft and sweet, there's a woodwind grouping that will do it. If you want hard and rocking, there's a different woodwind grouping available. The family is that versatile. Virtually any sound you want can be found somewhere in the woodwind section.

Understanding the Woodwind Family

Some woodwind instruments are made of brass; some are made of wood. But all (except the flute and piccolo) use a vibrating wooden reed to produce their sound. (The flute and piccolo produce sound when you blow across an open hole, kind of like blowing across a soda bottle.)

There are many different woodwind instruments, including flutes and piccolos, at least four different types of saxophones, a variety of clarinets, the unique-sounding oboes and bassoons, and even the less-common English horn (which isn't a horn and isn't even English—it's actually an alto version of the oboe). Woodwind instruments primarily use the treble clef, although the bassoon and contrabassoon both use the bass clef.

Woodwind instruments fall into three main groupings—flutes and piccolos, double reeds (oboes and bassoons), and single reeds (clarinets and saxophones).

Note that saxophones are a clearly distinct subfamily from their fellow wood-winds, with unique characteristics among all types of saxes.

Ranges and Transpositions

With the exception of flutes, piccolos, and oboes, woodwinds are transposing instruments. The following table describes the ranges and transpositions of these woodwind instruments.

Table 9.1   Woodwind family ranges and transpositions

Instrument	Range (as sounds)	Range (as written)	Transposition
Piccolo			Write one octave below concert pitch
Flute			Sounds as written
Alto flute			Write a perfect fourth above concert pitch
Bass flute			Write one octave above concert pitch
Oboe			Sounds as written
English horn			Write a perfect fifth above concert pitch
Bassoon			Sounds as written
Contrabassoon			Write an octave above concert pitch
E♭ clarinet			Write a minor third below concert pitch
B♭ clarinet			Write a major second above concert pitch
A clarinet			Write a minor third above concert pitch

Instrument	Range (as sounds)	Range (as written)	Transposition
Alto clarinet			Write a major sixth above concert pitch
Bass clarinet			Write a major ninth above concert pitch (using the treble clef)
Soprano saxophone			Write a major second above concert pitch
Alto saxophone			Write a major sixth above concert pitch (on treble clef)
Tenor saxophone			Write a major ninth above concert pitch (on treble clef)
Baritone saxophone			Write an octave and a major sixth above concert pitch (on treble clef)

Common Techniques

Some woodwind instruments, such as flutes and oboes, are rather quiet. Other woodwinds, such as saxophones and clarinets, have a very broad dynamic range. That said, the tone color of most woodwinds remains fairly constant across all registers, although the intensity may vary from register to register.

There are many interesting instrument combinations available within the woodwind family. Consider voicing clarinets and flutes, clarinets and saxes, flutes and oboes, and various combinations within the same instrument family.

All woodwinds are typically found in both the orchestra and the concert band, except for saxophones, which are not orchestral instruments. Saxes are, however, members in good standing of concert, marching, and jazz bands.

When writing for the saxophone family, know that saxes in octave unison—alto and tenor in the top octave, baritone on the bottom—can create a somewhat sinister sound. Close-voiced altos or tenors in the medium and high registers make for sweet melodic or accompaniment passages; you can voice harmony in parallel thirds for a very pleasant effect.

For the Glenn Miller big band sound, voice a clarinet lead on top of two altos and two tenors (A-A-T-T), in that order. More modern big bands get rid of the clarinet but keep the A-A-T-T voicing, often with a baritone sax beneath that.

For rapid repeated notes, all woodwinds can employ double and triple tongue effects. These are repeated notes articulated with the tongue, as notated in Figures 9.1 and 9.2.

Figure 9.1

Double tonguing on woodwind instruments.

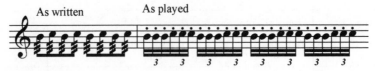

Figure 9.2

Triple tonguing on woodwind instruments.

Another interesting effect is flutter tonguing, which sounds a little like the rolled-r "drrrr" sound. It is notated as shown in Figure 9.3.

Figure 9.3

Flutter tonguing on woodwind instruments.

Examining Individual Woodwind Instruments

As noted previously, there are three distinct types of woodwind instruments—the flutes, the single reeds, and the double reeds. Each type of instrument has a slightly different sound and performance technique.

Piccolo

The piccolo is a soprano version of the flute, extending the flute's range up an octave. Not nearly as warm as the flute, it has a somewhat piercing quality, especially in the top half of its range. It's not very capable in its lowest octave, however, due to its very soft (yet somewhat haunting) tone.

The piccolo is quite easy to play, especially for scale-wise passages. It produces a whistling-type sound when multiples are played in unison. It also blends well with trumpets.

Flute

The various flutes (and the piccolo) are the only nonreed instruments in the woodwind family. It's a very agile instrument, also capable of great sensitivity. It mixes well with other woodwinds, and it's also good for ensemble work across sections. Flute parts are common in all types of ensembles, from orchestras and concert bands to marching bands and jazz bands.

The flute produces a beautiful warm tone in the lower octaves. The upper range, on the other hand, is extremely brilliant in tone. Due to its soft volume, solo lines are best accompanied by sparse instrumentation.

Alto Flute

The alto flute is a slightly longer version of a normal flute. The longer instrument enables a slightly lower range, with a slightly breathier tonal quality. It's a slightly more common instrument than the similar bass flute.

Bass Flute

The bass flute, although an uncommon instrument in the modern band or orchestra, has a very pleasing and somewhat "cool" sound, ideally suited for sustained passages. It's a very quiet and windy instrument, and takes a lot of breath to play; as such, you shouldn't write short notes or staccato passages for this instrument. Also, because of the air requirements, avoid long, sustained passages, unless you want to see the bass flautist keel over from lack of oxygen.

Oboe

The oboe is our first double-reed instrument, very warm-sounding and lyrical with a unique nasal sound. It sounds particularly distinctive (and melodic) in its top octave, while it tends to "honk" in the low part of its range. Avoid notes below the D.

The oboe blends well with flutes and clarinets, especially when doubling the flute line at the octave. Its penetrating quality keeps it from blending well with other woodwinds when employed in inner voicings. As such, it's better used when playing or doubling lead lines.

The tonal quality of the oboe contrasts well with that of its cousin the flute. Where the flute gets more brilliant as it goes up in register, the oboe loses its edge as it goes up. Conversely, the flute is weakest in its lowest octave, while the oboe's sound gets thicker and richer the lower it goes.

Tip

Skilled oboists often have the ability to sustain notes for an extended period of time, which lets them play lengthy passages with a single breath.

English Horn

The English horn is not a French horn made in England; it's a double-reed instrument, similar to an oboe. It's less agile than the oboe, however, due to its larger size. Think of the English horn as the alto voice of the double-reed family.

This instrument produces a very deep and distinctive sound that gets thinner as it gets higher. It sounds most melodic in its top two octaves, although the lowest part of the range is particularly rich and expressive. (You should avoid notes below the G, however.) It's commonly used as a solo instrument, where it has an expressive, almost brooding quality.

Bassoon

The bassoon is the bass voice of the woodwind section. It produces a somewhat comical sound, especially in its lower registers. That said, the bassoon blends surprisingly well with other woodwinds. It's expressively melodic in its middle and medium-high range, and also versatile in staccato passages.

Contrabassoon

The lowest of the woodwinds, the contrabassoon plays an octave below the bassoon. Its size makes it less articulate than its smaller brother, however. Very low, sustained tones have a "buzz" because of their slow vibrations.

E♭ Clarinet

The E♭ clarinet is a kind of "piccolo" clarinet. This smaller instrument is more difficult to play than the B♭ clarinet; players require frequent rest periods.

This instrument works best in the upper register; its lower range is quite thin. It's often used as a solo instrument due to its penetrating tone in its high range.

B♭ Clarinet

The B♭ clarinet is the workhorse of the woodwind family. It's a very flexible instrument with wide pitch and dynamic ranges.

The clarinet has a somewhat woody quality to its sound. This lets it blend well with other woodwinds, as well as with both open and muted brass. In addition, the instrument has a dry and sharp staccato—less edgy than the oboe, but more articulate than the flute.

The color of the clarinet varies quite a bit across its range. The instrument is easier to play in lower ranges than comparable saxophones, and it has lots of sustaining power. These characteristics make it ideally suited for both solo and ensemble passages—where it adds body to the voicings.

In concert and marching bands, clarinets tend to occupy the same space as strings do in orchestras. Most bands include several B♭ clarinets, divided into two or three sections with two or more players per section.

In the jazz world, the clarinet was a key component of both big bands and small ensembles in the 1930s and 1940s, as witnessed by the popularity of swing clarinetists Benny Goodman, Woody Herman, and Artie Shaw. You'll still see writing for clarinets in vintage bands, but the clarinet's role has been replaced by soprano and alto saxophones in more modern jazz ensembles.

Caution

Be aware of one peculiarity of fingering on the clarinet. The B♭ above middle C is played with no keys depressed, while the adjacent B-natural is played with all keys depressed (except for the vent hole). The fingering transition between these two notes presents difficulties for all but the most skilled players.

A Clarinet

The A clarinet is becoming more popular in the modern orchestra. It has a similar tone and range to the traditional B♭ clarinet, although a tad thicker and less brilliant.

Which clarinet is used often has more to do with the key signature than with anything else. The B♭ clarinet is more often used for flat keys, whereas the A clarinet works better for sharp keys. That said, the A clarinet is definitely a subsidiary instrument to its B♭ sibling.

Alto Clarinet

The alto clarinet is an E♭ instrument. It's not often used in the orchestra, but is increasingly common in concert bands and wind ensembles. Due to its unassertive sound, it's best used for harmony parts or soft solo passages.

Bass Clarinet

The bass clarinet is the lowest voice of the clarinet family. It sounds an octave lower than the normal B♭ clarinet. It's often written with open or muted trombones.

The lowest register on this instrument is the most distinctive, with the warmest tone. Above middle C, the sound thins out, and it can sound "pinched" in higher registers.

In older literature, the bass clarinet was most often written in the bass clef. More modern music tends to notate the instrument in the treble clef (with pitches sounding a major ninth below what is written).

Soprano Saxophone

Now we move to the saxophone family, all of which are transposing instruments written on the treble clef—no matter how low the range.

Of course, low range isn't an issue with the soprano saxophone, which is the highest voice in the family. It has a high, piercing, sound, although it can also be quite lyrical in its middle range. The soprano sax is quite popular in jazz settings, where it's sometimes used instead of the clarinet.

Alto Saxophone

The alto sax is a real workhorse in both concert and jazz bands. It has a sweet, sentimental sound that blends well with other saxes, especially tenors. It also blends well with trumpets, and is often used as a solo instrument in jazz ensembles.

Tenor Saxophone

The tenor sax is another workhorse instrument that can be played sweetly or with a rougher edge. It blends well with other saxes, especially altos, as well as most brass instruments. The tenor is the backbone of the sax section, and is also often used as a solo instrument in jazz, rock, and blues music.

Baritone Saxophone

The baritone sax most often functions as the bottom voice of the sax section. It's often voiced with the trombone section, typically in rhythmic patterns against a higher melody.

This instrument produces a very sharp, "honking" type sound when played staccato. It can also be used for low-bass sustain. Avoid the very lowest notes of the range (below F).

Bass Saxophone

Finally, we have the very lowest sax, the bass saxophone. This instrument is used only occasionally. It's written two octaves and a second below concert pitch—an octave lower than tenor sax. As you might suspect, it's a very slow-speaking instrument, so it shouldn't be used for faster passages. It's most often used to provide a pedal point, and for special effect.

The Least You Need to Know

- Flutes and piccolos produce sound by blowing across an open hole on the instrument.

- Single-reed instruments, such as clarinets and saxophones, utilize a large single reed in the mouthpiece.

- Double-reed instruments, such as oboes and bassoons, use a small double reed to produce a more nasal sound.

Chapter 10

Keyboard and Electronic Instruments

In This Chapter

- ◆ Understanding different types of keyboard instruments, from pianos to accordions
- ◆ Writing for both acoustic and electronic keyboards
- ◆ Discovering how synthesizers and samplers work

Depending on who is doing the deciding, keyboard instruments are either string instruments, because they have internal strings, or percussion instruments, because the strings are struck rather than plucked or bowed. To my mind, keyboard instruments are actually a little of both—and thus justify their own instrument category.

Understanding Keyboard Instruments

There are many different types of keyboards. The piano, of course, is the most-used keyboard instrument, but you can't forget about the organ, or the harpsichord, or even the humble accordion. And then there's the whole family of electronic keyboards, from Wurlitzer and Rhodes electric pianos to the latest synthesizers and samplers. It's a big family.

Ranges and Transpositions

Most keyboards have fairly wide ranges, as exemplified by the 88-key piano. Almost all keyboards sound in concert pitch, as well, which makes them relatively easy to write and arrange for.

That said, it does help to know the precise ranges of each instrument. For that, refer to Table 10.1, which details the ranges and transpositions of the primary keyboard instruments.

Table 10.1 Keyboard family ranges and transpositions

Instrument	Range (as sounds)	Range (as written)	Transposition
Piano (acoustic and electric)			Sounds as written
Organ			Sounds as written
Harpsichord			Sounds as written
Clavichord			Sounds as written
Celesta			Write one octave lower than concert pitch
Accordion			Sounds as written

Common Techniques

When writing for any keyboard instrument, the most important thing to remember, and I know this sounds blatantly obvious, is that keyboard players only have two hands. That means you don't want to write more than 10 simultaneous notes—and you want those notes to stretch no more than an octave or so per hand. Obviously, you can stretch the octave (and write more notes) when writing a run of notes, but when you're writing block chords, remember that you're writing for relatively normal, two-handed, ten-fingered human beings.

That said, keyboard instruments are relatively easy to write for, since all the keys are laid out in front of you—from A♭ to G# and over again. Unlike string or wind instruments, where different pitches are created by pressing combinations of frets, keys, or valves, you can easily visualize the shape of your music on a keyboard.

While all keyboard instruments share a common keyboard layout, they don't all share the same number of keys. The 88-key piano has the widest range, but you'll also run into truncated keyboards of various shapes and sizes. It's not uncommon to find 76- or even 61-key electronic keyboards, with notes lopped off both the top and bottom of the traditional 88-key layout; some organs only have 44 or 49 keys per bank. Know the range of whichever instrument you're writing for.

> **Note**
>
> Some pianos have more than 88 keys. For example, Bösendorfer makes models with up to 97 keys.

In addition, different keyboard instruments require slightly different playing techniques, beyond basic keyboard fingering, that is. For example, to play louder on a piano, you simply press the keys harder and faster. But on the pipe organ, loudness is affected by the flow of air from the bellows and the stops selected. And on the harpsichord, you can't change the volume much at all; the internal strings are plucked with the same force no matter how hard you strike the keys.

That said, keyboard instruments are quite versatile. With a few exceptions, keyboards have a dynamic range from extremely soft to room-fillingly loud. They're equally adept at unobtrusive accompaniment as they are at playing the lead. And you can write both linearly or in block chords—or for both styles at once, one in each hand. Glissandi, broken chords, arpeggios, all are easily accomplished on a keyboard instrument.

Examining Individual Keyboard Instruments

While all keyboard instruments have a similar-looking keyboard (give or take a few keys) that is played with two hands, that's where the similarities end. Each keyboard instrument has its own distinctive sound and musical capabilities, as you'll soon discover.

Piano

The acoustic piano (short for *pianoforte*) is the workhorse of any instrumental ensemble, ideal for both solo and ensemble passages. This instrument has an incredible dynamic range; it can be played lyrically or percussively. It also has the widest pitch range of any instrument in the orchestra, which means it can play lines that span too wide for any other instrument to reproduce.

It's important to remember that there are actually several different types of acoustic pianos. The grand piano has the richest sound, due to the size of the frame; the bigger the grand, the bigger the sound. (Concert grands are bigger than baby grands.)

Then there's the upright or "tack" piano, which has a more compact frame and a slightly tinnier sound. While you might think that the grand piano is the one you always want to write for, know that an upright might sound more appropriate in some rock or blues settings; the more trebly sound does a better job of cutting through the clutter of a loud ensemble than do the rounder tones of a grand.

You can write a piano to play backing chords or single-note leads. As with all keyboard instruments, don't write more or wider notes into a chord than can be physically accomplished.

While it's easy to think of the piano as an accompanying instrument, it's also effective when doubling other instruments in an ensemble. Having the piano double a melody or countermelody line adds a bit of an edge to the original line, and provides added articulation to the passage. It's particularly effective when doubling woodwinds and high strings.

When writing a piano accompaniment, there are several different styles you can employ. These include:

♦ Sustained chords (sometimes called a *pad*). These are typically whole notes played at the beginning of a measure, sometimes enhanced by tremolos or rolls between two important notes of the chords.

♦ Block chords, typically repeated in a rhythm.

♦ Bass line in the left hand, with block chords in the right hand. Some variations of this style are *stride*, in which the left hand plays the bass in two while the right hand plays chords on the backbeat, and *boogie*, where the left hand plays in four with right-hand chords on the backbeat.

♦ Arpeggios, either ascending or descending.

Note
Learn more about writing for piano in the rhythm section in Chapter 13.

How you notate a piano part depends on the type of music you're writing, and the particular player(s) involved. In more formal or classical settings, as well as for choral accompaniment, it's appropriate to write out all the notes of the piano part. But in rock, jazz, and other popular music, it's acceptable to simply indicate the underlying chords and, if necessary, the desired rhythm. This lets the piano player determine the exact voicing of the chords, as well as any other notes to play.

Electric Piano

Starting in the 1940s, the piano went electric. That's when Harold Rhodes combined the principles of the celesta with the electric guitar, and developed the Rhodes electric piano.

An electric piano looks and feels like a regular piano, but it works (and sounds) a bit different. On an acoustic piano, sound is produced when felt-covered hammers strike a set of strings. On an electric piano, felt- or rubber-tipped hammers strike a set of metal bars, called "tines." This produces a pinging sound, which resonates the tone bars that sit over each tine, thus creating a mellow, bell-like ring. This sound is then amplified via an electronic pickup, and often processed through various effects, most typically a stereo tremolo or vibrato.

An electric piano can sound soft and mellow or hard and chimey. It's the sound of the laid-back slow grooves you hear on late-night FM radio, as well as the hard-edged rhythms of funk and jazz-rock jams. It all depends on how the instrument is attacked, and how its sound is processed and amplified.

The Rhodes electric piano sound was particularly popular in the 1970s and 1980s, in both pop and jazz-fusion music. After a period of submersion, the electric piano is seeing a resurgence in various forms of popular music, from hip hop to jam bands to neo-soul.

The traditional Rhodes electric piano has the same 88-key keyboard layout and range as an acoustic piano. Some other types of electric pianos, however, have a shorter 76-key keyboard. In addition, today's electric piano sound is often reproduced by digital synthesizers and samplers—which are easier for working musicians to haul around than those bulky old Rhodes suitcases.

> **Note**
>
> When the Rhodes piano was acquired by the Fender company, it became known as the Fender Rhodes. During the 1960s and 1970s, the Wurlitzer electric piano—which had a slightly softer sound than the Rhodes—was also popular.

Organ

After the piano, the most popular traditional keyboard instrument is the organ—both acoustic (pipe) and electric.

Large pipe organs have the largest range of any instrument, due to the extended bass notes played by the pedals. The sound of a pipe organ is produced by forcing air through whistles and reeds called *pipes*. Pipe organs range in size from portable instrument with just a few dozen pipes, to large church organs with tens of thousand of pipes. Almost all pipe organs have more than one keyboard; two keyboards and a separate pedalboard are typical. This type of organ is a very powerful instrument—and the larger the pipes, the bigger the sound.

Different "stops" on a pipe organ produce different sounds. A stop is literally a stoppage of sound, affected when a vibrating tongue is pressed against the end of a pipe, thus stopping the sound. An organ with two banks of keyboards can be configured to produce different sounds on each bank.

Electric organs aren't quite as impressive, but they're equally—if not more—versatile. There are actually two types of electronic organs today. The most

> **Tip**
>
> One of the nice things about the organ is that it can sustain pitches almost indefinitely. This makes it an ideal instrument to provide sustained chordal accompaniment.

Tip

In Black gospel music, the Hammond B3 is nearly always present and played through a spinning Lesley speaker. Use of the Lesley is typically not notated, but rather left to the organist's discretion.

common type of electric organ isn't limited to pipe organ sounds, but contains other voices that imitate additional instruments. (And, in some instances, electronic sounds that have no acoustic equivalent.) The other type of electric organ is meant as a pipe organ replacement; the so-called *pipeless organ* is primarily designed for church use.

In popular music, probably the best-known electric organ is the Hammond organ, in particular the Hammond B3. Today, organ sounds tend to be produced digitally via electronic keyboards or samplers; this makes it easy to incorporate an organ sound without having to lug a massive organ around on stage.

Harpsichord

The harpsichord is actually a plucked string instrument. Instead of being hit by hammers, the strings are plucked by crow quills or leather tabs. This produces a delicate tone that is easily overwhelmed by other instruments.

The other side-effect of this approach is an almost total lack of dynamic range. No matter what force you use to press a key, the string is plucked in the same manner. This limited dynamic range makes the harpsichord unsuited for use in louder ensembles, or with music that varies considerably in volume.

The harpsichord was widely used in the Baroque era, both as a solo instrument and to provide continuo within that era's smaller orchestra. As the orchestra expanded, the harpsichord was replaced by the more versatile piano.

If you write for harpsichord, take into account its dynamic limitations. It's easily overwhelmed, so arrange accompanying instruments accordingly.

Clavichord

The harpsichord was predated, musically, by the clavichord, which was used from the late Medieval era through the Baroque era. The clavichord produces music by string brass or iron strings with small metal blades, which are tied to the keyboard.

Note

The clavichord was the inspiration for the electronic clavinet.

Like the harpsichord, the clavichord has a very limited dynamic range. The size of the instrument is such that it's suited for playing in small rooms, and not much more. If you want to include the clavichord in your arrangements, you might want to consider mic'ing or amplifying a traditional instrument, as was done on the song "For No One" on The Beatles' *Revolver* album.

In Table 10.1 I showed a five-octave range (GG to d3) for the clavichord, which is typical but not universal. Given the era in which the clavichord was popular, there was no such thing as a "standard" instrument; different instruments have different ranges. For example, a particular 50-key harpsichord might have a range from C to c3, while a 61-key model might range from FF to f3. With this variability in mind, clavichord music is best written with a specific instrument in mind.

Celesta

Many musicians classify the celesta as a percussion instrument, as it utilizes steel plates struck by hammers. The metal plates are suspended over wooden resonators, for a fuller sound; pedals are used to either sustain or dampen the sound.

The celesta sounds a little like the percussion section's glockenspiel, but with a much softer sound. Although you typically write the celesta part in or near the percussion section of a score, the instrument itself is played by a pianist, and the part is written on two bracketed staves, just like a piano part.

Given the delicate nature of its sound, the celesta is best used to double other instruments, especially mallet percussion (xylophone, vibes) or high woodwinds. While it can be used to carry a solo melody, its sound is easily overwhelmed by other instruments.

Accordion

While you might think of it only in terms of polkas, the accordion is a wonderfully versatile instrument. It can contribute to just about any form of music, from Cajun and French chanson music to contemporary folk and rock.

The accordion is a squeezebox that works by compressing and expanding a bellows. This generates air flow across a series of reeds; the attached keyboard controls which reeds receive the air flow, and thus which notes are produced.

Most accordions have both a keyboard and a series of buttons. The keyboard is a small one, anywhere from 25 to 41 keys. (The 41-key accordion is most common.) The buttons are used to play both bass notes and complete chords, without having to finger the notes on the keyboard.

A concert accordion has four sets of reeds, called *treble shifts*. The second set of reeds is tuned an octave higher than the first; the third set is tuned an octave lower; and the fourth set is tuned just slightly higher than the first.

The sound of the accordion is very rich and reedy, almost organ-like. This makes it ideal for chordal accompaniment, although melodic lines are also possible—typically doubling other instruments.

Know that the strength of a note or chord depends on how much air is flowing from the bellows. Loud dynamic levels and full chords require more air; these loud or long tones cannot be sustained for more than a few seconds without a break. Softer dynamic levels or nonchord notes can be sustained longer.

One neat effect on the accordion is the *bellow shake*, which is a rapid in-and-out movement of the bellows. You notate this by putting a double-ended arrow over the shake area. The end of the shake is notated as *B.N.* (for "bellow normal").

> **Note**
> Treble shifts extend the accordion's range an octave higher and lower than the range described in Table 10.1.

Synthesizers and Samplers

Then we have the newest category of keyboards, those electronic instruments known as synthesizers and samplers. These electronic instruments can be either analog (creating new sounds via oscillators and other electronics) or digital (typically sampling and then reproducing the real-world sounds of other instruments). Digital synthesizers can be programmed to resemble other instruments or to create wholly new sounds of a virtually unlimited nature.

A synthesizer is so-named because it synthesizes sound. It doesn't recreate existing sound; instead, new sounds are created using various synthesis techniques.

Today's synthesizers can either be freestanding instruments or software programs operated by computer. Most synthesizers come with a variety of preset sounds, which eliminates the need for constant experimentation. You can, however, tweak these presets—or still generate your own unique sounds, if you like.

> **Note**
>
> An early example of a sampler, using analog technology, was the *Mellotron.* Developed in the 1960s, the Mellotron used taped samples to reproduce various instruments, played back via a piano-type keyboard.

Sibling to the synthesizer is the digital sampler. A sampler takes a sample of an existing instrument, and reproduces it digitally—either exactly, or with effects added. Samplers are typically used to reproduce a variety of instruments onstage, or to reproduce orchestral or concert instruments when recording. As with synthesizers, samplers can be either freestanding instruments or, more typical today, software programs that tie into other computer programs.

The toughest thing about writing for synthesizers and samplers is describing the sound you want. It's easy enough to write out the notes; most electronic instruments have a range similar to a piano, although sometimes achieved with a smaller keyboard. But there's no standard whatsoever for specifying a particular synthesized sound. You can notate something like "orchestral strings," or "rounded tone with soft attack," but what you get in return is a crapshoot. If doing both the arranging and playing, of course, you get to find your own sounds; but when specifying synthesized sounds in an arrangement for others, it's almost impossible to guarantee that someone else will be able to recreate the sounds that you hear in your head.

For these reasons, if you intend to include synthesizers in your arrangements, its best to either hire a competent programmer or to learn how to program them yourself. Otherwise, you're at the mercy of whoever is doing the playing at any given point in time.

The Least You Need to Know

- The most popular and versatile keyboard instrument is the piano; organs, electric pianos, and synthesizers are also widely used.

- Most keyboards sound in concert key and have a wide range.

- The sounds of many formerly freestanding electronic keyboard instruments, such as the organ and electric piano, are now reproduced on separate electronic keyboards or samplers.

- A synthesizer creates new sounds from scratch, by generating and manipulating electrical signals; samplers reproduce existing instruments that have been digitally sampled.

Chapter 11

Percussion Instruments

In This Chapter

- ◆ Learn how to write for the pitched percussion instruments—xylophone, marimba, vibes, and timpani
- ◆ Find out about the drums and cymbals that are indefinite-pitch percussion instruments
- ◆ Learn how to write a drum-set part for jazz or popular music
- ◆ Discover all the different Latin percussion instruments—from cabasas to congas

When you talk percussion, you're talking about a lot of different instruments. Percussion instruments make noise when you hit them or shake them, so the family includes everything from snare drums and cymbals to marimbas and timpani. Most percussion instruments are of indefinite pitch—that is, although they make a noise when you hit them (or shake them), that noise isn't associated with a particular pitch. Other percussion instruments, such as timpani and the mallet family, do produce a definite pitch (or pitches).

We'll look at the pitched percussion instruments first, followed by the things you shake or hit.

Understanding Pitched Percussion

There are two main types of pitched percussion instruments. The so-called mallet instruments, such as the xylophone and marimba, have a series of bars in a piano keyboard-like arrangement, and are struck with hard or soft mallets. Timpani, while struck with mallets, produce sound like any other drum, but are tuned to specific pitches. As you might expect, the mallet instruments are more nimble than are timpani, and they're completely different in context and sound.

Note
Another way to classify percussion instruments is by the way they produce sound. *Idiophones* (marimba, cymbals, etc.) produce sound when their bodies vibrate, while *membranophones* (drums, timpani, etc.) produce sound when a membrane or head is struck.

Pitched Percussion Ranges and Transpositions

Before we get into the different pitched percussion instruments, let's look at their respective ranges and transpositions, as defined in Table 11.1:

Table 11.1   Pitched percussion instruments ranges

Instrument	Range (as sounds)	Range (as written)	Transposition
Glockenspiel			Write two octaves below concert pitch
Xylophone			Write one octave below concert pitch
Marimba			Sounds as written
Vibraphone			Sounds as written
Chimes			Sounds as written
Timpani (20")			Sounds as written
Timpani (23")			Sounds as written
Timpani (25"–26")			Sounds as written

Instrument	Range (as sounds)	Range (as written)	Transposition
Timpani (28"–29")	𝄢	𝄢	Sounds as written
Timpani (30"–32")	𝄢	𝄢	Sounds as written

Common Techniques for Pitched Percussion

All pitched percussion instruments are struck by a mallet of some sort. Different instruments—and different sounds—require different types of mallets.

In general, the higher-pitched the instrument, the harder the mallet. So for example, the high-pitched glockenspiel is typically struck with hard rubber or metal mallets, while the lower-pitched marimba is struck with soft rubber or yarn-covered mallets. You can specify different types of mallets for any instrument, to produce specific sounds. In general, a harder mallet produces a sharper-edged sound than a softer mallet.

To sustain a note on all pitched percussion instruments except the chimes, that note must be *rolled*. This is accomplished by hitting the right and left mallets in rapid succession over the duration of the note; the faster the roll, the more seamless it sounds. A roll is notated by placing three slashes through the stem of a note, or above or below a whole note, as shown in Figure 11.1.

Figure 11.1

A timpani roll.

On timpani, a roll is played on a single note on a single drum. On mallet instruments, a roll can be on a single pitch or between two (or more, with a four-mallet approach) notes. In this instance, the roll alternates strokes from one bar on the instrument to the other. For example, a four-mallet marimba part can roll a four-note chord, as shown in Figure 11.2.

Figure 11.2

A four-mallet roll on a marimba.

With many mallet instruments, sustain is not an issue; there is no such thing as a legato note on a xylophone, for example. Some mallet instruments, however, do have a natural sustain, and thus must be dampened for staccato notes. These sustaining instruments include the glockenspiel, vibraphone, chimes, and timpani. Simply notate the staccato as you would on any other instrument, and the player will manually dampen the note as necessary.

Examining Pitched Percussion Instruments

Now let's spend a few minutes examining the most common pitched percussion instruments, from highest to lowest in pitch.

Glockenspiel

The glockenspiel is the soprano voice of the pitched percussion section. It consists of a series of metal bars, arranged in piano keyboard order.

> **Note**
>
> Glockenspiels are sometimes called *bells*.

A concert glockenspiel is played horizontally, typically placed on a stand at about waist height. In marching bands and drum and bugle corps, the glockenspiel is played somewhat vertically, held in front of the player with the lowest notes at the bottom and the highest notes at the top.

When hit with metal or hard-rubber mallets, a glockenspiel produces a piercing, high-pitched sound. The notes ring for some time after being hit, unless dampened. In concert band and orchestral settings, the glockenspiel is typically played with two mallets. In marching band settings, it is played with a single mallet, as the left hand is used to help steady the instrument while marching.

Because of its piercing sound, the glockenspiel is not an instrument that fits well into the background. It's best used to double melodic lines with other high-pitched instruments, such as flutes, high woodwinds, and the piano (in its higher registers).

Xylophone

The xylophone is also a soprano voice in the pitched percussion section, often functioning in a piccolo-like role. It is built from a series of small wooden bars that produce a very sharp, high-pitched biting sound.

The xylophone is typically played with two mallets. The instrument has no natural sustain, so longer notes must be executed via rolling.

The high pitch and distinctive, almost comical sound of the xylophone makes it ideal for playing staccato figures. Like the glockenspiel, it's best used to double melodic lines with other high-pitched instruments.

Marimba

The marimba is a lower-pitched instrument than the xylophone. It is a larger instrument, with more notes and larger wooden bars that produce a richer tone. This tone is also affected by the use of large metal resonators beneath the wooden bars, which help to both round off and slightly amplify the sound.

The marimba is also a more versatile instrument than the xylophone, with varied colors across its entire range. In its lower registers, the marimba produces an almost mellow tone. In contrast, its top octave has a similar sound to the xylophone. Notes sustain slightly longer than with the xylophone, but still not quite like that of the glockenspiel or vibraphone; you'll want to roll any longer notes.

The marimba can be played with either two or four mallets. In four-mallet playing, two mallets are held in each hand; a good player has about an octave range between the two mallets. Mallets are typically soft rubber or yarn-covered rubber; softer mallets produce a rounder tone with softer attack. Notation can be on either the treble or bass clefs, or on two staffs.

You can find the marimba in all genres of music, from classical to jazz and beyond. It blends well with clarinets and French horns, and even with saxophones and low-register strings, to some degree. It can be used for sustained chordal accompaniment (via rolled chords) or for doubled or solo melodic lines.

Vibraphone

The vibraphone differs from other mallet instruments, in that the bars are made of metal. It also incorporates an electronic motor that rotates metal plates within the instrument's resonators, which creates a pulsating type of vibrato. The instrument can be played with or without the motor running. Without the vibrato, the sound is very clear and bell-like.

Unlike other mallet instruments, the vibraphone has a sustain pedal, like that on the piano, which enables the use of sustained notes (with or without the vibrato turned on) without rolling. Individual notes can also be dampened by hand, or by pressing a mallet against a ringing bar. The instrument can be played with either two or four mallets; the mallets are typically yarn-covered, of various degrees of hardness. Vibes parts are typically written in treble clef.

Vibes are used in both jazz and popular music. The instrument can be used like a piano, to provide comping chordal accompaniment, or to play straight melodic lines. A good player can do both at the same time, playing the melodic line with the right hand while comping with the left, just like a piano player. It's not uncommon to find the vibes filling the piano or guitar accompaniment role in jazz groups, or adding color to the rhythm section in popular music.

> **Note**
>
> The vibraphone is also referred to as *vibes*. For some good examples of how vibes are used in popular music, listen to just about any classic Motown recording, where vibes are used to double the piano, bass lines, and even provide countermelodies for other instruments.

Chimes

The chimes are a unique instrument within the percussion family. A set of chimes consists of an octave and a half's worth of long metal tubes, each tube tuned to a specific pitch. The tubes are struck with wooden mallets—actually more like small hammers than marimba or xylophone mallets. The tubes have considerable sustain, unless dampened with the instrument's foot pedal.

> **Note**
>
> Chimes are sometimes called *tubular bells*.

The chimes produce a loud ringing tone that has the same slightly "out of tune" quality as a church bell. (This leads to a common use of the chimes to mimic the sound of church bells in a composition.) The instrument's sound is quite prominent within any sized ensemble, and should be used sparingly. Because of the long sustain, chimes are ill suited to fast passages.

Timpani

The timpani is a large drum that can be tuned to a specific pitch. Actually, most timpanists use a set of four or five separate drums, with overlapping ranges. Each drum has a range of a perfect fifth; for example, the middle drum (typically 25"–26" in diameter) can be tuned from B♭ to F. The drums are played with felt-headed mallets, which are available in a variety of hardnesses.

> **Note**
>
> Timpani (sometimes spelled tympani) are also referred to as *kettle drums*. Some smaller or school-based ensembles may only have two timpani instead of the traditional four.

Modern timpani are tuned by use of a foot pedal that rapidly tightens or loosens the head; older models are tuned via use of hand-operated T-shaped tension rods, which take longer to affect new tuning. However the timpani is tuned, it takes a bit of time to retune the drum to a new pitch. Although you can change notes in the middle of a composition, you should allow several measures of rest for the timpanist to do this.

The sound of the timpani is that of a thundering low end. (In fact, timpani are often used to simulate the sound of thunder.) Staccato notes are accomplished by manually damping the head with the hand. Undampened, the timpani has a short sustain, almost like a pitched bass drum. Longer sustain is accomplished by two-handed rolling, typically on a single drum.

Timpani are most often used for punctuation, sometimes in unison with string basses or tubas. If your not sure how to incorporate the instrument, consider tuning the timpani to the tonic, subdominant, and dominant notes of the piece; this lets the instrument emphasize the key cadences.

> **Tip**
>
> When writing for beginning or less-skilled timpanists, it's best to set a group of four notes (one for each drum) at the beginning of a piece and not change them.

For special effect, you can indicate a short glissando on a single timpani drum. This is accomplished by striking the head and then using the foot pedal to change the pitch upward or downward, as appropriate. The effect is more like a "bo-ing" than it is a true glissando, but it's interesting nonetheless.

While the timpani is primarily an orchestral or concert-band instrument, marching bands and drum corps that have a percussion pit can make use of the instrument. You can also find timpani used in some popular music, typically for limited effects.

Examining Indefinite-Pitch Percussion Instruments

The timpani excluded, most drums are of indefinite pitch—that is, they simply can't be tuned to a specific pitch. Thus we have the subfamily of indefinite-pitch percussion instruments, which includes drums, cymbals, and other things you hit and shake.

Snare Drum

Perhaps the most essential instrument of the percussion family is the snare drum. This is a relatively small drum (12"–15" in diameter, 14" being most common) with curled metal wires or gut cables stretched under the bottom head. The result is a snappy, cracking sound that produces the backbeat in popular music, the accents in jazz, the driving beat in marching bands, and the sustained rolls in orchestral pieces. It can play single-note accents as well as complicated rhythms, at volume levels from pianissimo to fortissimo.

> **Note**
>
> To learn more about writing for drums, check out my companion book, *The Complete Idiot's Guide to Playing Drums, 2nd Edition* (Michael Miller, Alpha Books, 2004).

Figure 11.3

Snare drum notation, using an indefinite-pitch percussion clef.

The snare drum part is typically written on the third space ("C") of the treble-clef staff, or using a special percussion clef, like that in Figure 11.3. To facilitate ease of reading, stems are typically placed above the notes, slightly contrary to standard notational practices.

There are several unique bits of notation that you need to know when writing for snare drum. The first is that of the *flam*, which is a short grace note before a primary note. The grace note is played lighter than the main note, with the opposite hand, and the resulting sound is that of "fa-lam," hence the name. Flam notation is shown in Figure 11.4.

Figure 11.4

A flam for the snare drum.

If one grace note is good, two or three are even better. Two grace notes before the main note (played with double strokes: LL-R or RR-L) is called a *drag*. Three grace notes before the main note (played with alternating strokes: LRL-R or RLR-L) is called *ratamacue*. Both are notated in Figure 11.5. These techniques are used primarily in marching or military music.

> **Note**
>
> Flams, drags, and ratamacues are just three of forty official *rudiments* that all snare drummers must learn. Other popular rudiments include the *paradiddle* (four notes with RLRR or LRLL sticking) and various types of rolls.

Figure 11.5

A drag and a ratamacue—two and three grace notes, respectively.

Then there's the roll—the drummer's way of sustaining a note. In orchestral and concert band music, rolls are most always closed, or "buzz" rolls, played by pressing each stick against the head to produce multiple bounces and a relatively smooth sound. Closed rolls are notated by placing two slashes through the stem of a note, or three slashes above or below a whole note, as notated in Figure 11.6.

Figure 11.6

A buzz or closed roll for the snare drum.

In marching or drum corps music (and in some other forms, as appropriate), rolls are played open rather than closed. An open roll consists of a single bounce per hand, for an effect that replicates individual thirty-second notes rather than a single sustained note. Open rolls are typically notated the same as closed rolls, but with a number over the note to indicate the number of strokes. For example, an open roll on an eighth note is a *five-stroke roll* (the fifth stroke is the ending note on the next beat), and is notated and played as shown in Figure 11.7. Other common open rolls are the *seven-stroke roll* (on a dotted eighth note), the *nine-stroke roll* (on a quarter note), and the *seventeen-stroke roll* (on a half note). Unlike closed rolls, all open rolls have a distinct, and sometimes accented, ending note.

Figure 11.7

A five-stroke roll—as written, and as played.

Tip

Unless you're a drummer yourself, leave the sticking to the individual players.

Also important to the snare drum is *sticking*—that is, which hands play which notes. In most instances, you should leave the sticking up to the individual drummer. But for particular effect—especially when writing for marching band or drum corps—you might want to specify sticking underneath the notes, as shown in Figure 11.8.

R L R R L   R L R R L   R

Figure 11.8

An example of a snare drum part with specific sticking noted.

In jazz and some popular music, the snare drum can be played with *brushes.* These are sticks that end in a brush-like fan of thin metal wires, instead of the normal wooden bead. Brushes produce a softer sound than sticks, and are typically brushed across the head to produce a "shushing" sustain sound. Use is common in ballads, where the brushes created a bit of soft background noise instead of a harder backbeat.

Bass Drum

The bass drum is the bottom voice of the percussion section. It is typically used to reinforce the beat, or to provide an added "oomph" to key rhythms. It is used in both orchestral and marching settings. The bass drum can be written either in bass or percussion clef, typically on the bottom space of the staff.

Don't overdo the bass drum part. In particular, try to avoid rapid repeated notes or rhythms, unless for effect. Think of the bass drum as your music's pulse, and use it accordingly.

Cymbals

Cymbals are used in both concert and marching settings. You can write for a single cymbal, typically mounted on a stand, or for a pair of handheld cymbals, which are typically crashed together by the cymbal player. A mounted cymbal—called a *suspended cymbal*—can be played with sticks or mallets; it's most often used to achieve a swelling effect caused by using the mallets to roll the cymbal in a crescendo.

Gong

You can think of a gong as a very large specialty cymbal, struck with a large felt mallet. Like a traditional cymbal, a gong is made of brass (or similar metal compound), but is much larger in size and has a distinctive, very powerful sound. The gong's sound is uniquely sustaining; in fact, large gongs have to be "warmed up" by the player to facilitate a more immediate attack. Use sparingly.

Marching Percussion

In marching bands and drum corps, you have more drums than just the snare and bass. For example, you're likely to incorporate more than one snare drum part as well as two or more bass drums—sometimes tuned to approximate actual pitches. When you're writing for multiple bass drums, you typically split a single part into two or three parts; when the bass drums play their individual parts together, the entire part is reproduced.

Then there are the *tenor drums*, which are single-headed drums, much like the tom-toms on a drum set. A tenor setup typically consists of three to five individual drums (sized 10"–14" in diameter, sometimes with smaller drums added) on a single harness, so that the drummer can play between multiple drums. Tenors are tuned to different indefinite pitches, and are typically played with hard mallets rather than sticks.

Note
Tenor drums are sometimes called *toms, trios, quads,* or *quints*—depending on the number of drums attached to a single marching harness.

Most small marching bands have only one or two tenor players in the lineup. Larger marching bands and drum corps incorporate lines with four or five tenors.

Marching bands and drum corps also utilize cymbals and glockenspiels, of course. Some bands and corps have a separate percussion "pit," which is a non-marching section located directly in front of the audience. The pit lets the band use nonmarching percussion, such as timpani, xylophones, marimbas, drum sets, and the like.

Drum Set

When you're writing for jazz or popular music, more often than not you'll be writing for a single drum set rather than individual drums and cymbals. A drum set consists of a snare drum, bass drum, two or more tom-toms, one or more ride cymbals (used for playing constant eighth or quarter notes), one or more crash cymbals (used for accents), and a pair of hi-hats (two cymbals that are "chinked" together via a foot pedal). All of these drums and cymbals are played by a single drummer, using both hands and both feet.

The different elements of the drum set are notated on different lines of the staff, typically using the percussion clef, as shown in Figure 11.9. Elements played with the hands (snare drum, cymbals, hi-hat, toms) are notated stems up; items played with the feet (bass drum, hi-hat pedal) are notated stems down.

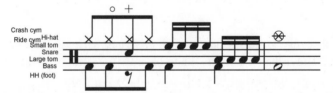

Figure 11.9

Drum set notation.

To notate a "ride" pattern on the hi-hat or ride cymbal, use closed note heads, or Xs. To indicate a cymbal crash, use an open note head. And to notate open and closed notes on the hi-hat, use the same notation as for brass muting—+ for closed, and ○ for open.

When writing jazz or pop music, you don't have to compose a detailed part for the drummer. Instead, it's common to let the drummer figure out his or her own part—unless you have a specific beat or rhythm in mind. All you have to do is notate how many measures there are in each section of the piece and let the drummer make up his or her own part along the way. You can, of course, notate specific rhythms and accents as necessary; this is most prevalent when writing for big band, where you want the drummer to "kick" accents played by the rest of the band.

Tip

If you want to notate additional elements—more toms or different cymbals or auxiliary instruments such as a cowbell or woodblock—you should notate these outside the clef, and label them accordingly.

Latin Percussion Instruments

When writing popular and ethnic music, it's not uncommon to include various Latin percussion instruments. These are instruments derived from traditional African, South American, or Cuban instruments. The most common of these instruments include the following:

- **Bongos,** a set of two small single-headed drums, typically 6" and 8" in diameter, played with the hands and fingers. These are high-pitched drums, used to create a constant rhythm or provide specific accents.

- **Congas,** deep single-headed drums that are played with the hands and fingers. Different sounds are produced by slapping or tapping the heads in different places. A conga player might play a single drum, or a set of two slightly different-sized drums. Congas are typically used to produce a constant rhythm.

- **Timbales,** a pair of shallow single-headed drums tuned to different pitches, played with sticks. Timbales are used to both create a constant rhythm and to provide accents and solo parts. Many timbale players play the shells of the drums as well as the heads, and typically use one or more cowbells in conjunction with the timbales.

- **Cowbell,** a medium-sized metal bell of indefinite pitch and very slight sustain, typically played with a stick to produce a constant rhythm.

- **Agogo bells,** a set of two pitched bells, like small cowbells, used to set up a static rhythm.

- **Castanets,** a small hand-held instrument consisting of two wooden halves that are clicked together.

- **Claves,** two wooden cylinders that are clicked together, typically to produce accented rhythms.

- **Guiro,** a cylindrical gourd with grooves cut around its circumference. It is played by scraping a stick across the grooves to produce a repeating rhythm.

- **Cabasa** (sometimes called the afuche/cabasa) is a small handheld corrugated cylinder covered by strings of metal beads. It can be shaken with one hand, or played with two hands by pressing the beads to the cylinder and then moving them back and forth. It is typically used to steady quarter-note or eighth-note background beat.

- **Maracas,** typically played in pairs, are constructed from gourds with dried seeds inside and handles attached. Maracas are shaken to produce a steady quarter- or eighth-note rhythm.

Note
Maracas are just one of many different shakers used in Latin and Afro-Cuban music. Other shakers are created from hollowed-out cylindrical gourds, or from hollow metal tubes, with dried seeds or small metal beads inside.

Other Percussion Instruments

There are other instruments in the percussion family that have their origins in European and Asian music. These instruments are most often used in orchestral music, although some are widely used in popular music, as well. These instruments include the following:

♦ **Tambourine,** a narrow wooden ring studded with multiple metal disks. The metal disks jingle when the tambourine is shaken or hit. Orchestral tambourines typically have a head that can be played with sticks, or rolled with a wetted finger. In popular music, the tambourine is typically shaken in a constant quarter- or eighth-note rhythm.

♦ **Triangle,** a three-sided bent metal bar that is struck with a small metal beater. It produces a uniquely ringing, high-pitched tone.

♦ **Finger cymbals,** which look like small (3" or so in diameter) brass cymbals. When struck (not crashed) together, they produce a ringing, bell-like tone.

♦ **Wood block,** a hollowed-out block of wood that produces a resonating note of indefinite pitch.

♦ **Temple blocks,** a set of hollow wooden or hard-plastic blocks of various sizes, thus tuned to an ascending series of indefinite pitches—typically to approximate the pentatonic scale.

♦ **Sleigh bells,** just like the kind horses used to wear, mounted on either a handheld harness or a piece of wood. Typically shaken to produce a constant rhythm.

And there's more than that—lots more, including a variety of Indian and Middle Eastern ones, such as the tabla and dumbek, and even more that we simply don't have space to discuss here. All the different percussion instruments provide lots of interesting colors you can use in all types of arrangements.

The Least You Need to Know

♦ There are two primary types of percussion instruments—those that have a definite pitch, such as xylophones and timpani, and those that don't.

♦ The glockenspiel is the highest-pitched mallet instrument, followed by the xylophone, the marimba, and the vibraphone.

♦ Most timpanists work with a set of four or five different drums, all of which can be tuned to a variety of definite pitches.

♦ Writing for snare drums requires a knowledge of different types of rolls, both open and closed.

♦ You can write out a specific drum set part, or just indicate general rhythms and let the drummer do his or her own thing.

♦ Added color can be provided by the use of Latin percussion instruments, as well as traditional orchestral percussion, such as the tambourine and triangle.

Chapter 12

Voices

In This Chapter

 ◆ Mastering ranges for all voices—from soprano to bass

 ◆ Discovering how to write for younger singers

 ◆ Incorporating common vocal characteristics

It might seem odd to apply the words orchestration or instrumentation to voices, but a singer's voice is his or her instrument. When writing for voices, one has to consider the same factors as when writing for any other type of instrument—range, transposition, tonal characteristics, and the like. Even when one masters this basic vocabulary, I find writing for voice more challenging than writing for other instruments. That's because the vocalist has to actually *sing* the part you write. It's not just a matter of mechanically reproducing notes as written; the vocal lines you write have to make sense melodically—that is, they have to be *singable*. And that takes some work.

Understanding Vocal Orchestration

When you're writing vocal music, you typically have two female voices and two male voices at your disposal, with an optional third male voice (baritone) available. Obviously, you don't have to use all these voices in all situations; for example, if you're writing background vocals for a pop tune, you may only work with two or three voices, instead of the entire choir. But you still have to know *which* two or three voices to use, and how they work—which is where vocal orchestration comes in.

Ranges and Transpositions

Compared to an instrumental ensemble, a vocal ensemble is fairly easy to write for. That's because all the voices reproduce exactly what you write, with absolutely no transposition—except for the tenor, that is, which sounds a simple octave lower than written.

The challenge when writing for voices is the relatively narrow range of each voice—at least among normally skilled singers. (Exceptional talents can somewhat exceed these ranges, as you might suspect.) If you exceed the singable range, the part simply can't be sung. In fact, as you near the extremes of each range (top or bottom), the singing begins to sound strained. So range in vocal writing is particularly important.

Table 12.1 describes the range and transposition of each of these voices.

Table 12.1   Vocal ranges and transpositions

Voice	Range (as sounds)	Range (as written)	Transposition
Soprano			Sounds as written
Alto			Sounds as written
Tenor			Write one octave above concert pitch on the treble clef (unless sharing a staff with the basses)
Baritone			Sounds as written
Bass			Sounds as written

Common Techniques

Vocal music can be written on either two staves (soprano and alto on the treble clef, tenor and bass on the bass clef), four separate staves (one for each voice), or some combination of the two approaches (such as soprano and alto on separate staves with tenor and bass sharing a staff). When using the four-staff SATB notation, the tenor line is on a treble clef with a small "8" below the clef, as shown in Figure 12.1; this signifies that the notes sound one octave lower than written. (This is sometimes called the *vocal tenor clef.*) Piano accompaniment is always placed below the vocal parts.

Figure 12.1

The vocal tenor clef—sounds one octave lower than written.

One of the most common vocal techniques is the use of *vibrato*. This is similar to instrumental vibrato, in which a sustained note wavers somewhat. Vibrato is typically a part of an individual singer's vocal characteristics, and is not normally indicated in the music except to eliminate the vibrato for special effect (i.e., "no vibrato").

Another characteristic that you can notate, if you like, is the use of *melisma*. This effect occurs when the singer swoops up and down in pitch while singing a constant syllable. (Think Mariah Carey here—or Aretha Franklin, if you want the real deal.) Melismatic singing comes from gospel music via R&B and soul, and typically takes its alternate notes from the blues scale.

A less-common vocal technique, sometimes used in popular music (and also in some classical works), is the use of the *falsetto* voice. This is a register above a male singer's normal range, typically with different vocal characteristics than the singer's normal range. Falsetto is best used by solo singers, and not by ensembles.

When arranging for voices, close voicing is often better than open voicing, especially between similar voices. Try not to voice notes more than an octave between soprano and alto or alto and tenor. (You can have a larger gap between tenor and bass, due to the different vocal characteristics of these two voices in the extremes of their registers.)

That said, you may want to accentuate the differences between voices when one voice carries the melody and the others sing harmony. For example, you might write the soprano with the melody in the upper part of her range, while keeping the alto with harmony notes in the lower part of her range. This wide voicing helps to set the melody apart from the harmony.

Arranging for Younger Voices

Special consideration should be given when arranging for younger voices. Less-mature voices simply don't have the same range as more mature voices, and you have to take this into account when arranging for specific groups.

When arranging for the elementary school level, it pays to keep it simple. Avoid complicated rhythms and large leaps; stick to easy step-wise lines. Most elementary-level choirs have just one or two vocal parts—and the younger the choir, the more likely they are to sing (or attempt to sing) in unison. You should keep both parts within the relatively narrow range detailed in Figure 12.2.

Figure 12.2

Vocal range for elementary school choirs.

When you get to middle school (grade six through eight), the singers have a bit more training under their belts—but now have to face the challenge of changing voices. And it's not only the boys' voices that change; the girls' voices are maturing, as well.

Boys whose voices have not yet changed could be classified as tenors, although the current "correct" term for this voice is *cambiata*. Whatever you call it, this voice sings in the female alto range, with music notated on the treble clef, with no transposition.

Those boys whose voices *have* changed don't quite graduate to bass status just yet. Instead, they're more apt to sing in the baritone range, notated on the bass clef.

Girls' voices at this age are starting to mature, but still tend to fall in a generic middle—they haven't yet separated into true higher (soprano) and lower (alto) ranges. For this reason, it's best to write girls' voices in the low soprano range, typically in two parts. These parts can be noted soprano I and soprano II, just I and II, or (more rarely) soprano and alto.

This adds up to a four-voice choir comprised of soprano I, soprano II, cambiata (tenor), and baritone. The ranges for each voice are detailed in Table 12.2.

Table 12.2   Voice ranges for middle school choirs

Voice	Range (as written and sounds)
Soprano I	
Soprano II (alto)	
Cambiata (tenor)	
Baritone	

By the time you get to high school, most of the voices have changed, and you can write in traditional soprano, alto, tenor, and bass voices. However, high school vocal ranges are not quite as wide as the fully developed ranges detailed in Table 12.1; instead, you should use the slightly more limited ranges detailed in Table 12.3. (Remember, the tenor voice is either written on the vocal tenor clef, or an octave higher on the regular treble clef.)

Table 12.3   Voice ranges for high school choirs

Voice	Range (as written and sounds)
Soprano	
Alto	
Tenor	
Bass	

When writing for any elementary, middle, or high school choir, try to avoid the extreme registers of any voice. Youthful voices at the extremes not only tire easily, they sound thin, strained, and dynamically weak. For the best tone, write in the beefy part of each range.

Examining Individual Voices

The general conception is that voice classifications are based on vocal range or pitch abilities—that is, how high or how low one can sing. While this is true, more factors need to be considered when classifying a particular voice type. For example, tone quality is equally important in making this determination. Other factors—such as *tessitura*, *timbre*, and *passaggio*—can also come into play.

def•i•ni•tion

Tessitura is the range within which most tones of a voice part fall. **Timbre** (pronounced "tamber") is the distinctive character of a voice—in other words, its tone quality. **Passaggio** is that point where the vocal quality switches from one register to another; the two registers are commonly referred to as *head voice* and *chest voice*. This transition point is also called a *lift* or *break*.

Soprano

The soprano is the highest female voice, and is typically assigned the lead or melody line. The typical soprano range starts at middle C and goes up at least one and a half octaves, to the first G above the treble-clef staff.

Sopranos are further subdivided into types according to their differing timbres, ranges, and technical abilities. The highest, lightest, and perhaps most "agile" soprano is called the *coloratura*. Coloraturas are typically assigned highly ornate songs and arias, sung mostly on one-syllable nonwords somewhere in the upper stratosphere.

The most familiar or generally accepted soprano voice is the *lyric soprano*; this is the "standard" soprano voice. Another subdivision of soprano is the *mezzo soprano* (mezzo means "middle"), with the same overall range and quality of the lyric but with a little more power in the lower range.

Whichever soprano we're talking about, the highest notes in the range often sound quite shrill, especially with younger or less-skilled singers. The soprano will also sound strained at the bottom of her range.

Alto

The alto is the lower female voice, with a deep and resonant tone. The range of a typical alto starts on the G below middle C, and goes up one and a half octaves, which results in substantial overlap with both the male tenor and the female soprano voices.

In classical singing, the alto voice can be quite heavy and dark, sounding almost like a tenor. In popular singing (especially in jazz), this type of voice sounds warm and rich in its depth of tone.

Altos tend to sound strained at the top of the vocal range. It's best to keep the alto lower, and to write in unison or parallel harmony with the tenor voice.

Tenor

The highest and probably most common of the male voices—especially in popular music—is the *tenor*. The tenor range overlaps significantly with the range of the female alto, and with the male bass.

Most of the famous male popular singers—now and in the past—fall under the category of *lyric tenor*. The *dramatic tenor* has a similar range to the lyric tenor, but displays a heavier or perhaps more resonant quality. There is an additional, rarely used, type of tenor called the *countertenor*. This is a falsetto part above the regular tenor.

When writing for male choruses, the tenor typically is assigned the lead or melody line. The tenor voice blends well with both basses (at the top of the range) and altos.

Baritone

Bridging the gap between the tenor and the bass is the *baritone*—sometimes referred to as Bass I. (The traditional bass voice is then designated Bass II.) Although rarely broken out separately in choral music, it is a very "listen-able" voice, being rather lyric in quality. It lends itself well to a lot of popular repertoire.

> **Note**
>
> Mezzo sopranos are sometimes designated Soprano II or "second sopranos," and are typically assigned a harmony part a few notes below the main melody.
>
> Alto is short for *contralto*—a designation you'll find in some classical music.

> **Note**
>
> Remember, when the tenor part is written on the treble clef, it sounds an octave lower than written.

Bass

The lowest and heaviest of the male voices is, of course, the bass. The bass voice can be very powerful, capable of overwhelming many lighter voices. Note, however, that at the low end of the bass range, the sound gets a tad rumbly. At the high end of the range, the sound is somewhat strained and sometimes shrill.

The bass voice is typically used to provide the foundation to any harmony, most often assigned the root notes of chordal accompaniment. Basses blend well with tenors, but less well with higher female voices.

Note
Most high school "basses" are actually baritones—and only become true basses as their voices deepen over time.

The Least You Need to Know

- ◆ The four most common voices are soprano, alto, tenor, and bass—with the baritone voice being an occasionally used option.

- ◆ Younger choirs require different arranging techniques—including the use of different vocal ranges.

- ◆ You can arrange vocal music on either two shared staves (treble and bass), four individual staves (one per voice), or some combination of the two.

- ◆ Voices are best kept in the middle part of their ranges; voices at the extremes can sound thin and strained.

Part 3

Real-World Arranging

Now that you've mastered the skills and know how to use each instrument, it's time to put those skills to use—by creating your own arrangements. Read on to learn how to create specific types of arrangements, for rock band, big band, marching band, orchestra, choir, and popular recording.

13

Arranging for a Rhythm Section

In This Chapter

- ◆ Discovering what the rhythm section does—and how
- ◆ Learning how to write individual rhythm-section charts
- ◆ Mastering different types of beats
- ◆ Creating an arrangement for a rock band

The nucleus of any rock, country, blues, or jazz band—and of most Broadway musicals, show choirs, and the like—is the rhythm section. This is the core group of musicians who keep the beat going, over which you arrange all the melody and harmony parts.

Writing for the rhythm section is an essential skill required of any serious arranger. And it's not as easy as it seems; there are specific techniques you need to learn to make it work.

Elements of the Rhythm Section

Just what instruments are in a typical rhythm section? Well, if there was such a thing as a typical rhythm section, this would be an easier question to answer. In reality, the instruments present depend on the genre and the specific ensemble, and can include any or all of the following:

- ◆ Piano and other keyboards, including synthesizers and samplers
- ◆ One or more guitars (either electric or acoustic)
- ◆ Bass (either electric bass guitar or acoustic string bass)

◆ Drums (drum set, that is)

◆ Percussion (various auxiliary and Latin percussion instruments, from congas to tambourine)

This core group is sometimes augmented by multiple players on any instrument (two or three guitars, for example, or two keyboard players), and sometimes by related instruments, such as vibes or organ.

There are some common combinations used in specific types of ensembles, as detailed in Table 13.1.

Table 13.1   Common rhythm section combinations

Ensemble	Rhythm section
Rock band	Rhythm guitar(s), keyboards (optional), bass, drums
Country band	Rhythm guitar(s), mandolin (optional), keyboards (optional), bass, drums
R&B/soul band (classic)	Rhythm guitars(s), keyboards (typically electric piano or organ), bass, drums
Hip-hop section	DJ (scratch), rhythm guitars (optional), keyboards, bass, drums, percussion (optional)
Jazz ensemble (small)	Piano, bass, drums
Big band	Piano, rhythm guitar (optional), bass, drums, percussion (optional)

Naturally, these are not hard and fast configurations. For example, some small jazz ensembles use an organ/guitar/drums configuration instead of piano/ bass/drums, with the organ handling the bass part of the equation. And rock bands can be anything from a simple three-piece outfit (guitar/bass/drums) to monster groups with three or more guitars, a couple of keyboards, and double drums. It's variable.

Roles of the Rhythm Section

The rhythm section is there to back the other musicians. It provides not only the underlying beat (typically via repeated rhythmic patterns), but also the basic harmonic background to a piece.

Within the rhythm section, there are three primary roles:

◆ The beat or groove, which is typically supplied by drums and percussion.

◆ The bottom or bass line, which is (not surprisingly) supplied by the bass guitar.

◆ The chordal accompaniment, which can be provided by either guitar or keyboard.

The beat is accomplished via rhythmic repetition. This may be nothing more than a simple two-and-four backbeat with an eighth-note ride, or it may be something more complicated, like the clave pattern used in Latin music. In most cases, the beat is the responsibility of the drums, supported by the other instruments.

On slower tunes, the beat is less important and becomes less prominent; on some ballads, the pulse can evaporate to the point where the drummer either plays with brushes or drops out altogether. Conversely, in some genres (dance music, hip hop, etc.) the beat is all there is, to the point where the rest of the accompaniment becomes something akin to a rhythmic chant.

A piece's rhythmic foundation is also enhanced by comping from the keyboard and rhythm guitar players. On piano, this is typically accomplished by playing block chords in a rhythmic pattern. On guitar, this is also accomplished by playing chords in a rhythmic pattern. Sometimes the piano and guitar will play the same pattern; other times they'll play complementary patterns.

The bass line reinforces the beat and grounds the piece harmonically, typically by playing the root notes of the underlying chords. Rhythmically, the bass line can be straight-ahead "four on the floor" (common in jazz), a two-beat (playing only on beats one and three, as with some country and older dance music), a doubling of the drummer's bass-drum pattern, or something outside the norm. The more rhythmic the music, the more likely it is that the bass line will closely follow what the drummer is doing.

The final function of the rhythm section is to fill in the background of a piece, by playing background chords. Naturally, the bass line implies the chords by playing the roots; the full chords are provided by the keyboard(s) and/or guitar(s). The chords may be provided in a rhythmic fashion (the patterns played by the rhythm guitarist, for example), by more free-form chordal comping (typically played by the keyboardist), or by longer sustained chords (provided by a synthesizer, organ, or even vibes).

Put together, the instruments of the rhythm section can create the sound of a complete ensemble—minus only the melody.

Rhythm-Section Notation

Here's the most important thing to know about arranging for a rhythm section—in most forms of jazz and popular music, you don't actually write out all the notes. That's right, most rhythm section parts are just sketches; you rely on the individual players to essentially ad lib their own parts.

That doesn't mean that you're completely off the hook, or that the rhythm section is a total free-for-all. One way or another, you have to provide the following information to each player.

♦ Which instruments you want to be played

♦ Where in the piece you want each instrument to play, and where you want any instruments to rest

♦ The chords that must be played

♦ The overall style or rhythm of the piece

♦ Specific rhythms you want played

♦ Specific melodic lines or figures you want played at certain points

Beyond this combination of both general and specific instructions, the individual players are free to improvise their own parts. This is actually a good thing, as it frees you from trying to come up with natural-sounding parts for instruments that you probably don't know how to play. After all, the specifics of creating a measure-long drum fill are probably best left to a drummer, who can do that sort of thing in his sleep.

That said, there are some general guidelines you can use when writing for the instruments of the rhythm section. Read on to learn more.

Writing for Piano and Keyboards

The "piano" in a rhythm section can be an acoustic piano, or one of any number of keyboard instruments—electric piano, organ, synthesizer, you name it. If you have a particular instrument in mind, say so; otherwise, leave the choice of instrument to the player.

When writing for a synthesizer, sampler, or even an organ, you'll need to specify the type of sound you want. While it's almost impossible to dictate exact sounds, you can provide a verbal description of the sounds you'd like to hear—and then let the keyboardist use her best judgment in picking an appropriate sound.

There are a few ways to notate a keyboard part in a rhythm-section environment. You can simply write slashes for each beat, with the chord symbols above, as shown in Figure 13.1. You can also write out the desired bass line on the bottom clef, with chord symbols on the treble clef, as shown in Figure 13.2. Another option is to write slash rhythms, as shown in Figure 13.3, which is necessary if you want the pianist to pick up a particular rhythm pattern. Or you can indicate the melody line on the upper staff, with chord symbols above, as shown in Figure 13.4. This gives the piano player an indication of what's going on where, which can better help him put together his part on the fly. (It also helps the pianist, as accompanist, cue the lead instrument or vocalist.)

> **Note**
>
> The keyboard part is typically notated on the grand staff, although sometimes a single bass-clef staff is used instead.

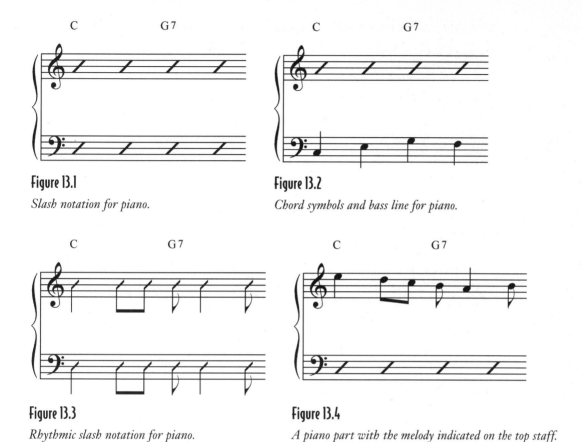

Figure 13.1

Slash notation for piano.

Figure 13.2

Chord symbols and bass line for piano.

Figure 13.3

Rhythmic slash notation for piano.

Figure 13.4

A piano part with the melody indicated on the top staff.

However you notate the piano part, don't expect the pianist to take your part literally; it's only a guide—unless you have specific voicings or patterns that you want the keyboardist to play, that is. In that instance, write out the complete part, even if it's only for part of a measure.

It's also useful to notate horn parts on the top line of the piano part when you're writing for big bands and similar ensembles. It's also a good idea to indicate key ensemble passages, so that the pianist can either double or stay out of the way of these passages.

Writing for Guitar

As with the keyboard part, the "guitar" part in a rhythm section can mean a lot of things—acoustic six-string guitar, acoustic twelve-string, solid-body electric, hollow-body electric, electric twelve-string, you name it. And when you're dealing with electric guitars, there is an almost limitless number of sounds available, resulting from the combinations of different guitars, amplifiers, tone pedals, fuzz boxes, and the like. Unless you have a particular sound in mind, it's often best to let the individual players choose their own instruments and sounds.

That said, you may wish to employ more than one guitarist in a rhythm section. One approach is to use two rhythm guitarists, one playing staccato two and four backbeats, the other playing a more complex rhythmic pattern. Another approach is to supplement the rhythm guitar(s) with a lead guitar, playing short single-note lines and countermelodies. If you use multiple guitarists, strive for some sort of sonic variety among the instruments; this can be accomplished by the use of different instruments (acoustic vs. electric, solid-body vs. hollow-body) and by the use of different amplification and processing.

When writing a guitar part, you don't have to—and shouldn't—notate all the notes of a chord; instead you can use slash marks to indicate background comping (as shown in Figure 13.5), specific rhythmic patterns (as shown in Figure 13.6), or the top note of a line to indicate specific voice leading (as shown in Figure 13.7). In all instances, simple chord symbols are written above the measures. Unless a particular rhythm is specified, it's up to the guitarist to determine which rhythmic patterns and chord voicings to use.

Figure 13.5

Typical free-form guitar rhythm, with chords above the slash marks.

Figure 13.6

Indicating a specific rhythm in the guitar part.

Figure 13.7

Indicating a specific voice leading in the guitar part.

This type of notation is used because the voicing of the individual notes in a chord is best left to the guitarist. (Unless, of course, the arranger is an accomplished guitarist in his own right.) There are so many different ways to play any individual chord, it's appropriate to simply note the chord symbol and let the guitarist figure out which fingering to use.

Writing for Bass

In much jazz and popular music, creation of specific bass parts is best left up to the bassist, unless you have a definite bass pattern in mind. As with the guitar part, the bass part can be notated with just the chord symbol and slash marks; specific lines can be notated within this structure.

That said, there are two specific types of bass lines that are common in certain types of music.

The *two to a bar* bass style is used in some country and older dance music. In this style, the bass plays half notes on beats one and three of each measure (or quarter notes separated by quarter rests), as shown in Figure 13.8. If there are two chords per measure, the bass always plays the root of each chord. If a single chord extends the length of a measure, the second note (on beat three) is typically the fifth of the chord.

Figure 13.8

A two-to-the-bar bass line.

The second common bass style is the *walking bass line*, typically used in jazz and blues music, in both the swing and shuffle styles. A walking bass line is a string of straight quarter notes that move in step-wise motion up and down the scale, often incorporating accidentals outside the scale, as shown in Figure 13.9.

Figure 13.9

A walking bass line.

If you simply notate chord symbols for the bass part, the bassist will compose her own walking bass line on the fly. If you feel comfortable composing your own walking bass line in the score, however, you can do so.

To compose a walking bass line, follow these general rules:

> **Note**
>
> Listen to Track 12 on the CD to hear an example of a walking bass line in a jazz setting.

- ◆ Always place the root of the chord on the beat where the new chord first appears.

- ◆ Lead into each root with an approach note that is a half step above or below the root. (You can also lead into the root with whole-step movement, but the half step provides a stronger leading tone.) This approach note may not be part of the underlying chord—or even of the underlying scale. That's okay; the more unstable the approach note, the stronger the push into the next chord.

- ◆ Fill the gaps between the root and the next approach note with both chord and nonchord tones, using primarily step-wise movement with a combination of half steps and whole steps.

- ◆ You can vary the step-wise movement with selected intervals, including thirds, fifths, and octaves. You can also repeat the root, as appropriate.

- ◆ Avoid leaping into a nonchord tone. It's okay to move step-wise to a non-chord tone, however.

The key to writing an effective walking bass line is to listen to it. Let your ears be the final judge as to what does and does not work.

Writing for Drums

When you write a drum part, you have a choice. You can write out a specific beat (and then use repeat signs to show the beat across multiple measures, as shown in Figure 13.10), or you can simply indicate a general feel and how many measures you want the drummer to play. If you employ the latter approach (which is most common; most arrangers aren't drummers and don't know how to write viable drum parts), you should break up the drum part in sections, with the number of measures in each section noted.

Figure 13.10

A notated drum part, repeated over multiple measures.

There are three variations to these approaches. One that some musically inclined drummers seem to like is to write the melody or lead line into the drum part. This lets the drummer follow along with what's happening in the rest of the ensemble—although it only works if the drummer can read music.

The second variation, quite common in big-band music, is to notate "kicks" and accents in the drum part, as shown in Figure 13.11. In big-band jazz, the drummer has to set up these ensemble patterns and accents, and knowing where they are in the music is helpful. It also helps to label each cue with the name of the section or instrument that will be playing, so the drummer will know what to listen for.

Figure 13.11

A big-band drum chart with kicks and accents notated.

The third variation comes when you want a particular pattern to be played, but you don't care on what drums the drummer plays it. In this instance, you simply write the rhythm into the drum part, as shown in Figure 13.12, without noting a particular drum or series of drums. You can use either standard or slash notation.

Figure 13.12

A drum part with a desired rhythm notated; the drummer can choose how to play it.

Naturally, you need to note at the beginning of the chart the desired style and tempo for the piece. You should also notate any changes in dynamics throughout. And if you want the drummer to play a fill at a given point, put that into the chart as well, as shown in Figure 13.13.

Figure 13.13

A basic drum chart with fills indicated.

Arranging Different Feels

Whether you're writing for a jazz, rock, or country group, the entire rhythm section needs to know what feel they're supposed to play. Some feels are easier to describe or notate than others.

Straight-Ahead Rock

Let's face it. When you're arranging popular music of all types, the most common feel you'll write is the good old straight-ahead rock beat. This is a 4/4 beat that can be subdivided into equal and steady quarter, eighth, and sixteenth notes. There are plenty of variations on this beat, of course (that's what makes even rock music interesting), but the generic version is notated in Figure 13.14.

Figure 13.14

A few bars of a basic rock beat, for bass and drums.

Track 7

What's interesting about this beat is how versatile it is. It can be played at slow tempos for power ballads or extremely fast tempos for death metal. It is utilized in classic rock, alternative rock, heavy metal, country/rock, country, R&B, classic soul, and even some smooth jazz. It is, without a doubt, the most popular basic beat in popular music.

It's also the easiest beat to indicate. You can write out the beat, as shown in Figure 13.14, or you simply write "Rock beat" or "Straight eighths" or "Basic rock" at the top of the chart. The musicians will know what to play.

Country Two-Beat

Much of today's country music is just pop or rock music gussied up with a few fiddles and steel guitars. (And with a twangy-voiced singer wearing cowboy boots, of course.) Listen to any contemporary country station, and you'll hear a basic rock beat supplemented with a few unique Nashville touches.

There are other types of country music, however. When you edge toward more traditional country or Bluegrass, you often hear the classic country two-beat. Think of this as a basic rock beat played twice as fast, or a basic beat with the accents on the upbeats, or a variation on old-time two-beat dance music. (Think polka.) Whatever you call it, it looks and sounds like the example in Figure 13.15.

Figure 13.15

A few bars of a classic country two-beat.

Track 8

The bass line, of course, is the same two-beat line that we discussed previously in this chapter—it plays the root and the fifth on beats one and three. The guitar can pick a single-note line or strum chords in a constant pattern. The drum part can be a simple quarter ride with two-beat bass and two and four backbeats (sometimes played with rimclicks), or it can be gussied up into a "train" beat by playing accented eighth notes on the snare with brushes, as shown in Figure 13.16.

Figure 13.16

A country "train" beat on drums.

This country beat is not a heavy beat. It's light and rhythmic, with a gentle drive—the sort of beat that would feel right at home behind anyone from Johnny Cash to Patty Loveless.

Dance Groove

When you want a heavier beat, you're talking dance music. There are lots of different styles of dance music, from old-school disco to modern techno, but what they have in common is a relentless pulse, as demonstrated in Figure 13.17.

Figure 13.17

A few bars of a modern dance beat.

Track 9

The pulse of a dance groove is achieved, first and foremost, by a heavy four on the floor bass drum. The electric bass (sometimes supplemented by synthesized bass) can follow along, or play something a little funkier. The drummer typically plays sixteenth notes on the hi-hat (sometimes with open notes on the upbeats, especially in disco-like styles), and the guitar (when there is a guitar) plays a chucka-chucka muted rhythm or, in techno music, something a little spacier. The whole thing, especially in more contemporary forms, is supplemented by lots and lots of synthesizers, some playing rhythmic patterns and some adding chordal "pads" that create a constant texture above the beat.

When you're arranging dance music, you definitely have to specify the beats per minute (120 bpm is quite common), and you should think about all the different ways you can reinforce the beat and the rhythm. And that rhythm is all straight sixteenths—and lots of them.

Latin Beat

Another popular beat falls outside the realm of American rock and pop music. World music, particularly Latin music, is increasingly popular among the general populace. As such, it's important to learn how to write a basic Latin beat.

Of course, there's no such thing as "the" Latin beat. So-called Latin music (hailing from Mexico, South America, Cuba, and similar environs) is as diverse and as complex as American rock music. That said, there is one Latin beat that is arguably more common and more popular than the rest—so popular that you even find it in rock and pop music.

This beat is called the *clave*. As you can see in Figure 13.18, the clave is a two-bar pattern, typically played on the drum set (with rimclick on the snare drum) or other percussion instrument, superimposed over a pulsing bass guitar. The basic rhythm is often augmented by other percussion, such as maracas, shakers, congas, cowbell, and, yes, claves.

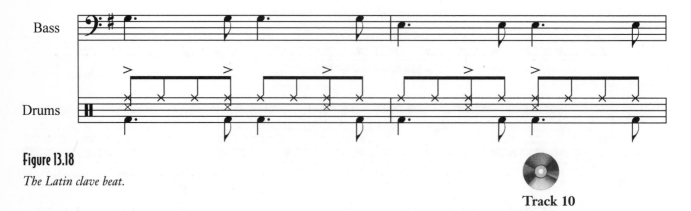

Figure 13.18

The Latin clave beat.

Track 10

You can use the clave beat in big-band writing, as a rhythmic accompaniment in marching band or drum corps music, or as the groove in various rock and pop songs. It comes up less frequently in orchestral and country music, and not much at all in the core choral repertoire.

Shuffle Beat

So far, all the beats we've discussed have had a straight-eighths or straight-sixteenths foundation. But not all beats are so straight ahead. When you're talking blues and some rock, you often use a shuffle beat, which is anything but straight.

The shuffle is based on a background of eighth-note triplets. In a shuffle, the bass player typically plays a walking bass line, either in straight quarters or in repeated shuffled eighth notes. The drummer can also play a quarter-note ride or a shuffled eighth-note ride, with either straight-quarter bass drum or a simple two-beat bass. (The snare is a traditional two and four backbeat, of course.) Depending on the speed of the shuffle, the rhythm guitar can play "chunk" chords on two and four, or play a shuffled eighth-note pattern.

Track 11

Notating a shuffle beat gets a little tricky. To be precise, you'd notate it with triplets, as shown in Figure 13.19, although it's seldom notated this way. More often it's notated as a dotted eighth- to sixteenth-note rhythm, as shown in Figure 13.20. It can also be notated as straight eighths, with the instruction "Shuffle" noted at the top of the chart, as shown in Figure 13.21. However it's notated, it's played the same way—with an eighth-note triplet pulse.

There are lots of variations to the basic shuffle beat for all rhythm-section instruments, but the key is to retain a laid-back, shuffling feel. That's where the beat gets its name, after all.

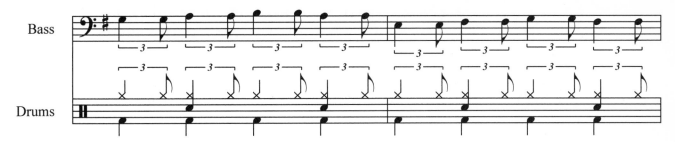

Figure 13.19

A shuffle beat notated with triplets.

Figure 13.20

A shuffle beat notated with dotted eighth and sixteenth notes.

Figure 13.21

A shuffle beat notated with straight-eighth notes.

Swing Beat

All of the previous beats are used in popular music. But when you move into the jazz realm, you have a quite-different groove to deal with.

The basic jazz beat is called swing, and like the shuffle, it's based on a triplet feel. Jazzers know how to swing like they know how to breathe; if it doesn't come naturally, it doesn't come at all. The swing beat is played on all types of jazz music from Dixieland to big band to bebop to cool (smooth jazz and jazz-rock excepted, of course).

A swing beat is easier to play than it is to notate. As with the shuffle, how it's played is often different from how it's dictated.

Track 12

The signature rhythm of a swing beat is the "spang spang-a-lang" played on the ride cymbal or hi-hat. While this is properly played with an eighth-note triplet pulse, as shown in Figure 13.22, it's often written with dotted eighth and sixteenth notes (as shown in Figure 13.23), or with straight-eighth notes (as shown in Figure 13.24). To be safe, indicate "Swing" at the top of the score, or add the type of note equivalency notation as shown in Figure 13.25.

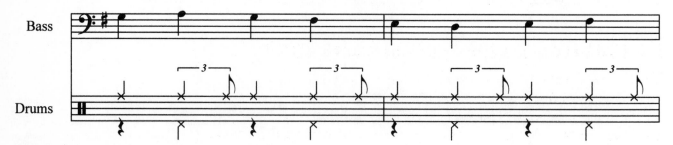

Figure 13.22

A swing beat notated with triplets.

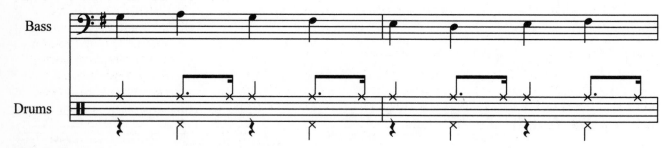

Figure 13.23

A swing beat notated with dotted eighth and sixteenth notes.

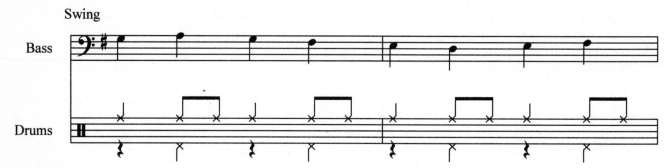

Figure 13.24

A swing beat notated with straight-eighth notes.

Figure 13.25

A note-equivalency notation, sometimes written at the top of a jazz chart.

However it's notated, the drummer almost always plays the "spang spang-a-lang" rhythm with her right hand, two and four with her left foot on the hi-hat, and then uses her left hand (snare) and right foot (bass drum) to play comping patterns and accents. The bass player (can be either electric or acoustic, depending on the group) plays a walking bass line. The piano player comps through the chord changes, and the rhythm guitarist (when there is a guitar—in jazz, it's very much an optional instrument) typically plays straight quarters.

Working from a Lead Sheet or Chord Chart

Whatever type of music a rhythm section is playing, it's not uncommon to work from either a *lead sheet* or *chord chart*. Although the two terms are sometimes used interchangeably, a lead sheet technically includes chords, melody, and lyrics, whereas a chord chart typically includes only chords (and sometimes melody—but never lyrics). There are examples of both in Appendix B.

The use of lead sheets and chord charts is especially prevalent in the studio environment. When a musician walks into the studio for a session, he's typically handed a chord chart of the song to be recorded; that's what everyone works off of.

Chord charts can be notated in several different ways. The traditional chord chart has the actual chords (C, Am, G7, and so forth) written out. Some chord charts have the chords written in Roman numeral notation (I, vi, V7, and so forth); this makes it easier for nonreading musicians to follow along, and to transpose the chords to different keys.

And in Nashville, so-called Nashville notation is sometimes used; this depicts the chords as simple numbers (1 for the I chord, 2 for the ii chord, and so forth). Chords are modified with "m" for minor and numbers for extensions, so that a ii7 chord is written as **2m7**. In addition, Nashville notation is seldom written on music paper; it's just a chord number followed by a number of slashes, with one slash for each beat of the chord, as shown in Figure 13.26.

Tip

When arranging for a recording session, check with the producer to determine what materials are required and the expected notation style.

1/// | 2m/// | 4/// | 5/// |

Figure 13.26
Nashville notation.

The point is that when you're arranging a rhythm section for a rock or country recording, you don't have to do a lot of arranging. In most instances, you can create a simple chord chart, using whatever type of notation is appropriate, and let the musicians work from that.

Creating a Rock Arrangement: "Love Waits"

Now let's get down to practicalities. Throughout the balance of this section of the book, we'll be working with a single composition, and arranging it for different types of ensembles. The piece is called "Love Waits," and the lead sheet for it is included in Appendix B.

Track 1

"Love Waits" is a relatively short composition, with a 12-bar verse (played three times) and an 8-bar bridge. The chord progression contains a few interesting chords and a fairly lively set of changes, while the melody plays among the extended chord notes. There's enough raw material there to play with, which is what we'll do—and what I encourage you to do. I've included this composition as something for you to work with to create your own arrangements; the arrangements I've included are just examples of what can be done.

Our first arrangement will be a simple one. We'll take the lead sheet (or corresponding chord chart, also found in Appendix B) and give it to a basic five-piece rock band with vocalist. The five instruments are keyboards, lead guitar, rhythm guitar, bass, and drums.

What we end up with is a very basic arrangement, which you can hear on Track 1 of the accompanying CD. The bass plays steady eighth notes throughout, in sync with the drummer's eighth-note hi-hat pattern. The rhythm guitarist plays a similar eighth-note pattern, and the drummer plays a basic rock beat with heavy snare-drum back beat, and a few fills at the end of selected phrases. There's also an organ part that comes in on the last half of the first verse, playing sustained chords.

The variety in the instrumental arrangement comes from the lead guitar. You first hear the lead guitar during the song's intro, then it drops out when the vocalist starts singing the first verse. It pops back in at the end of that verse, then continues into the second verse, playing echoing notes to the vocal. This addition in the second verse is what helps the piece to build. The building continues in the bridge, where the lead guitar plays whole-note *power chords* at the start of each measure. Then it's back to a more prominent solo line for the third verse and the out-chorus (the bit after the final verse), which helps the piece end on its highest point.

Instruments aside, the real key to a rock arrangement is the singer. In the recording of this piece, you can hear how vocalist Joanna Jahn takes liberties with melody as written, to create a more effective performance. The singer has to make the song her own, which means you as the arranger have to arrange around the performance. This sometimes means altering the arrangement *after* the vocal tracks have been laid down—or making sure the other musicians are versatile enough to adapt during a live performance. Let the singer sing, and then create the most effective showcase for his or her vocals.

Expanding Your Arrangement

If you want to add more tonal interest to this type of rock arrangement, you have to add more instruments. While this is difficult to do live (you only have so many musicians in the band), it's a very real option when you're in the recording studio. You can add more keyboards, or extra percussion, or background singers, or even horns or strings—the sky (and your budget) is the limit.

def•i•ni•tion

A **power chord** is a chord with just the root and the fifth. This type of chord is common in guitar-based rock music—but much less common on other instruments.

Of course, to add these extra instruments to a rock or pop recording requires a knowledge of arranging for those instruments—which is what we'll get into in the following chapters. We'll start (in Chapter 14) with arranging for big band (lots of horns), follow (in Chapter 15) with arranging for marching band (more horns and some additional percussion), lead from there (in Chapter 16) to arranging for orchestra (here come the strings), and end (in Chapter 17) with arranging for choir (vocal arranging). Once you've mastered the techniques for arranging for all those different instruments and voices, then you're ready to return to the studio and create a full-featured commercial popular recording—which we'll do in Chapter 18. There's lots of music ahead!

The Least You Need to Know

- Although the individual components of the rhythm section differ from style to style and from group to group, the basic instruments include keyboard (piano), guitar, bass, and drums.

- Individual rhythm-section parts can be fully notated, or sketched out with chords and slash notation.

- Different styles require different types of writing; for example, jazz pieces typically include a walking bass line.

- Studio musicians are comfortable working from lead sheets or chord charts, which display chord symbols for the piece being recorded.

Chapter 14

Arranging for a Jazz Big Band

In This Chapter

- ◆ Discover the elements of the different big-band styles
- ◆ Master the big-band form
- ◆ Learn how to create unison, two-, three-, four-, and five-part big-band voicings
- ◆ Find out how to voice for different sections, and for the full ensemble
- ◆ Create your own big-band arrangement

Maybe it's just my background, but I find arranging for big bands especially fun and challenging. There are a surprising number of colors available from the dozen and a half instruments you have to work with; it's exciting to discover new sounds by creating new combinations of these instruments.

In addition, big bands today play a wide variety of styles. What other ensemble can you write for that plays straight-ahead jazz, blues, rock, Latin, even avant-garde compositions? As a genre, big-band writing has few restrictions; it encompasses everything from Benny Goodman's classic swing to Count Basie's smooth blues to Stan Kenton's contemporary concepts to Maynard Ferguson's jazz/rock to the Big Phat Band's driving modern sounds. It's truly a medium where you can write pretty much whatever you want, and expect the musicians to be able to pull it off.

Of course, the bread and butter of big-band music is jazz. Which means you need a thorough grounding in jazz concepts—including improvisation—before you get started. You need to be comfortable using extended chords, reharmonizing existing progressions with various chord substitutions, and writing in all manner of sophisticated block harmony. You have to have your seventh and ninth chords mastered, and know your way around the blues scale. Then, and only then, will you be equipped to arrange your first big-band chart.

Big-Band Orchestration

While the numbers of players within each section may vary somewhat, the orchestration of a big band is fairly standardized. From top to bottom, here are the instruments you'll be writing for:

- **Saxophones:** Three to five players, typically two altos, two tenors, and a baritone sax. One or more altos typically doubles on soprano sax, and one or more of the altos or tenors may also double on flute.

- **Trumpets:** Three to five players. The lead trumpet and the solo player are typically two different musicians. Some or all of the players may also double on flugelhorn.

- **Trombones:** Three to five players. The fifth player may be a dedicated bass trombonist, or may simply double on the bass bone.

- **Rhythm section:** At a minimum we're talking piano, bass (either amplified acoustic or electric), and drums. May be supplemented with rhythm guitar, vibes, and/or percussion (typically congas and other Latin percussion).

And that's it. Anywhere from 12 to 20 players, all capable of playing section parts or solos. It's amazing how versatile this combination of instruments really is.

Big-Band Styles

I mentioned previously that today's big bands can play in a variety of styles. The most common styles are classic 1940s swing (Benny Goodman, Glenn Miller, Artie Shaw), straight-ahead jazz (Thad Jones/Mel Lewis, Woody Herman), hard-driving jazz (Buddy Rich, Big Phat Band), blues (Count Basie), Latin/jazz (Stan Kenton, Dizzy Gillespie), jazz/rock (Maynard Ferguson), and ballads (any and all). A given band may specialize in a particular style, or may have a book that encompasses multiple styles.

Specifics of each style are detailed in Table 14.1.

Table 14.1   Big-band styles

Style	Beat	Tempo	Dynamics	Voicings	Other Factors
Classic swing	Swing	Moderate	Varied	Block voicings, counter-melodies, melody with block chord accompaniment, liberal use of independent section playing	Emphasis on melody and harmony, emphasis on sax section (sometimes supplemented with one or more clarinets), fairly simple rhythmic approach

Style	Beat	Tempo	Dynamics	Voicings	
Straight-ahead jazz	Swing	Moderate	Varied	Block voicings, counter-melodies, melody with block chord accompaniment	Em... and harm... on sax section, ... use of solos
Hard driving jazz	Swing	Fast	Loud	Ensemble voicings, mixed sections, liberal use of unison lines, section treatments of melody and accompaniment	Liberal use of rhythmic figures and punches, emphasis on brass sections (trumpets especially)
Blues	Swing	Slow to moderate	Varied	Conventional voicings, sectional voicings, little use of mixed sections	Liberal use of blues scale, emphasis on riff backgrounds
Latin/jazz	Latin	Moderate to fast	Moderate to loud	Sectional orchestration, reduced emphasis on harmony, typical 3–5 part voicings	Very rhythmic, liberal use of extended percussion, emphasis on brass sections
Jazz/rock	Rock	Moderate	Moderate to loud	Sectional orchestration, liberal use of unison and octaves, little use of sophisticated harmony and voicings	Emphasis on modal and blues scales, liberal use of repetitive patterns
Ballads	Swing or rock	Slow to moderate	Soft to moderate	Lush block voicings, 4–5 part open voicings, section and ensemble backing of lead melody, little mixed-section writing	Often used as solo vehicles, drums using brushes

Big-Band Form

Most big-band music adheres to an established-yet-flexible form. You start with some sort of an introduction, move into a series of verses and chorus (some of which are used as sections for improvisation), perhaps play through a short interlude, ramp it up for the shout chorus, and then drive through to the ending.

Introduction

Most, but not all, big-band charts have some sort of introduction. The introduction may be as simple as a 4 to 8 bar *vamp* from the rhythm section, or as complex as a 16 to 32 bar section that mirrors themes from the piece's verse or chorus. Most introductions use some melodic, harmonic, or rhythmic ideas from the primary composition, in order to foreshadow, set up, and, yes, introduce the main piece.

def•i•ni•tion

A **vamp** is typically a chord pattern repeated over a pedal point—more often than not, the tonic or dominant of the key.

Verses and Choruses

The body of the chart consists of the composition's verses and choruses. These sections can be arranged as simple melody with accompaniment or block-voiced ensemble passages. One or more of these sections are generally given over to instrumental soloists, which we'll discuss next. Know, however, that you need to strike a balance between written and improvised sections. While jazz is all about improvisation, it's not really a big-band piece unless the whole band plays.

Solo

Most big-band charts devote at least one verse or chorus (or combination of the two) to one or more instrumental soloists, playing with either the rhythm section or with some sort of instrumental backing.

One popular approach is to give the soloist one verse with just the rhythm section, and then add instrumental backing for the second pass. These backgrounds should be used sparingly, as they tend to inhibit the soloist.

It's best if the instrumental backing complements the soloist. For example, if it's a trumpet solo, use woodwinds in the background. If it's a tenor sax solo, write trumpet figures into the background. And if the solo instrument and the backing instruments are similar or play in a similar range, create contrast by using other devices—*punches* and *kicks* (as shown in Figure 14.1), muted unisons, open voicings, etc.

def•i•ni•tion

Jazz and big-band writing has its own peculiar vocabulary. For example, short rhythmic accents are variably called **kicks**, **punches**, **hits**, and **stings**. The word *sting* is also used to describe a tag ending. And the arrangement itself is, more often than not, called a **chart**. Learn the lingo!

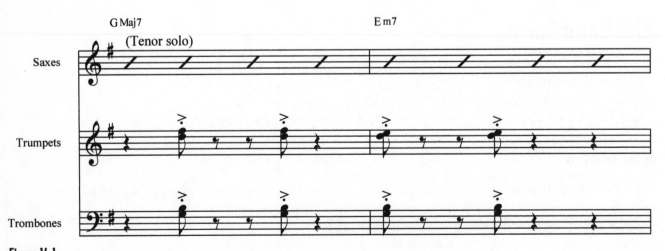

Figure 14.1

Behind a solo, punches and kicks from the brass section.

One more thing: you don't have to limit yourself to a single soloist in a piece. Many big-band *charts* include sections for two or even three individual soloists. You can dictate the length of each solo section, or insert repeat marks and let the solos go as long as they need to go when the piece is played live.

Interlude

Some big-band charts insert an interlude or bridge in the middle of the piece, either before or after an instrumental solo. An interlude is usually related to the piece's introduction or ending, either melodically or harmonically. On occasion, you can use an interlude to introduce brand new material, but it's better to use this section as a bridge between—and a break from—existing material.

Shout Chorus

Now we come to the "shout" chorus, a section somewhat unique to big-band writing. The purpose of the shout chorus, which comes near the end of the piece, is to provide a climax to the arrangement, and to synthesize all that has taken place before.

The shout chorus is either the penultimate or final chorus of the chart. It offers a little more of everything—it's louder, more rhythmically active, heavier on ensemble voicings, and has greater arranged density and complexity than the preceding sections. In other words, this is the section where the entire band stands up and "shouts." It's also where you, the arranger, pull out all the stops.

In spite of its name, a shout chorus can use material from either the verse or chorus (or both). It should be somewhere between a half chorus and two choruses long, just long enough to generate maximum excitement without becoming overbearing. The shout chorus typically builds on existing material within the piece, often paraphrasing the melody.

Ending

The chart doesn't end with the last note of the shout chorus—at least not usually. In most instances you'll want to tack on some sort of ending to the piece, a short section that puts a "period" or "exclamation point" on the entire chart. It's common for an ending to repeat some or all of some part of the piece, most often the introduction or interlude. You can also use harmonic or melodic material from the chorus or shout chorus, stretch the final phrase with an added turnaround, or use a short and rhythmic "tag" ending. The approach you use is up to you, as long as it works within the general nature of the piece.

Voicing in Big-Band Arrangements

When writing for a big band, you have anywhere from nine to fifteen instruments to work with (outside the rhythm section). You use these instruments to convey the melody and all harmony. To do this, you need to master the technique of voicing for saxes, trumpets, and trombones.

Most voicing for big band is in the form of *block voicing*. This is where the inside or harmony parts move in the same direction of the lead. The harmony parts can be literal harmony (based on the underlying chord) or harmony lines that follow the melody line.

General Voicing Guidelines

We'll get into specific types of voicings in a moment. But first, let's examine some general guidelines for voicing in the big-band environment:

♦ Denser four- and five-part voicings are more common than simpler two- and three-part voicings. It's easier to write for four or five voices, as you can simply use all the notes in the underlying chord. Writing for fewer voices forces you to choose which notes to leave out, and results in a thinner harmony.

♦ You don't have to follow classical voice-leading rules. For example, parallel movement is not only allowed but encouraged.

♦ When voicing for sections (that is, all saxes, trumpets, or trombones), the melody part is typically the highest part in the voicing. If you voice a harmony part above the lead, you need to specify dynamics that allow the lead to be heard distinctly from the higher harmony part.

♦ When voicing for mixed ensembles (a mixture of instruments from more than one section), the lead line doesn't have to be the top voice, but should be assigned to the loudest instrument—typically a trumpet part.

♦ Try to keep the melody higher than middle C, or the harmony parts (which are typically beneath the melody) will get muddy.

♦ Leading tones (notes of less than a beat that lead to a main note on the downbeat) are usually harmonized as part of the chord for the following note.

♦ Any bass notes you write into the instrumental voicing should be consistent with the notes played by the rhythm section's bassist.

Unison and Octave Voicing

You probably won't do a lot of unison and octave voicing in your big-band work. There are too many instruments at your disposal to focus solely on unison lines!

In general, you should use unison or octave lines only when there is ample harmonic support from the other instruments. For example, you might write for saxophones in octaves, against a background of trumpet punches or trombone block chords. Unless you're talking a true instrumental solo, you generally don't want a unison or octave line hanging out there without sufficient support.

Two-Part Voicing

When writing for two voices, you need to keep both voices within an octave. Two-part writing is typically all parallel lines, generally using thirds or sixths between the notes. Seconds and sevenths are also usable, but you should use fifths, octaves, and tritones only for specific effect—and avoid parallel fourths as much as possible.

If the melody note is a chord note, the harmony note should be a chord note, as well. Same thing with passing notes; if the melody is a passing note, make the harmony note a passing note, too.

As with most voice writing, you should try to avoid voice crossing. And if a chord changes across the barline while the melody line stays static, try to change the harmony note at the measure.

Three-Part Voicing

Three-part writing is an interesting tool for the big-band arranger. Believe it or not, using three-part voicings gives even the biggest big band a lighter, small-band feel.

When writing for three voices, keep all three voices within an octave. You should avoid the use of simple triads, except in *modal* compositions, where triads may be used freely. You should also avoid the use of parallel fourths. It's okay, however (and sometimes desirable), to introduce dissonance between two of the three voices.

One interesting approach to three-part voicing is to treat it as melody plus two-part harmony. With this approach, you can use parallel movement in the bottom two voices; thirds, seconds, and sixths are best. You should also experiment with contrary movement between the top (melody) voice and the bottom two voices.

When you're voicing a four-or-more-note extended chord for three voices, one or more notes will have to be left out. As to which chord tone to omit, here are some guidelines:

def•i•ni•tion

A **modal** composition is one where all melody and harmony is based on the notes within a specific mode, such as the Aeolian or Dorian modes.

♦ When voicing any extended chord, you must voice the third and the seventh—unless the root of a major seventh chord is in the lead voice, in which case you should voice the third and the fifth (or sometimes the sixth), instead.

♦ You don't have to voice the fifth, as it's the least important tone when defining a chord's harmonic nature. (Unless the chord has an altered fifth, in which case the fifth probably should be included in the voicing.)

♦ You don't have to voice the root, as it's typically present in the rhythm section.

Four-Part Voicing

The most common types of writing in big-band music uses four- and five-part voicings. Four-part voicing is particularly popular when writing single-section parts.

When creating four-part voicings, you must have four different voices—no doubling. In addition, all four voices should be within an octave.

You can create four-part voicing by taking a melody line and adding three other notes from the chord beneath the top line. You can also create a fourth voice from a simple triad, by adding the closest extensions—sixths, sevenths, or ninths.

Most four-part voicings are "rootless" voicings, where the root of the chord is not included in the voicing. This requires the used of extended chord notes, even if the chord is not initially notated in that fashion.

But what do you do when you're writing four-part voicings with extended chords that have more than four notes (ninth chords and above)? It's actually quite easy:

Tip

To create an open four-part voicing, simply drop the second voice down an octave.

- For ninth chords, omit the root.

- For eleventh chords, omit either the fifth or the third, or both.

- For thirteenth chords, omit the fifth and the root.

It's important to note that four-part voicing should not consist solely of triad stacks. Instead, vary the inversions to create more interesting intervals between voices.

Five-Part Voicing

Add one more voice and you get a five-part voicing. Five-part voicing is typically used when writing for the saxophone section, for mixed sections, and for the full ensemble.

While you can try to keep all five voices within an octave, this isn't always possible. This is especially so when the fifth voice is a low bass part that represents the root of the chord.

To create a five-part voicing, you start by using all available chord tones. If you still need another note, you can double the lead voice an octave lower, or use the next available extension. For example, you can turn a seventh chord into a ninth chord, or a simple triad into a sixth or seventh chord. But make sure you keep the lead line in the top voice, for clarity.

Voicings for Different Instruments

In addition to dealing with the number of voices, you also have to deal with the types of voices. Writing for saxophones is different than writing for trumpets, which is much different than writing for mixed sections or the full ensemble. Read on to learn more.

Saxophone Voicings

Because of the large range and easy blending of the saxophone section, from the alto (or soprano) down to the baritone, the saxophone section works well with all types of voicings.

When writing for the sax section, it's common to double the lead alto an octave lower in the bari sax. You can also move what would normally be the second alto part down an octave to the baritone, which forces you to revoice the inner parts and double the melody an octave lower in the second tenor part. This is called *drop-2* voicing. (A similar *drop-2-4* voicing drops both the second note and the fourth notes down an octave.)

However you voice the sax parts, make sure you keep the upper extensions—ninths, elevenths, and thirteenths—in the treble-clef range. Also try to voice thirds and sevenths immediately above the chord roots.

Trumpet Voicings

Unless you have an expanded section, you'll probably be writing for four trumpets. If a band has a fifth trumpet, he typically doubles the fourth trumpet part or is held in reserve for solos.

You seldom use open voicings in the trumpet section; if the notes are spread too far apart, you diminish the power of the section. In addition, notes written in the lower register do not balance well with higher parts—another reason to use closed or semi-closed voicings.

If you're writing the section in unison, there's no reason to write for more than three trumpets at a time, as three trumpets are as loud as four. Use the opportunity to let the lead player rest his or her lips.

Trombone Voicings

The trombone section sounds equally good in either closed or open voicings. Because the bones serve as the harmonic foundation of the band, you should almost always use the third and seventh chord tones in their voicings. You don't, however, have to include the chord root in the trombone voicings.

As to register, try to keep the lead trombone part above middle C. This leaves space beneath the lead for the other bones playing harmony notes, and it gives a little more bite to the most important line. You should also try to write any extended notes (sevenths and above) above the clef, to avoid creating a muddy sound.

Mixed Sections

Writing for mixed sections means writing for instruments in two (not three) different sections—saxes and trombones, trumpets and saxes, or trumpets and trombones. Mixed-section writing gives you a lot of flexibility, as the different combinations can create a large number of interesting and unique sounds.

Note, however, that a mixed section doesn't have to include all the instruments in each section. Some of the more popular mixed section combinations include the following:

- Unison trumpets against harmonized, rhythmically contrasting trombones

- Alto and tenor sax melody and harmony against rhythmically contrasting trombones, accompanied by bari sax

- Two or three trumpets playing contrasting rhythms against the remaining trumpets and the trombones

- Bass trombone or bottom two trombones in a rhythmically contrasting bass line with the other brass

Tip

When voiced with trombones, trumpets contribute certain "color" notes, such as altered tones and extended harmonies.

Ensemble Writing

For the utmost flexibility, you have the option of writing for the entire ensemble—all the instruments playing at a single time. Not necessarily playing a single note, of course, although this sort of unison playing is permissible.

When writing for the entire ensemble, here are some interesting approaches to try:

- **Block voicing,** where you combine the instruments into five distinct voices—with the lead voice typically doubled an octave lower, as shown in Figure 14.2.

- **Stacked voicing,** where you write closed voicing for the trumpets on top of the stack, closed or open voicing for the trombones immediately below, and open voicing for the saxes—with the lead alto doubling the second or third trumpet, as shown in Figure 14.3.

- **Big chords,** where you add chord tones downward from the lead, as shown in Figure 14.4. You should employ smaller intervals at the top of the chord stack, and larger intervals down lower. You can double roots and fifths, but try to avoid doubling the thirds. Make sure you place upper chord extensions in higher registers.

- **Melody plus chords,** where one instrument or section plays the melody, and the other instruments play simple block chords, as shown in Figure 14.5. Make sure that the lead line of the chordal accompaniment moves smoothly from note to note, creating a kind of simple countermelody that follows voice-leading principles. When you employ this approach, take care not to overwhelm the melody; use dynamics and smart instrument choices to make sure the melody always has prominence.

◆ **Melody plus rhythmic accompaniment,** where the nonmelody instruments play rhythmic "punches" or "stabs" instead of sustained chords, as shown in Figure 14.6. This is a good way to keep the background from overwhelming the melody.

◆ **Melody plus counterpoint,** where you create a second melodic line to complement the main melody. You can divide the two lines between all the instruments, or add a chordal or rhythmic accompaniment in addition to the countermelody, as shown in Figure 14.7.

◆ **Unisons and octaves.** As I said, you always have the option of using all unison/octave writing, if you wish. As you can see in Figure 14.8, this provides a very powerful sound—and is especially impressive in fast, rhythmically agile passages.

Tip

When writing section or ensemble passages, you should always pay particular attention to the lead part in each section. Every chord is voiced down from the lead part, so it's essential that the leads are written in a realistic range.

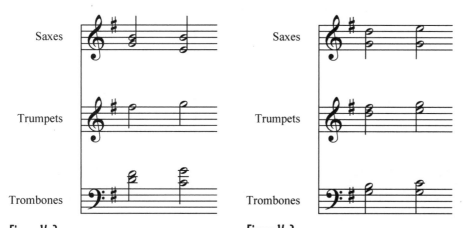

Figure 14.2

Five-part block voicing for the ensemble.

Figure 14.3

Stacked voicing for the ensemble.

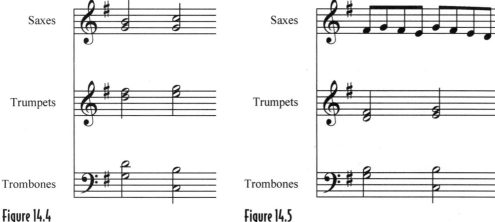

Figure 14.4

Big-chord voicing for the ensemble.

Figure 14.5

Melody plus chord voicing for the ensemble.

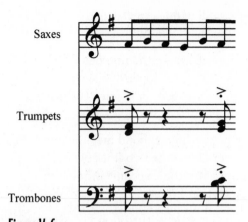

Figure 14.6

Melody plus rhythmic accompaniment for the ensemble.

Figure 14.7

Melody plus counterpoint (plus chords) for the ensemble.

Figure 14.8

Unison and octave voicing for the ensemble.

Creating Various Sounds and Effects

You can also vary the instruments and voicings in the band to create a variety of colors and effects. To this end, it's the saxophone section that's key. While the fourth trumpet always sounds a lot like the first trumpet, each voice in the sax section has its own unique sound. So don't treat the sax section as a single voice; instead, use the alto, tenor, and bari saxes separately and in combination with other instruments to create specific sounds and colors.

When looking for new sounds, the other important factor is in what order the instruments are voiced. The placement of specific instruments or sections within a voice stack dramatically affects the resulting sound.

We'll look at some examples.

Big Band as Reed Section

Let's say you want to harness the power of the full ensemble, but you want the band to sound like a reed section. It's doable, if you stack your instruments the right way.

To create the effect of a reed section, voice the instruments in the following top-to-bottom order: alto sax, trumpets, tenor sax, trombones, and baritone sax.

Tip

In general, when a brass instrument is in the lead, the ensemble takes the property of a brass section. When a saxophone is in the lead, the group takes the property of a reed section.

Big Band as Brass Section

Conversely, you can write the entire ensemble, saxes included, so that it sounds like a very powerful brass section. Just voice the instruments in the following top-to-bottom order: trumpets, alto sax, trombones, tenor sax, and baritone sax.

Big Band as French Horn Section

And here's a fun one. To create the effect of a French horn section (without any French horns), voice the instruments in the following top-to-bottom order: trumpets (in a bucket), alto sax, tenor sax, and trombones (in a bucket).

Note that for this effect, you leave out the bari sax—and you use bucket mutes on the brass.

Muted Brass

Which brings us to the last type of special effect, that produced when you use mutes on the brass. You can create a large number of colors and effects by noting different types of mutes for the trumpet and trombone sections. You can use straight mutes, Harmon mutes, buckets, plungers, hats, you name it. Mutes are also useful when you face balance problems, where the brass might overwhelm

Note

Learn more about brass mutes in Chapter 8.

softer woodwind instruments such as flutes and high saxophones. If nothing else, you can have some fun experimenting with all the different mute effects.

Employing Front and Back Phrasing

Because of the close-knit nature of the ensemble, most big bands are capable of playing very complex passages. That means you don't have to hold back on the syncopation, even when writing unison or ensemble passages; the big-band ensemble is small enough to play even tricky passages in perfect precision.

Coming from the jazz environment, big-band players are also adept at swinging a rhythm, and are actually somewhat uncomfortable playing a rhythm "straight." That means that you should phrase your melodic lines in a naturalistic fashion, as a jazz singer might sing them. For example, it's common to take a straight quarter-note melody and move the first note forward, to anticipate, or *front phrase*, the downbeat, as shown in Figures 14.9 and 14.10. You can also delay, or *back phrase*, the line, as shown in Figure 14.11.

def•i•ni•tion

When you move a note forward to anticipate the beat, it's called **front phrasing**, or "pushing" the beat. When you delay a note beyond the beat, it's called **back phrasing**, or "dragging" the beat.

Figure 14.9

A melody played straight.

Figure 14.10

The same melody with front phrasing—anticipating the beat in the previous measure.

Figure 14.11

The same melody with back phrasing—delaying the beat.

In both instances, it's the sort of subtle shifting of rhythm that a singer might do, and it's quite natural in the big-band environment. In fact, that's a good way to approach a big-band line; sing the line to yourself, in a swinging fashion, and then write it the way you sing it.

Creating a Big-Band Arrangement: "Love Waits"

Now it's time to create your own big-band arrangement. Your assignment: turn the "Love Waits" lead sheet (found in Appendix B) into a swinging big-band chart.

That's just what I've done on the second track of the accompanying CD. You can find the score for this arrangement in Appendix B.

Track 2

This is an up-tempo arrangement with a swing feel, somewhere between straight-ahead and hard-driving jazz. For time and space considerations, I've kept this arrangement short; there are no solo sections. However, as you attempt your own big-band arrangement of this piece, you should feel free to incorporate a few verses for instrumental improvisation, either with just the rhythm section or with some other instrumental backing. (Or both!)

The piece starts with an ostinato dotted quarter-note pattern from the rhythm section and trombones. The pattern builds over the introduction by adding extended notes on top of the basic chord.

The first verse starts with the melody in the saxes, over the ostinato pattern in the bones. Then, in the second half of the verse, the pattern breaks into straight-ahead four, with kicks in the brass. Note how the brass kicks continue in the trumpets after the end of the first verse, creating a polyrhythmic pattern against the trombone's return to the ostinato.

You should also listen carefully to the way the melody has been rhythmically altered. First, it's been augmented (doubled in rhythmic value) so that it fits better against the piece's fast tempo. Then, instead of straight quarter-notes or half-notes, the melody has been heavily syncopated—and syncopated differently in different parts of the chart. There's liberal use of front and back phrasing to impart a more swinging feel.

When we get to the second verse, the melody is passed off to the trumpets, with the saxes doing a smooth little answering counter figure and the bones continuing the ostinato pattern. Then, as the second verse winds down, the harmony opens up for some colorful extended chords, especially vibrant in the high trumpets and saxes.

The bridge provides a nice contrast to the rhythmically agile verses. The melody is kept relatively simple, the dynamics are dialed down, and we get a very straight-ahead feel with no ostinato patterns or punches. That's until the end of the bridge, of course; that's when the harmonies expand and the band kicks into gear for the final verse, or shout chorus.

The shout chorus is filled with kicks and countermelodies, lots of high-octane excitement. Once the climax is reached, everything dials down; the rhythms simplify, the dynamics decrease, the kicks and punches give way to smoother harmonies, and the original ostinato pattern returns. Then it's to a series of trading patterns as everything quickly ramps up again for the final sting.

There's a lot going on in this arrangement, especially given its short length. Listen carefully and analyze the chart to comprehend all the different techniques and voicings used throughout. Then try your own big band arrangement!

The Least You Need to Know

- The typical big band consists of three to five saxophones, three to five trumpets, three to five trombones, and a rhythm section.

- One of the key parts of any big-band arrangement is the shout chorus, which is the musical and emotional climax of the piece.

- Four- and five-part voicings are most used in any big-band chart, although you can also write for unison, one-, two-, and three-part voicings.

- For variety, you can arrange a mix of single-section, mixed section, and full ensemble passages.

- Create more sophisticated and swinging melodic lines by employing front and back phrasing, as well as other syncopated phrasing.

Chapter 15

Arranging for a Marching Band

In This Chapter

- ◆ Learn how the marching band differs from the drum and bugle corps
- ◆ Discover important tips for writing for marching bands
- ◆ Find out how to employ rudimental drumming
- ◆ Discover the particular challenges of marching-band writing—including creating complete shows

Bands are different from orchestras. Depending on how you look at it, a band can have both more and fewer colors available than a symphonic orchestra.

What do I mean by that? It's simple. Orchestras have strings, while bands don't. But bands have a greater variety of woodwind, brass, and percussion instruments than you typically find in orchestral music. So it's a little of this, a little of that, which creates a much different sound than you get with a symphonic orchestra—brighter and brassier.

Of course, there are several different types of bands. The jazz band or big band, as you learned in Chapter 14, is kind of like a small combo with a relatively small number of horns added. The concert band is more like an orchestra (minus the strings and plus the other instruments, of course), as the repertoire is of a similar nature. And then there's the marching band, which takes most (but not all) of the instruments of the concert band and puts them in motion, either down the street in a parade or on the field for a halftime show or competition. There is even a special instance of the marching band, called the drum and bugle corps, which has a more compact instrumentation (no woodwinds and only five types of brasses) and exists almost solely for competition.

As an arranger, you'll no doubt discover that there are lots of opportunities to practice your skills writing music for marching bands and drum corps. When you consider that just about every local high school has a marching band that needs music to play at football games, you can see the potential.

So let's take a special look at arranging for marching bands—how it differs from other types of arranging, and what tips and tricks you need to know to be successful.

Marching Band Orchestration

Let's start by looking at the typical marching band—if there is such a thing. That's because the size and composition of marching bands vary considerably from band to band. A band from a small school might have fewer than 20 members; a "pep" band organized for high school basketball games might have 30 to 40 members; a monster band from a large high school or college might have 200 members or more. So there's a lot of variety.

There's also variety in the ages and skills of the players. As we'll discuss later in this chapter, writing for a junior high marching band is going to be a lot different than writing for the average high school or college marching band. And the talent level (and interest) will vary depending on how focused the band is on competition, versus just playing at football games and a few local parades.

This is why, as with all types of writing for hire, you need to know exactly who you're writing for. Gear your arrangement to the age and skill level of a specific band. Don't assume expertise or interest beyond a basic level—especially when writing for younger or smaller bands.

Woodwinds

While the number of players per section may vary, most marching bands have similar woodwind instrumentation. The most common instruments include these:

- Piccolos
- Flutes
- Clarinets
- Alto saxes
- Tenor saxes

You typically have just one part per section—that is, you're not likely to find second flutes or third clarinets.

Larger woodwind instruments are less common, because their size and weight make them awkward or even impractical to carry around. We're talking bass clarinets, baritone saxes, and the like. Some bands have them, but most don't.

> **Note**
>
> So-called "pep" or athletic bands are smaller than the full marching band, and typically have more sparse instrumentation. That means fewer instruments on each part, and some parts omitted entirely (depending on the band, of course).

And here's another type of woodwind you seldom see in marching bands—double-reed instruments. That's right, for some reason you don't find a lot of oboes and bassoons in marching bands, so don't feature them in your arrangements.

Brass

While you seldom find precisely 76 trombones in any marching ensemble, the marching band is the province of the brass section. After all, the marching band evolved from nineteenth-century military brass bands, so almost all brass instruments are quite at home here.

What instruments are we talking about? Here's the short list:

- Trumpets
- Mellophones (or French horns)
- Baritones
- Trombones
- Sousaphones (or tubas)

In the typical marching band, mellophones are used interchangeably with French horns, and sousaphones are used interchangeably with tubas; the alternate instruments are often used because they're easier to carry and play when marching. Whatever the instrument, most sections have more than one part; for example, it's not uncommon for a band to have three trumpet parts within the section.

Percussion

You can't have a marching band without a marching beat—which is where the percussion section comes in. Marching percussion instruments are designed to be played while marching, which typically means attaching the drum to a special harness that is worn by the drummer. Marching drums are typically tuned higher than similar concert drums, for greater articulation and projection when played outdoors.

In true marching or parade bands, all the percussion instruments are carried. In show or competition bands, some of the drummers march while others play in a stationary "pit" facing the audience. The marching drummers are called the *drumline* or *back battery*; the stationary instruments are called the *pit* or *front ensemble*.

A typical marching drumline will include the following instruments:

- Snare drums
- Tenor drums (typically three to five toms carried together, also called *trios*, *quads*, or *quints*)

♦ Bass drums

♦ Cymbals (handheld, and crashed together)

♦ Glockenspiel

While pit instrumentation differs from band to band, a front ensemble might include the following instruments:

♦ Marimbas

♦ Xylophones

♦ Vibraphones

♦ Chimes

♦ Timpani

As always, make sure you know the precise instrumentation of a given band before you start the percussion arrangement.

Arranging—and Other—Considerations

There are many special considerations you have to keep in mind when arranging for marching band—and not all of them musical. The marching band is a very special beast, with its own traditions, opportunities, and limitations.

Know Your Marches

As noted previously, contemporary marching bands evolved from the military bands of prior generations. That military background is evident from the reliance on martial music—in other words, military marches. You need to familiarize yourself with popular marches from Sousa on down, and with the march form in general. That means learning to write in 2/4 and 6/8 and, as we'll discuss shortly, mastering the art of rudimental drumming.

Know Other Forms of Music

The march, however, is not the only musical form employed by today's marching bands. While marches are great for parades, they're less interesting or impressive for 10-minute-long halftime shows or formal competition.

When you're writing an extended show piece, you'll need to incorporate elements from a variety of different musical forms, from popular music and Broadway musicals to movie scores and classical pieces. You'll not only need to familiarize yourself with these other forms, but also learn how to best translate each form into the marching band environment. How, exactly, do you create a marching band arrangement of the latest hip-hop hit? That's a challenge you'll probably face.

Write in Band-Friendly Keys

Since you don't have to write for strings, you can tailor your arrangements for the woodwind and brass instruments found in the typical marching band. That means selecting keys that are "band-friendly"—that is, keys that are easy to play for all the horn players.

The best keys for bands are the flat keys—concert F, B♭, E♭, and A♭. You should avoid sharp keys, as well as keys with more than four flats.

Make It Easy to Remember

Here's something arrangers sometimes forget—but marching-band players painfully remember. While some bands use clip-on music holders when playing, many more bands require their musicians to memorize all their music. That means, of course, that the music you write should be easily memorizable. How do you create music that the players won't forget? By keeping the parts relatively simple, and by going where the musicians expect to go. A piece for a high school parade band is not the best place to stretch your arranging chops. Keep the parts easy to play and easy to remember, and everyone will be happy.

Keep It Simple

The concept of keeping it simple also comes into play when you consider that many marching bands are, how shall I put this, not comprised of the most talented musicians available. I'm not talking about the highly talented high school and college competition bands but, rather, the average junior high or high school parade band.

You see, in a lot of schools, the atmosphere is such that the marching band doesn't attract the most talented musicians. In smaller schools, of course, you don't have a large pool of musicians to draw from in the first place. And when you're talking junior high and high school bands, the skill level is naturally not as high as what you get on the college or professional level.

In addition, keep in mind that the band is playing the music *while they're marching*. If you have trouble walking and chewing gum at the same time, consider the difficulty of marching in a detailed formation while playing a complex musical arrangement. It's tough, even for the most talented musicians.

For all these reasons, it pays to keep your arrangements relatively simple—especially when writing for junior high and high school bands. That means a lot of unison or octave passages, passages with no more than two or three voices, and relatively simple rhythms (outside the drum section, of course). Don't get too fancy; go for the big, solid sound that comes from writing multiple sections en masse.

For example, instead of the syncopated and front-phrased melodies you find in big-band arrangements (and in popular music vocals), you want to simplify the melodic lines to be more downbeat-oriented. That's because it's difficult for a large ensemble to play such a line in perfect precision, especially when you're talking about younger or less-skilled players. You want to move the syncopated notes so that they occur on the downbeats. (Figure 15.1 shows a typical melody you might find in a popular tune; figure 15.2 shows the same melody rhythmically simplified, as suitable for the marching-band environment.)

Figure 15.1

A typical syncopated melody—too complex for some marching bands.

Figure 15.2

The same melody, rhythmically simplified by removing the syncopation.

This simplification also applies to the arrangement itself. Instead of writing multiple harmony lines, countermelodies, and rhythmic patterns, it's okay to write a complete section or even multiple sections playing in simple unison. Maybe you have a moving bass line in the tubas, the main melodic line played in the high brass and high woodwinds, and a single countermelody or rhythmic pattern in the low brass and low woodwinds. Three or four parts at the most is quite common in marching-band writing.

Of course, this sort of simplification is less necessary if you're dealing with a better-trained band, or with a precision drum and bugle corps. But whatever the ensemble, don't get too fancy; you want your music to be playable, not an unachievable challenge.

Write Comfortably

The bit about playing and marching at the same time also leads to the conclusion that you don't want to overly strain the players. This means avoiding extreme ranges, especially the high registers. Keep the instruments in the middle of their ranges, and the players will be more apt to last through an entire 10-minute routine—or 2-hour parade.

Do the Double

Because you want to keep your arrangements simple, you'll be doing a lot of instrument doubling. Of course, some doublings sound better than others. Here are some of the more popular doublings (or triplings) used in the marching band environment:

- Piccolo/flute
- Piccolo/flute/clarinet
- Clarinet/saxes
- Piccolo/clarinet/trumpet
- Piccolo/flute/trumpet
- Trombone/baritone
- Trombone/baritone/tenor sax
- Alto sax/mellophone
- Mellophone/trumpet
- Mellophone/baritone/trombone

Other instrument combinations are possible, of course—use your imagination to create interesting color combinations.

Write Rudimentally—for the Drums

One of the keys to successful marching-band writing is mastering the drum section. While the rest of the marching-band arrangement may need to be simplified somewhat, not the drums—even at the junior high or high school level.

During a parade, the drum section plays throughout, even between songs when the other instruments are resting. The same goes with show and contest performances, which are often driven by the drumline. That's why the drum parts are so important—the drums play more than any other instrument in the band.

Marching-band drumming is derived from military drumming. It's based on the core drum rudiments, which are combinations of grace notes, rolls, and stickings. Drummers play things like flams and seven-stroke rolls and paradiddles and double ratamacues. While this isn't the place to discuss all the details of rudimental drumming, if you want to arrange for marching bands, you need to spend the time and effort to learn the lingo and write the rudiments.

> **Note**
>
> Learn more about rudimental drumming in my companion book, *The Complete Idiot's Guide to Playing Drums, 2nd Edition* (Michael Miller, Alpha Books, 2004).

One of the things you may need to write (depending on the absence or presence of a percussion coach) is a drum *cadence*. This is the beat played when the band is marching, either between songs in a parade or to march the band on and off the football field during a show. Cadences are typically two or four beats long, and multiple cadences can be strung together in combination.

What does a drum cadence sound like? It's like any other musical phrase, except without a defined melody. It's usually fairly symmetrical, in that it can be divided in halves and quarters to create sub-phrases. The cadence itself typically ends on the third beat of the final measure, which can either be final or leave space for the lead-in to the next cadence.

Figure 15.3 shows a typical four-bar cadence for snare drum, bass drum, and cymbals, followed by what is called a *roll-off*. The familiar sound of the roll-off is used to signal the end of the cadences and the beginning of the arrangement. (Naturally, all cadences can be expanded to include additional percussion—typically nonpitched instruments, such as tenor drums.)

Figure 15.3

A four-bar drum cadence followed by a two-measure roll-off.

The style of writing used for cadences continues into the drum parts used in your marching-band arrangements. Drum parts can be rather elementary, with lots of eighth notes and five-stroke roles, or they can be rhythmically sophisticated, with complex syncopation and layered orchestration across the full range of available instruments. In fact, a weak drum part is the sign of an unskilled or inexperienced arranger; the best marching-band arrangers tend to build their work from the bottom up, treating the drum section as the key instruments in the mix.

If you're not yet comfortable writing complex drum parts, call in some assistance—in the form of the band's percussion coach. Or if the band has talented players, consult with the lead drummer(s). In any case, it won't reflect poorly on you if you ask the coach or the drummers for comments and advice, or even to contribute a first pass of the drum part. After all, if you're not a drummer yourself, the intricacies of rudiments and stickings can be quite foreign and very overwhelming. When you need a better drum part, ask a drummer.

Write for the Show

Here's something somewhat unique to show band writing. While one tune is as good as the next when marching in a parade, a halftime or competitive show is quite a different situation. The arrangements you write are just one component of the total show. The show consists not just of music, but also of choreography. Your music has to fit in with and complement the whole; it doesn't exist as music for music's sake.

Work Well with Others

Most larger marching bands, especially those focused on shows and competition, have a large support staff. You'll need to work with—and get along with—them. If not, you won't get additional assignments in the future.

The first person you'll probably be working with is the drill designer or choreographer. This is the person who puts together all the fancy footwork that you see on the field. In most instances, the drill designer works from your arrangement, developing the choreography to fit the music—although this can go the other way, as well, which would require you to fit the music to preset choreography.

In any case, you need to work closely with the drill designer, as the choreography can affect the sound of your arrangement. If your arrangement is complex and the choreography is, too, the musicians will have difficulty playing the notes you write. You should work with the choreographer to point out the more difficult spots in your arrangement, so the choreography can be simplified to help the musicians play through it.

You may also be working with a percussion specialist or coach. This is a drummer who works with the percussion section, not just to practice the parts in your arrangements, but also to develop the cadences and marching beats that are played between songs. You should work with this person to get a feel for the drumline's style and abilities, as well as to point out and work through particularly challenging sections of your arrangement. A good collaboration between the arranger and the percussion coach can result in really interesting drum parts.

Finally, you'll have to work with the conductor or band director. He's the boss, and you're an employee, which means he has to approve what you write. Work with the band director beforehand to find out what he really wants, and then do your best to provide it. You should also be available and flexible throughout the practice period, so that you can make any necessary changes—either on your own, or as requested by the director.

Get Permission

While there are a lot of original compositions for marching band, there are even more arrangements of existing works—either popular songs or classical pieces. It's important that before you attempt an arrangement of an existing piece, you get permission to do so.

As the arranger, it's your responsibility to seek a "permission to arrange" from the music publisher or composer who holds the print rights to the original music. Put more directly, you are required by law to acquire this permission to arrange.

By the way, the print rights holder may or may not be the same as the copyright owner. That's because the copyright owner may grant print rights to a music publisher (such as Hal Leonard or Alfred Publishing) to arrange music for band. In this instance, the music publisher has the power to grant or deny requests to arrange particular works.

Permission to arrange is usually granted to a specific arranger (you), for specific performances by specific bands. The period of permission is typically a single calendar or school year, or performance season.

When you receive permission to arrange an existing work, the arrangement you create typically becomes the property of the original copyright owner. That's right, when you arrange an existing work, you don't own the arrangement. That means you can't loan or sell the arrangement to another band, without first obtaining additional permission from the rights holder. And you'll probably have to provide copies of the arrangement (either the score or individual parts) to the rights holder.

How do you find out who to get permission from? The best place to search for copyright holders is at the Bands of America Copyright Resources database (www.bands.org/public/resourceroom/copyright/database/). This comprehensive database lets you search by song title, composer, or print rights holder.

Once you know who to contact, you can usually fax, mail, or e-mail a written request to use the composition. Contact the individual rights holder for specific instructions.

Know, however, that some composers and publishers don't easily give out permissions to arrange. This may be due to previous contractual obligations, or it may be that the composer simply doesn't want her work performed by marching bands. Again, this is a good reason why you want to seek permission before you begin the arrangement.

> **Caution** _____
>
> You should obtain permission to arrange _before_ you begin your arrangement. Do not wait until your show is finished, or you may be left on the hook without the right to proceed.

Tip _____

Find more detailed information about copyright issues pertaining to the marching band world at the Bands of America Copyright Resources page (www. bands.org/Public/resourceroom/copyright/).

Write to the Band's Strengths—and Avoid Its Weaknesses

Finally, as with any type of arranging, you need to know who it is you're writing for, so you can write to your band's strengths—and weaknesses. Your job is to make the band sound good, not to show off your arranging skills. Know the precise instrumentation you're working with, and any issues within individual sections. Don't assume that all bands have the same elevated skill level throughout; know when to pump it up, and when to make it easy. The better you know your band, the more effective your arrangement will be.

Writing for Drum and Bugle Corps

Beyond the traditional marching band is the creature known as the drum and bugle corps—or, in some circles, just the drum corps. As the full name implies, the drum and bugle corps consists of drums and bugles, of various shapes and sizes.

The world of competitive drum corps is both fun and demanding. It's all about the competition, which is at a very high level. Most drum corps travel around a region (or across the country) in summer touring circuits, performing their meticulously rehearsed shows on football fields before large crowds and panels of judges. The corps are judged not just on musical performance, but also on visual performance and general effect.

Putting Together the Show

At the beginning of each season, a drum corps prepares a new show. This single show is used throughout the entire season; while the contents of the show may be refined over the summer rehearsal period, it's unusual for a corps to break in a new show mid-season.

The show itself typically runs between 10 and 12 minutes long. The musical content can vary wildly both between and within shows, running the gamut from symphonic works to Broadway tunes to rock 'n' roll to Latin and other ethnic music.

Unlike most noncompetitive marching bands, drum corps music exists at a relatively high level of difficulty. The best corps pride themselves on the ability to play highly sophisticated charts; the difficulty of the music itself factors into the judges' scoring.

While the musical content is unpredictable, most shows share a common structure, consisting of multiple pieces connected together in larger whole. A show typically starts with an opener designed to grab the audience's attention, which then flows into a feature for the percussion section. This is, more often than not, followed by a ballad (typically featuring the horn line), which then builds into a closer, which is the climax of the show. Naturally, other shorter pieces may be inserted into this general framework.

The goal of a show is to showcase various elements of the corps, as well as to demonstrate a mastery of different musical concepts. A well-designed show should have a good balance of dynamics, tempos, and musical styles.

It's common for a single arranger to write an entire show. In some instances, however, multiple arrangers work as a team to create the different pieces of the arrangement. Seldom, however, is a show cobbled together from disparate works; more than with marching-band shows, a drum corps show has to hang together as a complete work, from start to finish.

Brass Orchestration

Within the drum and bugle corps brass line, there are five different instruments, all based on the basic bugle: the soprano bugle (soprano voice), the mellophone (alto voice), the baritone (tenor voice), the euphonium (baritone voice), and the contra bass (bass voice). Of these sections, the sopranos are typically divided into three separate parts, the mellophones are typically divided into two parts, the baritones can be divided up to three parts (or not; single-part sections are common), the euphoniums play one or two parts, and the contras play a single part.

Brass orchestrations for drum and bugle corps are more complex than typical marching band arrangements. You can write each section in unison (for five-part writing), or you can use divided sections to create a total of up to a dozen parts.

Drum corps brass can also deal with more sophisticated rhythms, which means it's okay to syncopate and use front and back phrasing. In fact, you can achieve interesting effects by mixing different rhythms in different parts of the brass section. For example, Figure 15.4 shows a rhythmic figure tossed around between the five brass parts—which creates a complex combined rhythm.

Percussion Orchestration

Drum and bugle corps also include more percussion than found in the typical marching band. There are two parts to drum corps percussion—the back battery (called the *drumline*), which marches on the field, and the front ensemble (called the *pit*), which is stationary at the front of the field. The back battery contains snare drums, tenor drums, and bass drums. The front ensemble contains all the nonmarching percussion, including xylophone, marimba, timpani, even hand percussion and chimes. Obviously, the front ensemble doesn't march.

Drum corps often contain extremely intricate percussion parts, branching off from traditional cadences to include fully harmonized melodies (thanks to the pit instruments). Even the cadences in drum corps are more complex; it's important for the corps drummers to show their chops somewhere in the show. Remember, the drummers in a drum and bugle corps are the cream of the crop, so they should be able to handle just about anything you throw at them.

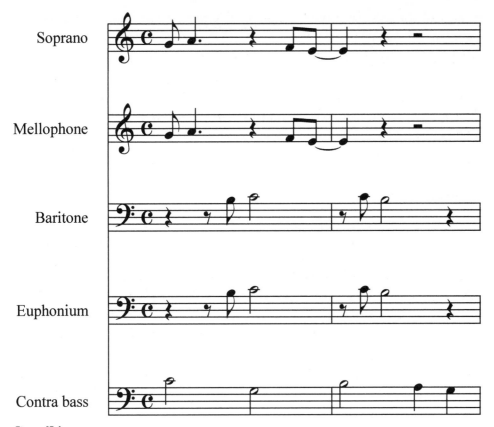

Figure 15.4

A rhythmic pattern arranged for drum corps brass.

Creating a Marching Band Arrangement

Now let's get down to brass tacks (pun intended) and start work on your own marching-band arrangement. As we've done throughout this section of the book, we're going to work with the "Love Waits" tune, as presented in Appendix B. My arrangement of this tune is showcased on Track 3 of the accompanying CD, and is also presented in Appendix B.

Track 3

A few things to note about this arrangement. It's for marching band, not drum and bugle corps, so I've opted to keep it both rhythmically and harmonically simple. The writing is primarily of the three- and four-part variety, with plenty of whole-section and ensemble passages. It's an interesting arrangement, but it won't tax high school-level players.

The drum part, on the other hand, has some complexity, especially in the interaction between the snare and tenor drums. But, as interesting as the drum part is, it doesn't get in the way; it's there to propel the band not to draw attention to itself.

The piece starts with a three-note pattern, B-G-D, which is repeated in various parts of the arrangement. These are the three notes of the underlying G major triad, and also of the classic bugle call; this pattern fits well with the G major-based melody.

The melody in the first verse is carried by the woodwinds, with some answering countermelodies by the brass. Later in the verse, the countermelody is actually split between the trumpets and the lower brass at the end of the phrase. Then, for a bit of fun, the first verse ends with an homage to Sousa's "Stars and Stripes Forever." A bit of fun, as I said.

In the second verse, the melody shifts to the brass section, with answering sixteenth notes (and later quarter notes) from the woodwinds. Then we get to the chorus, where things appear to slow down a bit, thanks to a smoother, simplified quarter-note melody, lack of rhythmic counterpoint, and some interesting drumplay between the snare and tenor drums.

Things perk back up in the final verse, where all the different pieces and parts come back together. The melody starts in the woodwinds, with the brass playing the opening three-note pattern in response. Then the melody shifts back to the brass for the big ending, which also incorporates the bugle call pattern. It all ends on a long held chord and a final cymbal crash.

So take a look at my chart, and then create your own marching band or drum corps arrangement from "Love Waits." How do you approach this assignment?

The Least You Need to Know

♦ The marching band differs from the orchestra in that there are no strings but more woodwinds, brass, and percussion.

♦ The drum and bugle corps drops the woodwinds, adds more percussion, and focuses on five types of brass bugles—sopranos, mellophones, baritones, euphoniums, and contra basses.

♦ Music for junior high and high school marching band should be rhythmically simple, within a normal register, and easy to memorize.

♦ Simple three- to five-part writing is common for marching band, with plenty of whole-section and ensemble passages.

♦ Music for drum and bugle corps can (and probably should) be more complex, both rhythmically and harmonically.

Chapter 16

Arranging for an Orchestra

In This Chapter

- Learning the instruments of the symphonic orchestra
- Mastering orchestral instrumentation techniques
- Applying composition techniques, including theme and variation
- Arranging for larger multi-section works

For many composers and arrangers, the pinnacle of the art is writing for the full symphonic orchestra. While smaller similar ensembles exist (such as the chamber and string orchestra), only the symphonic orchestra delivers such a compelling combination of tonal variety and sheer power. As such, it's worthy of your attention, even if you intend to write for smaller ensembles. Subsections of the orchestra crop up in all different types of pieces.

Orchestral Instrumentation

The modern orchestra is a very large ensemble. While it's not necessary to have every instrument playing at all times, you still have a large number of instruments to choose from for your orchestral arrangements.

Strings

The traditional orchestral string section consists of first and second violins, a single viola section, a cello section, and a section of double basses. In a large orchestra, you may have as many as 16 first violins, 14 second violins, 12 violas, 10 cellos, and 8 basses. Smaller orchestras use a similar ratio between sections, but with fewer individual instruments to start with.

Even with more than 50 string players at your disposal, the string section still has a difficult time competing dynamically with the much louder brass section.

The strings are delicate instruments, and don't have the power of most wind instruments. They do deliver a richness of sound, however, that the other instruments can't quite touch.

> **Tip**
>
> Strings are the heart and soul of the modern orchestra, they're also widely used in almost every other form of music, from sweetening pop and rock songs to adding fullness to R&B and hip-hop recordings. The techniques you use for arranging orchestral strings can also be used when writing string parts for other types of ensembles.

Woodwinds

Woodwinds have an important but limited role in the modern orchestra. Orchestral instrumentation typically includes piccolo, first and second flute, first and second oboe, English horn, first and second B♭ clarinet, bass clarinet, first and second bassoon, and contrabassoon. (Note the total absence of the saxophone family.)

This creates a large number of tonal colors, although the woodwinds are often relegated to a supporting role within the ensemble. That said, flutes and clarinets (and even oboes and bassoons) can be compelling solo instruments, as well as contributing important color in harmony passages.

Brass

The orchestral brass section is actually quite large, at least in number of parts. Typical orchestral instrumentation includes four French horn parts, three trumpets, three trombones, and a single tuba. You may have one or two instruments per part—although one instrument per part is most common.

Because of their power, relative to the softer strings and woodwinds, the brass instruments can easily overplay their parts in orchestral arrangements. Use the brass sparingly, especially in an accompanying role. They're better used to carry the melody or to provide added power to unison or ensemble passages shared with other instruments.

Regarding that power, the brass are often used to take the orchestra to new dynamic heights. When you want to ramp up the loudness, score for brass, either alone or in conjunction with other instruments.

Then there's the issue of rhythmic agility. While the trumpets can hold their own while doubling the equally agile strings and woodwinds, the lower brass are less agile, and often relegated to supporting roles that are less rhythmically demanding.

Percussion

The orchestral percussion section includes a wide variety of instruments played by a small number of players; a single player typically plays multiple instruments, as the piece requires.

Common orchestral percussion includes timpani, a range of mallet instruments (orchestra bells, chimes, xylophone, marimba, sometimes vibraphone), traditional percussion (snare drum, bass drum, suspended and crash cymbals), and a variety of hand percussion (sleigh bells, finger cymbals, triangle, tambourine, and so forth).

Percussion is typically less used in the orchestral setting than it is in concert, marching, and jazz bands. You're more apt to use mallet percussion, timpani, and selected hand percussion than you are the traditional snare and bass drums. That said, the drums (including timpani) are great for adding punctuation, while the mallets can double and reinforce melodic lines in other sections.

> **Note**
> Contemporary orchestras may also include harp and piano, although the latter is less common.

Orchestral Arranging Techniques

Arranging for orchestra is no different from any other type of arranging, save for the particular instruments involved—and the sheer numbers of those instruments. The full symphonic orchestra is a very powerful animal, yet still capable of breath-taking intimacy. It's all about the instruments involved.

Arranging as Orchestration

In a contemporary orchestra, you have an extremely wide variety of instruments in your palette. So wide is your palette that you'll seldom write distinct parts for each section simultaneously—there are simply too many different instruments to deal with. Instead, you'll do a lot of whole-section writing, as well as doubling between sections in an ensemble. As a guide, try to keep the number of distinct parts to six or fewer at any given time; use doubling (or, selectively, octave doubling) to add multiple instruments or sections to each part.

In terms of instrument choice and voicing, remember that you're dealing with a lot of instruments—and quantity and volume play a big part in the final sound. If you pit the melody in a single instrument or section against the rest of the orchestra playing a countermelody or accompaniment, the melody could easily get overwhelmed. You need to balance your instruments so that the most important line is easily heard over the power of the ensemble. That means giving the melody to either loud instruments (think brass) or large sections (think strings). If you want the melody played by more delicate instruments, arrange the rest of the orchestra so that the louder instruments are either resting or playing at a lower volume level.

> **Tip**
> One exception to the no-string-brass-pairing rule is to pair cellos with French horns, which results in a very rich mid-tone sound.

Whether doubling melodies or writing ensemble passages, it's important to experiment with different instrument combinations, as some instruments blend better with certain instruments—and less well, or not at all, with others. You can pair the clarinets and oboes with the violas, for example, or the trombones with the bassoons and low-register flutes. That said, you need to be aware of some less-desirable instrument pairings. In particular, strings don't always blend well with brass; when writing multi-section passages and voicings, pair the strings with the woodwinds, instead.

Arranging as Composition

When arranging for orchestra, you actually use a lot of composition chops. By that, I mean you'll be composing a lot of countermelodies and motifs, extending or enhancing existing melodies, and adding completely new sections to the original piece. Orchestral arranging is about more than assigning notes to specific instruments; it's about finishing a complete composition. You may start with a simple melody and chord progression, but there's a lot of filling in the blanks to do. You'll use all the music theory you've learned to date, and then some.

In orchestral music, you're more likely to adhere to traditional rules of voicing and voice leading. So although rules are always made to be broken, you probably don't want to use a lot of parallel fifths, for example. You will, however, need to brush up on your counterpoint and other classical techniques; traditional methods of augmenting the melody (including using ornamentation) are always effective.

Also necessary is a mastery of full-form compositional techniques, including *counterpoint* and theme and variation. The latter technique is used quite frequently, because theme and variation lets you take a single melody (also called a *theme* or *motif*) and use it as the basis for related musical ideas. This lets you work with a single melody throughout an arrangement, yet still make the piece more continuously interesting than you'd get with simple repetition.

These related musical ideas—the *variations*—can be created by altering a single note of the main theme, or by completely rewriting it. It's important, however, to retain enough of the main theme in each variation so that the variation remains recognizable.

There are several different types of variations you can employ. Some of the most common include …

- **Sequence**, where the original theme is replayed starting on a different pitch. (For this and following variations, we'll use the original melody as displayed in Figure 16.1.) In an *exact sequence*, as shown in Figure 16.2, the exact intervals of the original motif are retained, even if that means going chromatic. In an *inexact sequence*, as shown in Figure 16.3, the intervals are diatonic within the underlying key.

- **Inversion** (sometimes called a *melodic inversion*), as shown in Figure 16.4, which starts on the same pitch as the original melody, but then moves in the opposite melodic direction, using the same diatonic intervals (but reversed, of course).

---

def•i•ni•tion

Counterpoint is the art of creating a second, complementary melody that is played simultaneously with the main melody. There are many, many formal rules to the art of counterpoint—too many to discuss here.

Note

Learn more about theme and variation, as well as other compositional techniques, in my companion book, *The Complete Idiot's Guide to Music Composition* (Michael Miller, Alpha Books, 2005).

♦ **Retrograde inversion**, shown in Figure 16.5, plays the pitches of the original theme backward. (You can either use the same rhythm as the original, as shown here, or also reverse the rhythm.)

♦ **Permutation**, shown in Figure 16.6, which rearranges the original pitches in a somewhat random order.

♦ **Same rhythm, different pitches**, shown in Figure 16.7, retains the original theme's rhythmic values but assigns new pitches to each note.

♦ **Rhythmic displacement**, as shown in Figure 16.8, where the original phrase is started at a different place in the measure.

♦ **Augmentation**, shown in Figure 16.9, where the rhythm of the original theme is extended by lengthening each of the note values—in this instance, doubling them.

♦ **Diminution**, shown in Figure 16.10, which is the opposite of augmentation; you take the original theme and shorten the note values, thus speeding up the melodic line.

♦ **Truncation**, shown in Figure 16.11, which cuts short the original phrase by deleting one or more of the final notes.

♦ **Expansion**, shown in Figure 16.12, where you tack on new notes to the end of the original melody.

♦ **Thinning**, shown in Figure 16.13, where less-essential and ornamental notes are removed from the melody.

♦ **Ornamentation,** shown in Figure 16.14, which is the opposite of thinning; new ornamental notes are added to further "decorate" the melody.

Figure 16.1

Our original melody, or theme.

Figure 16.2

Exact sequence, where the exact intervals of the original melody are maintained, while starting on a different pitch.

Figure 16.3

Inexact sequence, where diatonic intervals are maintained while starting on a different pitch.

Figure 16.4

Inversion, which reverses the intervals of the original theme.

Figure 16.5

Retrograde inversion, which plays the original pitches backward.

Figure 16.6

Permutation, which rearranges the original pitches in random order.

Figure 16.7

A variation that uses the same rhythm but with different pitches.

Figure 16.8

Rhythmic displacement, where the original melody is started at a different place in the measure.

Figure 16.9

Augmentation, where the original rhythm is lengthened.

Figure 16.10

Diminution, where the original rhythm is shortened.

Figure 16.11

Truncation, where the original melody is cut short.

Figure 16.12

Expansion, where the original melody is added to.

Figure 16.13

Thinning, where the original melody is simplified.

Figure 16.14

Ornamentation, where the original melody has ornamental notes added.

You can also add variety to your orchestral arrangement without changing the theme, by simply reharmonizing the melody. Change the chords behind the melody, and you can make a subsequent section sound much different from the first. The original theme is maintained for familiarity, but is put in a different light due to the changed chords.

Finally, there is the ever-useful technique of ostinato, where a melodic or rhythmic pattern is repeated, typically in one or more of the accompanying parts. When an ostinato is repeated over an extended period of time, you create a type of minimalist effect, the ostinato serving as kind of a drone over which the main theme can be played.

Tip

Another useful arranging technique is *modulation*, where you take the entire piece into a different key. Modulations of a fifth or fourth are common, as are whole-step- and half-step-upward modulations.

Creating Multiple-Section Arrangements

Much orchestral music is longer-form—that is, it includes multiple related sections, often performed separately with space between. Think of the symphonic form, or of instrumental suites, and you know what we're talking about. And working in long forms is different from writing a single-section piece.

When a composition is long enough to warrant multiple sections, you have to work with each section as if it is a discrete piece. Yes, the individual sections have to relate to each other musically (and in service of the larger musical whole), but they also need to have their own individual structure and form. That may mean composing separate themes for each section, or employing separate keys, time signatures, and so on.

The traditional symphony is written in what is called the *sonata form*. The sonata form has four sections, or *movements*, as follows:

1. **First movement**, typically fairly fast (allegro), using the *sonata-allegro* form.

2. **Second movement**, typically slower (andante, adagio, or lento), using either sonata allegro form, theme and variations, or A-B-A song form.

3. **Third movement**, typically faster (scherzo), using A-B-A song form.

4. **Finale**, even faster (allegro molto or presto), using either sonata-allegro or *rondo* form. The finale almost always ends with a *coda*, a short section that ends the piece with a distinct finality.

Obviously, these movements are not written in stone. Some early symphonies only had three movements (dropping either the third or fourth movements); some symphonies reverse the order of the second and third movements; and some symphonies follow completely different guidelines.

def•i•ni•tion

The **sonata-allegro** form used in the first movement of many symphonies includes its own particular form—introduction, exposition, development, recapitulation, and an optional coda.

The **rondo** form alternates a recurring theme with other themes, in ABACA, ABACADA, and similar constructions.

Creating an Orchestral Arrangement

Track 4

With this knowledge under your belt, it's time to attempt your first orchestral arrangement. Your assignment? Take the "Love Waits" melody and chords, as found in Appendix B, and use it as the basis for a longer orchestral work.

My orchestral version of "Love Waits" is found on Track 4 of the accompanying CD. In this arrangement, the song has become a short single-movement tone poem for orchestra; there are no percussion instruments used.

At first listen, you may be wondering where the melody is. That's because I don't go directly to the melody of the original song; instead, I use a long introduction to build to the melody. The introduction is based on the three-note pattern (B-G-D) first used in last chapter's marching band arrangement. In fact, I use this pattern throughout the entire introduction. The pattern is passed around the oboes, clarinets, flutes, and French horn, in various permutations. The melody is stretched, rhythmically displaced, embellished, and otherwise used as a basis to build the tone of the piece. As the pattern begins to take its final shape, we introduce the rest of the instruments and the underlying two-bar chord change, which helps the piece to build in power, leading up to the introduction of the melody in section A.

The melody is initially carried by the string section—violins first, then the other strings joining in. This is effective because the violins were one of the few instruments not used in the piece's introduction. In the second half of this first verse, the three-note pattern changes into an answering countermelody, then returns at the end of the verse, where it shifts from the woodwinds to the strings.

At this point you think the verse is going to repeat, but instead the piece goes into what amounts to a two-measure vamp, building and building on the G-to-E minor chord change. When the melody starts up again, it's kind of in stealth mode, as it sounds like an extension of the preceding buildup. It's the trumpets who now carry the melody, with a beautiful ascending countermelody from the strings.

As the strings peak, the arrangement backs down into a contrasting soft section. The French horns take the melody in the bridge, with a very sparse chordal accompaniment from the low strings. This holds until the end of the bridge, when all the other instruments join in for a big build, both dynamically and harmonically. This build then tapers off, with a descending pattern in the strings.

The final verse sees the return of the original three-note pattern, with the melody shifting between groups of instruments. Everything stays low-key to the end, with the instrumentation of the signature three-note pattern becoming more sparse. Listen carefully to the final chord, played by the flute, oboe, clarinet, French horn, and double bass. It's a very effective combination of instruments.

Throughout, listen to how I've applied different types of variations to the main theme. These variations not only add variety to the work, but also help to extend it; the same theme played identically three times throughout would have been a bit boring in this context.

As always, it's not important how I've arranged the piece, but rather how you arrange it. My arrangement is meant only as an example of some of the ways you can proceed; you're free and encouraged to experiment with your ideas and techniques.

The Least You Need to Know

◆ The symphonic orchestra is a large, versatile, and powerful ensemble, consisting of instruments from all the major families—strings, woodwinds, brass, and percussion.

◆ With so many instruments available, it's important to experiment with different instrumental combinations to discover what does and doesn't blend well.

◆ It's not necessary—and often not wise—to write separate parts for each individual instrument or section; five- or six-part writing is most common.

◆ To extend a simple melody into a full-length orchestral work, you need to apply various composition techniques, including counterpoint and theme and variation.

◆ When creating longer works, you may want to write multiple sections; the symphonic form includes four movements, each with its own unique character.

Chapter **17**

Arranging for a Choir

In This Chapter

◆ Discovering different types of vocal ensembles

◆ Learning how to arrange for voices—both accompanied and *a cappella*

◆ Writing piano accompaniment

◆ Creating a choral arrangement

Arranging for voices is both similar to and different from arranging for instruments. The similarity comes in the application of common arranging techniques—voicing, voice leading, and so forth. The differences come from the fact that singing is different from playing; you have to make sure the parts you write can be easily sung.

That said, choral arranging can be both fun and artistically fulfilling. Whether you're writing for a two-voice grade school chorus or a hundred-person symphonic choir, it's great to hear the notes you write spring to life from the lips of sweet-voiced singers.

Types of Vocal Ensembles

A choir can contain singers of any level of expertise, and can embrace music from a variety of genres, from the classical repertoire to the latest pop hits. Of course, to be accurate, there isn't a single ensemble type called "choir"; there are actually many different types of vocal ensembles for which you can arrange. Some of the more popular forms are as follows:

◆ **Trio.** A vocal trio is just what it says—three voices. In the classical genre, trio music is typically written for female voices (soprano, second soprano, and alto), although trios in pop music can consist of all female, all male, or mixed voices.

- ◆ **Quartet.** A quartet is a four-voice ensemble. In classical music (and some pop and jazz) the breakdown is standard SATB—soprano, alto, tenor, and bass. Of course, you can have all-female or all-male quartets, like those in barbershop quartets. But the mixed-voice quartet is the most popular.

- ◆ **Chamber choir.** A chamber choir is a small choir, normally with 12 to 24 singers, typically performing repertoire from the sixteenth and seventeenth centuries. There are also some modern chamber choirs that sing everything from Renaissance music to jazz.

- ◆ **Madrigal choir.** Another common vocal chamber group is the madrigal choir. The madrigal is a form of choral music that was popular in Europe primarily in the sixteenth century. It is usually sung *a cappella*.

- ◆ **Swing choir.** A so-called swing or show choir is a mid-sized mixed-voice ensemble that performs various types of popular music, from Broadway show tunes to the latest pop songs. Swing choirs typically have a full rhythm-section accompaniment—piano, bass, drums, and sometimes guitar.

- ◆ **Large vocal ensembles.** This is the traditional large choir or chorus, encompassing everything from junior high or high school choirs to church choirs to community choirs and beyond. These choirs can be of any size and composition—while mixed-voice is most common, there are also many popular all-male and all-female choruses.

> **Note**
>
> When writing for younger voices, you have to deal with different vocal ranges and different voice parts. Learn more in Chapter 12.

To make it simple, a high school or adult mixed-voice ensemble typically has four voice parts—soprano, alto, tenor, and bass. (Occasionally, each of these parts are split, so that you have first and second soprano, first and second alto, and so on.) Women's choirs have three or four voice parts: soprano I, soprano II, alto I, and alto II (optional). And men's choirs have three or four voice parts—tenor I, tenor II (optional), baritone, and bass.

Writing for Voices

In addition to applying the technique you've learned previously in this book, you also have to deal with various issues specific to choral arranging. This ranges from the limitation of four-voice writing to the necessity of writing lines that can be easily sight-read and sung.

That said, let's look at some particular issues and advice.

Write Melodic Lines

The primary challenge in arranging vocal music is that you have to think both horizontally and vertically. Vertically, as you would with any instrument, to fill in the appropriate voices in the underlying harmony. And horizontally, to create a singable line—even when that voice is purely harmony, not lead melody.

Put simply, every vocal part you create has to be sung—and thus must be singable. The singer has to hear the note in her head before she sings it (she can't just press a valve or hit a key), so the intervals in your vocal lines have to make melodic and harmonic sense.

That's the theory. In practice, this means writing in steps rather than leaps. Use seconds, thirds, fourths, and fifths; avoid tritones, sixths, sevenths, and larger intervals. (This is especially true when writing harmony lines; the primary melody can jump around as much as necessary.)

Bottom line, you have to work hard to construct vocal lines that have a linear logic when sung, yet still fit together with the other voices to impart the chordal harmony of your piece. It's a challenge—but essential in arranging any type of vocal music.

> **Tip**
>
> After you've written a vocal line, go back and try to sing it yourself. If you have trouble singing it, so will the real singers—which means you need to rethink it.

Write for Four (or Fewer) Voices

This one is blatantly obvious, but needs to be addressed. A four-voice choir has four voices. That means no fancy five- and six-part voicings, just simple writing for four (or fewer) voices. That means if you have a five- or six-note extended chord, you need to pick and choose which notes of the chord get sung.

The four-voice limitation also means that you may have to double one or more notes of a standard triad, when you're writing for full ensemble. This isn't that hard, as most voices blend well; it's easy enough to write the women's or men's voices in unison, or to pair the similarly ranged altos with the tenors. As always, don't feel obligated to arrange every note in a chord; unison, two-, and three-part writing for a four-voice choir is quite common.

Vary the Texture

Another challenge to vocal writing is to avoid falling into the trap of homogenous texture—that is, constant and consistent four-part writing. If you keep all the voices in a particular range and use similar voicings and voice spacing over an extended series of measures, your piece will start to sound boring.

This means you need to vary the texture, voicings, and number of voices you use throughout a piece. You can do this in the following ways:

- **Vary the number of voices.** Don't always use all four voices; let some voices rest so that only three, two, or even a single part is singing at any given time.

- **Vary the way voices are used.** Don't have all the voices sing the same rhythm; give the melody to one voice and have the other voices sing sustained-note harmony, or create a rhythmically different countermelody to supplement the main line.

♦ **Vary the voice spacing.** Don't use the same intervals between voices over extended passages. Go for a less homogeneous type of harmony between the voices.

The goal is to avoid boredom and listener fatigue; the strategy is to mix it up from time to time, in whichever way best fits the arrangement.

Voice for Effect

When you're experimenting with different voicings and textures, know that certain voice combinations result in some quite interesting vocal effects. Some of the more common voicings and effects include the following:

♦ To create an intense mood, or to surge toward a vocal climax, use high groupings of voices, as shown in Figure 17.1.

♦ To create a serene or restful mood (or a sad mood), use low groupings of voices, as shown in Figure 17.2.

♦ To create a very resonant effect, use close voicings in the mid-range—the upper voices voiced low, and the lower voices voiced high, as shown in Figure 17.3.

♦ To build toward a climax, build from a single voice to multiple voices by consecutively adding voices, as shown in Figure 17.4.

♦ To reinforce the melody, double it (either in unison or at the octave) in a similar voice, as shown in Figure 17.5.

♦ To make the melody stand out, write the accompanying parts in a different range than the melody part. For example, you could put the melody in the high soprano and keep the harmony in lower-register alto, tenor, and bass parts, as shown in Figure 17.6.

♦ For a sophisticated, jazzy sound, use close voicing in the middle of a vocal stack (in this instance, between the alto and tenor) for the chord's extended notes, as shown in Figure 17.7.

♦ To create a slightly unsettled sound, don't put the root note in the bass; instead, use the third or the fifth in the bass—or get really daring and use the bass for the chord's extended notes, as shown in Figure 17.8.

Tip

Since extended notes are more difficult to vocalize, lead the voice to the extended note via a logical step-wise motion. Whatever you do, don't force the singer to leap to an extended note via a difficult interval.

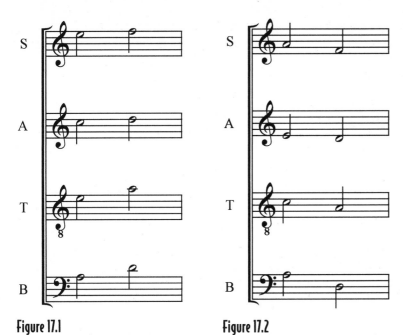

Figure 17.1

High voicings create an intense mood.

Figure 17.2

Low voicings create a serene or mournful mood.

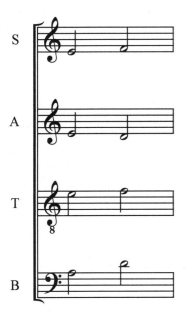

Figure 17.3

Close mid-range voicings create a resonant effect.

Figure 17.4

Add voices to build volume or intensity.

Figure 17.5

Reinforce the melody by doubling it in a similar voice—in this instance, soprano and alto.

Figure 17.6

Make the melody stand out by writing it in a different vocal range than the harmony.

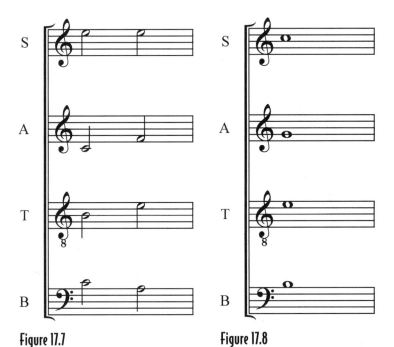

Figure 17.7

Extended notes in the middle of a voicing create a jazzy effect.

Figure 17.8

Extended notes in the bass create an unsettled effect.

Simplify the Rhythms

Don't confuse group vocals with solo vocals. A solo vocalist can easily handle complex rhythms, complete with syncopations and front-phrasings. Not so a large choir. The trickier the rhythms, the harder they are for a group to sing precisely. This means going through your piece and turning those syncopations and front-phrasings into downbeat-oriented rhythms. No matter how hard you try, you can't get a large choir to sound like a hip vocalist!

Write for Groups Within a Group

It's common to treat the choir as a single entity. Instead, you can break the large ensemble into smaller groups. After all, a large choir contains a complete women's chorus, as well as a men's chorus, as well as an alto-tenor-baritone vocal trio. You can also play one group against another, or treat the ensemble as lead vocal-plus-accompaniment. The combinations are numerous.

Note-Against-Note vs. Call-and-Response

When writing a two-part passage, you have a choice to make. You can write the second part note-against-note with the first part, or you can use a call-and-response approach. The first method, illustrated in Figure 17.9, creates a more traditional harmony vocal line—either with constant intervals or with a more versatile countermelody. The second approach helps to punctuate the main melody, by repeating or answering key pieces of the melodic phrase, as shown in Figure 17.10. Either approach is valid; pick and choose as appropriate.

Figure 17.9

A note-against-note harmony line.

Figure 17.10

A call-and-response harmony line.

Pass the Melody Around

It's tempting to always put the melody in the highest (soprano) part. Avoid the temptation. You should strive to pass the melody around all the parts, so that the basses, tenors, and altos get their share of the lead.

And you don't have to stay in a single voice throughout an entire verse or phrase. It's okay to start a phrase with the melody in one voice and then transfer the melody to a second point after a few beats or measures. Experiment with melody placement; it's a relatively easy way to add interest to a vocal arrangement.

The Top's the Top, and the Bottom's the Bottom

The previous advice to the contrary, there are some traditional roles for the various voice parts. Like it or not, the soprano is traditionally used to carry the melody or the top note of the chord in four-part writing. (That top chord note might be an octave doubling of the root, or the top extended note in an extended chord.) The bass is traditionally used to sound the root of the accompanying chords. And the alto and tenor are used to voice the interior notes of the chords.

All rules are made to be broken, of course, but these traditional voicings are always a good place to start.

Watch the Overlap

While you don't have to always keep your voicings in strict SATB vocal order, you do need to watch for issues arising from voice crossing and overlap.

One issue is that the same note sung by different voices will often sound different. For example, a middle C sung by a bass (near the top of his range) will sound higher than the same note sung by a tenor (in the middle part of his range). You get a similar effect with notes shared by sopranos and altos, and by altos and tenors.

And as with all types of writing, you probably want to avoid, as much as possible, instances of voice crossing. While it's almost impossible to avoid voice crossing when working within the limited range of a choir, you should still work to minimize it.

That said, the problem is less acute when the voices crossing aren't too similar in range; voice crossing works better when the voices crossing have different tonal properties. So you probably don't want to cross the soprano and alto lines or the tenor and the bass, but crossing alto and tenor is okay, as each voice retains its vocal characteristics.

> **Tip**
>
> Voice crossing is acceptable when one of the voices is carrying the lead and the other is providing some sort of accompaniment—the lead vocal line remains distinct from the backing oohs and aahs.

Use Neutral Syllables

To the issue of oohs and aahs, get used to writing these types of neutral syllables, especially for sustained chordal accompaniment. You can also employ nonsense syllables (doo wop de wop, dip dip dip dip, sha la la, and so forth) as vocal backing. Just make sure that the background accompaniment doesn't detract from the foreground lead—which is why the neutral syllable approach is often a better choice than more distinct nonsense syllables.

Don't Forget the Lyrics

The issue of neutral and nonsense syllables brings up the whole issue of lyrics. As an arranger, it's not your job to write the lyrics, but you do have to deal with how the lyrics are notated on the vocal parts.

When including lyrics for a voice part on a four-staff chart, position the lyrics directly below each note on each staff. When including lyrics on a two-staff chart (SA+TB), put the lyrics between the two staves, as shown in Figure 17.11.

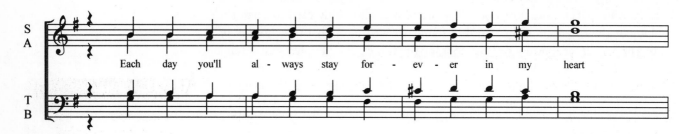

Figure 17.11

Lyric placement on a two-staff vocal chart.

As best they can, the notes accompanying the lyrics should follow the rhythm of the words. That means spacing the notes within a measure to reflect their rhythmic values. That said, you may need to take some liberties with this spacing to make the words more legible on the page.

You should break multisyllable words with a hyphen between syllables. The words should be broken into syllables as defined in a standard dictionary—not as you think they should be sung. And when a single syllable extends across multiple notes, indicate this with either dashes or an extended underline that flows across all the notes in the word. Use "oohs" and "ahhs" as appropriate.

Let 'em Breathe

There's one odd thing about singers—they need to breathe. While breath considerations are necessary for wind instruments, they're even more important for vocalists. Don't tie together four whole notes at a slow tempo, or the singers might pass out trying to make it to the end of a phrase. Try to arrange natural breathing places at the ends of phrases, and don't hesitate to insert a short rest after a few long notes. If you don't make it easy for them to breathe, they'll insert their own breaths—which might not be where you want them.

Accompanied or *A Cappella*?

A final consideration when writing for voices is whether you want the voices accompanied by another instrument (typically a piano) or whether you want them singing by themselves, in *a cappella* fashion.

A cappella writing has its own unique challenges, including the need to provide some sort of rhythmic drive, constantly outline the underlying chord, create a variety of textures from the available voices, and so on. And of course, not all types of music work well in an unaccompanied setting. But it is uniquely rewarding to hear the crystal-clear voicing without instrumental interruption—if the choir can pull it off.

Adding an accompaniment part is also challenging—so much so that we'll cover that in its own section, next.

Creating a Piano Accompaniment

When you're providing accompaniment to a vocal piece, you're most often talking about a piano accompaniment. You can, of course, arrange for other instruments—for example, a swing choir might have guitar, bass, and drum parts in addition to the piano—but the piano is the mainstay for most choirs.

At its most basic, the piano accompaniment can be simply a reduction of the vocal parts—that is, the vocal parts played together, verbatim, on the piano, as shown in Figure 17.12. This is most common when writing for younger singers, who need the assistance of hearing the notes they sing.

Beyond simple vocal reduction, the piano accompaniment should enhance, not overshadow, the vocal parts. Don't get too fancy, except perhaps in those sections where the voices are resting. Keep the piano part simple and subsidiary, so that it doesn't interfere with what's important—the choir itself.

To that end, you want to keep the piano part noticeably separate from the vocal parts, to let the vocal parts better stand out from the accompaniment. You can do this by writing the piano in a different range from the primary vocal parts. When the voices are in a lower range, write the piano with higher-register chords or figures. When the voices are in a higher range, go for a bass-oriented accompaniment.

Another way to distinguish the accompaniment from the voices is to emphasize textural or rhythmic differences. For example, if the choir is singing sustained notes, have the piano play arpeggiated chords. If the choir is singing rapidly moving figures, have the piano play sustained chords. You get the idea.

In addition, you can use the piano accompaniment to provide a bit of a breather for the singers. Keep the piano part simple until you come to the end of a phrase or the beginning of a brief interlude. Then, when the voices rest for a few bars or measures, make the accompaniment fuller and more complex, to fill the space. The piano can return to a less-dominant simplicity when the voices come back in.

> **Note**
>
> The accompaniment part goes beneath the voice parts on the score.
>
> A vocal reduction piano part is sometimes added to *a cappella* arrangements, for rehearsal purposes. In this instance, you should write "For rehearsal only" above the piano part.

Figure 17.12

A vocal reduction for piano.

And there's nothing wrong with having the piano rest from time to time. Even though a piece might be accompanied, it can still have *a cappella* passages. It's a nice effect to have the piano drop out and let the singers carry the piece for a while.

Creating a Vocal Arrangement

Track 5

Your assignment for this chapter is to create a four-part (SATB) vocal arrangement of "Love Waits." You can find the lead sheet for the song in Appendix B, which is also where you'll find my own "Love Waits" vocal arrangement. The choral performance of this arrangement is on Track 5 of the accompanying CD.

For my arrangement, I chose to take the *a cappella* approach. This helps to highlight the vocal harmonies, without them being hidden by any piano accompaniment.

The first verse of the arrangement builds intensity by the addition of voices; it starts with the tenors solo, adds a harmony line in the basses, and then adds the women's voices in whole-note harmony. The second verse gives the melody to the sopranos, with the other voices in more or less note-against-note harmony— with a little call-and-response thrown in from the men's voices in the second part of the verse.

The second part of the chorus (starting in measure 31) employs an interesting approach called *fanning*. This is where you start with a unison or close voicing (in this instance, everyone's on a B except for the tenor, who sings a close-third G), and then move the voices up and down to create wider and more complex voicings. It's a cool effect, as it results in very rich, spread-out sound.

The final verse opens with a bell-like effect, accomplished by having each voice come in with a new chord tone on different beats, all singing the word "love." This leads into a fully voiced, note-against-note harmony, and then to a decrescendo for the final chords.

Throughout, notice that I've simplified the rhythm a bit from that of the original song. By using straight quarter notes instead of the original syncopation, the piece is easier for a large ensemble to sing. In addition, I took substantial liberties with the original chords, in many instances extending them on a note-by-note basis to create more sophisticated harmonies. This is especially noticeable on the final chord, which is transformed into something like a G Major 9 with an added sixth (or a G Major 6 with an added ninth, depending on how you look at it). Note that I've led to these unusual harmony notes in simple, step-wise fashion, so the notes are easier for the singers to hit.

By the way, it's interesting to note how real-live singers interpret your vocal arrangements—where they take breaths, how they naturally crescendo over the course of a phrase, and so forth. For this recording, I didn't have the budget for a 100-piece choir, so I multi-tracked four talented singers from Minnesota's Zephyr Cabaret. They did an excellent job of interpreting the piece and bringing my arrangement to life; it's subtly different from what's in the written score, but without changing a single note on paper.

In any case, that's how I've approached this arranging assignment. I trust you'll come up with something totally different yet equally valid. Have at it!

The Least You Need to Know

- While there are many types of vocal ensembles, the most common is the four-voice (SATB) choir.

- The four-voice choir presents specific limitations (only four voices available) and challenges (extending simple triads into four-part voicings).

- Traditional SATB voicing puts the melody or highest chord tone in the soprano part, and the chord root in the bass part.

- The greatest challenge for vocal writing is ensuring that each part is easily singable; you can't include random leaps and expect singers to hit the notes.

- You don't have to arrange constant four-part harmony; you should vary the texture of your piece by using different voice groupings, voicings, and interval spacings.

- Vocal parts can be sung *a cappella* or accompanied by a piano or other instruments; piano accompaniment should support and contrast the vocal parts, without overwhelming them.

Chapter 18

Arranging for a Popular Recording

In This Chapter

◆ Learn the mechanics of arranging for the recording studio

◆ Discover the key elements of a popular recording

◆ Learn how to "sweeten" a basic recording

◆ Create your own recording arrangement

Arranging for a live ensemble is different from arranging for a commercial recording. That's because a live ensemble contains a set number of musicians; if you have two guitarists, a bass player, a drummer, and a singer, that's all you have to work with. The recording studio, on the other hand, can host an unlimited number of musicians, of all types—even if some of those musicians are virtual, provided by today's high-quality digital sample libraries. When you're recording, the entire musical world is at your fingertips—which lets you create any type of arrangement you can imagine.

That's why, by the way, I've saved this chapter for last. When you're arranging for a recording session, you have to employ all the arranging techniques you've learned to date. A commercial recording almost always includes a rhythm section (covered in Chapter 13) and vocals (covered in Chapter 17); depending on the type of tune being recorded, it might have a big-band backing (covered in Chapter 14) or an orchestral background (covered in 16). You need to master those types of arrangements before you head into the studio to record a densely layered pop track.

Arranging for the Recording Studio

The recording studio is an interesting place. The traditional studio is a big room full of microphones and baffles and isolation booths. The main studio room is then connected to the engineering room, itself dominated by the recording console laden with sliders and dials and meters. It's a place where talented musicians of all stripes gather to lay down tracks, taking whatever time is necessary to create the perfect take.

Today's home recording studios condense all of this into a much smaller space. The recording room might be a spare bedroom or basement, and the recording console has been replaced by the personal computer and computerized recording programs, such as ProTools and Cubase. Instead of armies of studio musicians, you have a MIDI keyboard and a battery of digital sample libraries; the libraries contain the instrument sounds you use to create your recordings.

The best of both worlds is a recording environment that accommodates live musicians but still offers digital samples for those instruments that are either impractical or impossible to record live. As useful as sample libraries are, there's nothing like the sound of a real-live musician playing your arrangements.

Whichever type of recording environment you use, as an arranger you still get the benefit of choosing from a wide variety of instruments for your arrangements. Instead of being limited to a four-piece rock band, you can augment the band with strings, woodwinds, brass, background vocalists, whatever. If you want traditional sweetening, add the sound of a string section; if you want something more esoteric, go with nontraditional or ethnic instruments, or with unusual combinations of common instruments. (A bassoon and accordion on a pop song? Why not!)

In the pop music world, the role of the arranger is often taken by the record's producer. It's the producer who's responsible for the final sound of the record, so becoming a producer/arranger lets one person control the entire process.

That said, traditional arrangers still have a place in some forms of pop recording. Arrangers are typically recruited to create orchestral backing for selected tracks; you arrange the string or wind sections that are used to "sweeten" the basic group tracks.

When you're working with rock or pop musicians, be prepared for some unusual working arrangements. That's because a lot of the musicians you'll run into aren't classically trained; some can't even read or write music. It's not unusual for a nontrained musician to describe the type of parts she wants using very unmusical terms. You'll have to learn how to interpret.

When you do translate those instructions into a formal arrangement, be prepared for change. The recording process is a long and interactive one, which means that things have a tendency to mutate over time. You might get into the studio, your real or virtual orchestra in hand, and discover that the group has added another verse or changed the chords in the chorus or totally scrapped a section. You have to be able to go with the flow, and redo your arrangements

Note
Famous musicians without formal musical training include John Lennon and Paul McCartney, as well as Benny Andersson and Björn Ulvaeus of ABBA. The lack of formal training didn't seem to hinder them; of course, it helps to be loaded with natural talent.

on the spot. It's your job to serve the process and the other musicians; you (and your arrangements) have to be flexible.

Some producers and musicians like to hear your arrangements before you get into the studio. That means working with a notation program, such as Finale or Sibelius, and a good sample library. You play your arrangements through the notation program or a separate sequencing or recording program, using the instruments in the sample library. This way, people who otherwise can't interpret a written chart can hear what you've written.

The other benefit of writing with a sample library is that you can quickly and easily hear what you're writing. Think that a trumpet would sound nice on the chorus? Then write it in and play it back using the sample library. You'll get immediate feedback, and be able to make any changes as necessary—even if you ultimately intend to have your arrangement played by real musicians.

Remember—using a combination of sample libraries and live musicians, just about any sound you can think of is now in your arranging toolkit. Use them wisely.

Elements of a Pop/Rock Arrangement

Despite what it might sound like when you listen to the radio today, no two popular recordings are alike. Even though many recordings utilize a set of common elements, the precise makeup of those elements is what distinguishes one recording from another.

That said, let's look at the common elements, and how you can use them in your recording arrangements.

Rhythm Track

Most commercial recordings are built from the bottom up—literally. Whether you're talking rock, country, or R&B, most recordings are built upon a basic groove. This groove is supplied by the rhythm section, of course. At its most basic, we're talking rhythm guitar, keyboards, bass, and drums, although this instrumentation can (and often is) augmented by additional guitars, keyboards, and percussion instruments.

You'll benefit by spending as much time as necessary to build the most effective rhythm track for the recording. Experiment with different combinations of instruments; don't limit yourself to the basic four-piece rhythm section. For example, you might want to try some or all of the following:

♦ **Use multiple guitars.** This is a hidden secret in all types of recordings. For example, the classic Motown recordings, while not necessarily sounding guitar-based, typically used three guitars in the rhythm section. One guitar played chunk chords on two and four, another played open chords in a strumming pattern, and a third played short melodic lines. The use of multiple guitars is an effective way to fill out the background sound of a recording.

◆ **Use multiple keyboards.** Just as multiple guitars help to fill out the sound, so do multiple keyboards. Consider starting with an acoustic piano, then layer on some sort of electric piano in a rhythmic pattern, a synthesizer pad playing whole notes, and maybe another synthesizer playing short melodic lines. You can create quite a lush sound with the right combination of keyboards.

◆ **Use auxiliary percussion.** Drums alone don't always make the scene. Create a more driving rhythm by employing a variety of percussion instruments—tambourine, congas, bongos, claves, maracas, even sleigh bells or triangle. Consider any instrument that can play a repeating rhythmic pattern.

◆ **Use synthesizers as a percussion instrument.** In many forms of music (dance music, especially) you can use synthesizers to provide the rhythmic background. Just program the synthesizer to produce an interesting rhythmic pattern, using your choice of chords, single-line patterns, or simple white noise. More often than not, the synthesizer plays an eighth- or sixteenth-note pattern, mimicking a shaken percussion pattern.

◆ **Don't use drums.** This is sacrilegious for a drummer to say, but you don't have to use all the instruments in the traditional rhythm section. In particular, drums aren't always the best way to provide a background rhythm. For example, a tune with a slow groove might not need a background rhythm at all, or might benefit from the softer sound of a shaker or congas. Think outside the box, and don't be afraid to write the drums (or other instruments) out of the mix.

◆ **Augment—or replace—the bass.** Pop, rock, and R&B records typically have a strong reliance on the bass line. You can use a solo electric bass, of course, or use other instruments instead of, or in addition to, the bass guitar. Popular instruments to use as bass replacements/additions include acoustic bass, synthesizer, guitar (played on the lower strings), tuba, baritone sax, and so on.

◆ **Consider other instruments.** Don't limit yourself to guitars, keyboards, and percussion; other instruments can also provide a background rhythm. In country music, consider mandolins, banjos, steel guitars, fiddles, and the like. In rock or country music, consider accordions, bass harmonicas, vibes, and the like.

Vocals

Once you have your rhythm tracks laid down, you should think about the vocal tracks—lead and backup. You don't have to do much arranging for the lead vocals, save noting where the vocalist does and doesn't sing. The backup vocals, however, are another story.

We talked about vocal parts in Chapter 17, and all the techniques discussed there apply in this setting, as well. Background vocals can be either note-against-note harmony or call-and-response counterlines, depending on the song and genre. The note-against-note harmony (typically in thirds, either above or below the melody) works fine in most rock, pop, and country settings. The call-and-response approach is part and parcel of uptempo soul and R&B, and also common in some rock music.

As to how many voices to arrange for, note-against-note harmony can work with either one or two voices (in addition to the lead voice, of course). Call-and-response backing works better with two or more voices. You can use either single-gender or mixed voices, depending on the sound you want.

Sweetening

Beyond the rhythm and vocal tracks, you have everything else on the recording—what we'll call the sweetening. These parts may include lead guitar or other solo instruments, a horn section, strings, or other combinations of instruments that are used to fill in the gaps and "sweeten" the sound.

The most common type of sweetening is the solo lead instrument, typically used to provide an instrumental solo in the middle of the piece, do some call-and-response mini-solos at the ends of phrases, or simply augment the vocal line throughout. In rock music this is almost always provided by a lead electric guitar, although other instruments (saxes, synthesizer, even trumpet or trombone) can also fill this role.

Bringing in other instruments helps to widen the musical palette of the song. For example, strings are often used in pop, rock, and country music, especially slower tunes. Often written in ensemble unison, sustained notes are the most common approach—although rhythmic patterns can also be effective (think Elton John's "Levon" or Train's "Drops of Jupiter").

In R&B, soul, and blues music, sweetening is most often provided by a horn section. The typical horn section consists of a tenor sax, trumpet, and trombone—although this configuration can be beefed up by doubling one or more of these instruments. The parts are typically accented rhythmic patterns (riffs and stings) that complement the vocal line.

Other types of sweetening can be provided by flutes, solo cello, accordion, and just about any type of instrument you can imagine. The sweetening can be simple block chords (or whole-note lines) behind the vocals, countermelodies that weave in and out of the vocal line, or rhythmic patterns that provide accent and contrast to the vocals.

Creating a Recording

Remember the simple rock-band arrangement of "Love Waits" back in Chapter 13? Well, when you move the band into the studio, the arrangement doesn't have to stay simple: you can sweeten the basic recording with all sorts of instruments and voices.

Track 6

To that end, your final assignment is to take "Love Waits" (found in Appendix B) and arrange it for a recording. The recording can be in any style and use any combination of instruments you want. Think of yourself as the producer/ arranger of the track, and go to work.

My take on this task appears on Track 6 of the accompanying CD. The chart for the arrangement is at the end of Appendix B. I opted to go for a mellow, laid-back kind of groove, kind of like the Rascals meets the 5th Dimension. And when you're talking about rock and pop recordings, the groove is the thing.

First off, the groove itself. The bass line is simple and somewhat repetitive, but that's what makes it effective. It just kind of glides along, pushing the song forward. To get just the right sound, I pulled out an old Phil Spector trick and used two different basses doubling the same line—one acoustic, one electric. To further help propel the rhythm, there's a trebly chunk-rhythm electric guitar, playing on the two and the "and" after three; acoustic piano, playing on one and the "and" after two; and an acoustic guitar, which contributes an eighth-note strumming pattern.

The other key element of the groove is the percussion, led by the drums playing a straight-ahead eighth-note rock beat. The drums are augmented (deep in the mix) by a cowbell, congas, and triangle. The triangle, while almost subliminal in its application, is important in that it contributes a much-needed high end to the mix. And note this—subsidiary instruments like the triangle don't have to be explicitly heard to be effective.

Just to show that I learned a thing or two from the Motown three-guitar approach, there's one more guitar in the mix, a tremolo guitar playing whole-note chords. It enters in the middle of the first verse, where it's used to continue the texture previously supplied by the background vocals; when the vocals drop out, that space is filled by the tremolo guitar.

Providing additional texture is an instrument you don't hear a lot these days, the vibraphone. It enters in the second part of the first verse, where it echoes the vocal line. From there on, it doubles the background vocalists throughout most of the rest of the tune, with a few block chords thrown in as appropriate. I like vibes; the instrument has a nice tonal quality that works well with all sorts of other instruments.

The background vocals are used primarily to provide a doo-wop style accompaniment. Notice how the "sha la las" alternate between straight quarters in the first measure to a syncopated rhythm in the second. This straight/syncopated rhythm helps to establish the song's basic groove.

This main mix is augmented by the use of some interesting orchestral instruments. In the second verse, there's a fun little countermelody provided by flute and oboe. These two instruments combine to create a very cool color, especially in their lower registers. You get a completely different sound from the two instruments in their higher registers, which you can hear in the final verse. In both cases, the sound is supplementary without being overwhelming; it adds color to the piece without drawing attention to itself.

The chorus sees the entry of a full string section (minus the double basses). It's a mainly homophonic texture from violins I and II, viola, and cello, although in places the cello splits off from the rest to double the flute/oboe line.

Then, in the final verse, we have the strings and the woodwinds playing patterns against each other. Their two figures are complementary in a somewhat call-and-response approach. Note how the lines play around the lead vocal line; they fill in the spaces without getting in the way of the main melody.

Finally, the ending—what we call the out-chorus—repeats the piece's signature two-bar phrase until the fade-out. Fading out the ending of a song is a luxury you have only with recorded works; it's almost impossible to achieve an effective fade-out in a live performance. To create this type of fade-out, you have your musicians keep on playing for a half-minute or so, which gives the engineer enough time to do the fade. (If there's not enough raw material there, the fade may need to be accelerated—or the listener will hear the unwanted final notes.) The out-chorus is also the place where you might choose to take the reigns off your musicians; the vocalist can wail a bit, the drummer can let loose on the skins, and any instrumental soloist can do his thing. If that's what you want, of course.

And here's a treat. The final track on the accompanying CD is a bonus track that shows you how all these instruments build up to create the perfect backing track. You hear one instrument added to another, one at a time in four-bar phrases, until the final track is complete. In order, listen to the acoustic bass, electric bass, cowbell (with lots of reverb!), triangle, drums, congas, electric rhythm guitar, electric tremolo guitar, acoustic piano, acoustic rhythm guitar, vibes, background vocals, strings, and flute/oboe. Yes, it sounds a little sparse at first, but just listen to how it builds and to how all the differing parts fit together into a cohesive whole. This is how you create a commercial recording!

Track 70

But this is just one approach to making a recording from this particular song. Now it's your turn—pick any style you like, and then start the process. What kind of recording can you arrange?

Final Words

When you've completed your recording arrangement, you're done with this book—but you're not done learning about arranging and orchestration. No matter how much you know or how talented you are, there's always more to learn. There are new instrument combinations to try, new musical approaches to explore, new sounds to experience. Even the best arrangers and orchestrators are constantly learning; you should do the same.

How do you learn more about your craft? You should explore the texts I listed in the introduction to this book, of course, but the best way to learn more about arranging and orchestration is to listen. Listen to all the music you can get your ears around and deconstruct what you hear. Listen for colors that you like, and figure out how those sounds were achieved. Listen for passages that are particularly effective, and take apart the arrangements to discover how they're done. Learn from what you hear; learn from other arrangers.

If you're an arranger/producer of rock or pop music, that means listen to all the commercial CDs you can get your hands on, from both current and classic artists. Listen to Phil Spector's classic Wall of Sound recordings, listen to Brian Wilson's marvelous *Pet Sounds*, listen to all of the later Beatles records, and try to figure out how all those wonderful sounds were created. Then listen to the best of today's music to learn more contemporary approaches—and even to some less-than-stellar songs, to learn what *not* to do.

The same goes if you're interested in choral, big-band, marching-band, or orchestral arranging. Listen to the best and most popular pieces in the genre, and learn from them. Learn how individual instruments and voices are used, learn how different instruments are combined, learn how whole pieces are structured for best effect. Listen and learn.

And when you listen, write down what you hear. Use your ear training skills to transcribe whole arrangements, so you can see what it is that you hear. Transcribing an arrangement is one of the best ways to learn specific techniques; when you write down each note for each part, you get inside the original arranger's brain and learn how he or she thinks and approaches a piece of music. It's a great way to learn.

That's what it's all about. Learning the techniques, you need to reproduce the sounds you hear in your head. Listen, learn, and then experiment. And always—always—keep writing. The more you write, the better your arrangements will become. You improve over time; there's nothing like sheer experience to grow your talents.

So now's the time to close this book (at least temporarily; you can still use it as a reference), open your ears, and venture forth into the real world of arranging and orchestration. It's fun, it's artistically fulfilling, and it's something you know you can do well. Just start putting one note after another—and keep writing!

The Least You Need to Know

- When you arrange for a recording, you have an almost-limitless variety of instruments and voices at your disposal.

- You can use digital sample libraries to help in the arranging process, to demonstrate your work to producers and musicians, and to provide virtual instruments for the recording itself.

- The three key components of a commercial recording are the rhythm track, the vocals, and the sweetening—provided by lead guitar, strings, horns, or other instruments.

- The basic rhythm track is typically provided by one or more guitars, keyboards, bass, and drums—although this instrumentation can be supplemented by additional instruments.

- The one unique structural element available to recording arrangers is the fade-out, where the song doesn't have a distinct ending; instead, the song simply decreases in volume throughout the out-chorus until there's nothing left to hear.

Glossary

a cappella   Singing without accompaniment.

altered bass chord   A chord with some note other than the root in the bass. The altered bass note is typically notated after a slash, like this: Am7/D.

alto voice   The lower female voice; short for *contralto*.

approach note   A note that leads up or down to a structural tone; an *approach note run* contains two or more approach notes.

arpeggio   A chord that is broken up and played one note at a time.

arrangement   A fully-arranged and orchestrated piece of music.

arranger   A person who creates arrangements

arranging   The process of adapting an existing composition for instruments or voices other than those for which it was originally written.

augmentation   A type of variation in which the melody is restated in longer note values.

back battery   See *drumline*

back phrase   The act of playing the notes of a melody later than originally written.

baritone voice   An optional male voice, positioned between the tenor and bass.

bass voice   The lowest male voice.

big band   A large jazz ensemble containing a mixture of trumpets, trombones, saxophones, and a rhythm section.

big chord voicing   A type of voicing for big band where chord tones are added downward from the lead.

block chord   A type of accompaniment consisting of simple sustained chords, without moving harmony.

block voicing   A type of voicing for big band where instruments are assigned five distinct voices.

blues   A type of music built on the blues scale and the blues progression.

blues progression   A 12-bar sequence of chords common in blues and jazz music, as follows: I-I-I-I-IV-IV-I-I-V7-IV-I-I.

blues scale   A seven-note scale (counting the octave) used when playing blues progressions; in relation to a major scale, the scale degrees (not counting the octave) are 1-♭3-4-♭5-5-♭7.

brass   The family of instruments, typically made of brass, that produce sound when air is blown through a mouthpiece. The brass family includes the trumpet, trombone, tuba, and French horn.

break   See *lift*

bridge   A short section that links two important sections of a piece of music. Sometimes called the C-section.

cadence   (1) A pause or stopping point, typically a short chord progression at the end of a phrase or piece of music. (2) A rudimental drum beat, typically used in marching band and drum and bugle corps music.

call and response   A melodic technique in which a phrase is stated in the first part of the melody and then answered in the second part.

cambiata   The unchanged male voice, similar in range to that of the female alto voice.

capo   A device placed on the fretboard of a guitar or similar instrument to transpose the instrument to a higher key.

chamber orchestra   A smaller version of the full orchestra.

chart   Colloquial term for a score or arrangement. Used frequently by jazz and rock musicians.

choir   A large vocal ensemble, typically with soprano, alto, tenor, and bass sections.

chord chart   A method of notating music using only chords and chord symbols.

chord leading   The concept that certain chords in a scale naturally want to move to certain other chords.

chord progression   A series of chords over a number of measures.

chord substitution   The art of substituting one chord in a harmonic progression with a convincing alternative.

chord voicing   See *voicing*.

chorus   In popular music, the part of the song (typically following the verse) that recurs at intervals; also known as the B section of a song.

clave   (1) A repeating two-measure Latin rhythm. (2) A percussion instrument consisting of two wooden cylinders that are struck together.

close voicing   Chord voicing where the notes are only a second or third apart.

closed voicing   See *close voicing*

cluster   A close collection of notes, typically each a second apart.

coda   A short section at the end of a composition that reinforces the final resolution.

common tone   A note that is shared between two adjacent chords.

comp   The process of repeatedly playing one or two chords, typically in a similar rhythm.

composer   A person who creates music.

composition   (1) The process of creating a new piece of music. (2) An original piece of music.

compound chord   Two chords sounded together. Typically notated with a vertical slash between the two chords.

concert band   An instrumental ensemble that includes virtually all the brass, woodwind, and percussion instruments from the larger orchestra, but without the strings.

concert key   See *concert pitch*

concert pitch   The actual (nontransposed) pitch of a piece of music.

consonance   Harmonious combination of tones. The opposite of *dissonance*.

contralto   See *alto voice*

contrapuntal   See *counterpoint*.

contrary motion   Two voices moving in opposite directions.

copyist   A person who manually copies individual parts from the master score.

countermelody   An accompanying melody sounded against the principle melody.

counterpoint   Two or more simultaneous, independent lines or voices.

countertenor   An optional falsetto voice above the normal tenor voice.

détaché   In bowed string instruments, the technique where consecutive notes are played without the bow leaving the string.

diatonic   Notes or chords that are in the underlying key or scale.

diatonic substitution   Replacing a chord with a related chord either a third above or a third below the original.

diminution   A type of variation in which the note values of the original theme are shortened.

dissonance   A combination of tones that sounds discordant and unstable, in need of resolution to a more pleasing and stable harmony. The opposite of *consonance*.

dominant   The fifth degree of a scale, a perfect fifth above the tonic; also refers to the chord built on this fifth scale degree.

double   Using a second voice or instrument to duplicate a particular line of music, either in unison or an octave above or below.

drop 2   A type of voicing, common when writing for jazz saxophone sections, where the second note in the chord is dropped down an octave to the baritone sax part.

drop 2-4   A type of voicing, common when writing for jazz saxophone sections, where both the second and fourth notes in the chord are dropped down an octave.

drum and bugle corps   A specialized form of competitive marching ensemble. Includes only brass and percussion instruments.

drumline   The marching drums in a marching band or drum corps.

dynamics   Varying degrees of loud and soft. For example, *forte* signifies a loud dynamic, while *piano* signifies a soft dynamic.

embellishment   Melodic decoration through the use of additional notes added to a structural tone.

expansion   A type of variation in which new material is added to the original melody, typically to the end of the phrase.

extended chords   Chords with additional notes (typically in thirds) added above the basic triad.

falsetto   A voice that sounds a register above a singer's normal range, typically with different vocal characteristics than the singer's normal range.

four on the floor   A form of bass playing that employs straight quarter notes.

front ensemble   See *pit*

front phrase   The act of playing the notes of a melody earlier than originally written.

glissando   A mechanism for getting from one pitch to another, playing every single pitch between the two notes as smoothly as possible.

guitar tab   See *tablature*

half-time shuffle   A shuffle beat where the backbeats are on the third beat of each measure; a way to apply a triplet feel to a standard rock beat.

harmonic   A vibration frequency that is an exact integer multiple of the fundamental frequency. The fundamental pitch is called the *first harmonic*; the *second harmonic* is an octave above the fundamental.

harmonize   The process of choosing chords to accompany a melodic line.

harmony   The sound of tones in combination; also used to refer to the accompanying parts behind the main melody.

idiophone   A percussion instrument, such as the marimba, that produces sound when its body vibrates.

instrumentation   The choice of instruments used in an arrangement. See also *orchestration*.

interlude   A short section of music that serves to connect two major sections within a piece, often blending themes contained in both sections.

inversion   (1) A chord in which the bass note is not the root of the chord. The *first inversion* indicates that the third of the chord is played as the bass note; the *second inversion* indicates that the fifth of the chord is played as the bass note; the noninverted status is referred to as *root position*. (2) A type of melodic variation that starts on the same pitch as the original melody but then moves in the opposite direction—but by the same intervals. Also known as a *melodic inversion*.

jazz band   See *big band*

lead sheet   A piece of sheet music that contains a single staff for the melody, with the accompanying chords written above the staff.

leading tone   The note that is a half-step below the tonic of the scale that leads up to the tonic note.

lift   The transition point from one register to another.

lyric soprano   The most common soprano voice, with a uniquely lyrical quality.

mallet instrument   A pitched percussion instrument, such as the marimba or vibraphone, that produces sounds when wooden or metal bars are struck with a mallet.

marching band   An ensemble with similar instrumentation to the concert band, structured for best effectiveness when marching in a parade or show.

melisma   In vocal music, the technique of singing multiple notes over a constant syllable.

melodic outline   The underlying skeleton of a melody, built from the melody's structural tones.

melody   The combination of tone and rhythm in a logical sequence.

membranophone   A percussion instrument, such as a snare drum, that produces sound when a membrane or head is struck.

mezzo soprano   A slightly lower soprano voice.

MIDI   Short for *musical instrument digital interface*, a protocol for storing and transmitting musical information and instructions in digital format.

minimalist   A type of contemporary music, popularized by composer Philip Glass, in which simple ostinatos and themes are repeated throughout the piece, effectively stripping down the music to its barest essentials.

modal music   A type of composition based on one or more modes.

mode   A set of scales, based on centuries-old church music that preceded today's major and minor scales. These include the *Ionian, Dorian, Phrygian, Lydian, Mixolydian, Aeolian,* and *Locrian* modes.

modulation   (1) A change of key. (2) A type of variation in which the original theme is repeated exactly, but in a different key.

motif   A brief melodic or rhythmic idea within a piece of music. Sometimes called a *figure* or *motive.*

motion   The upward or downward movement of a melody.

movement   Self-contained part within a larger musical work.

mute   (1) An external device inserted into the bell of a brass instrument, designed to alter the instrument's sound. Common mutes include the *cup mute, straight mute,* and *Harmon mute.* (2) A device used to dampen the strings on a bowed instrument.

Nashville notation   A way of notating chords using simple numbers (1, 2, 3, and so forth) to represent chords played on specific tones of the scale.

neighboring tone   A tone one diatonic step away (either above or below) a structural tone.

notation   The art of communicating musical ideas in written form.

notation program   A software program that facilitates the composition, arranging, and notation processes.

open voicing   Chord voicing with notes a fourth or more apart.

orchestra   A group of instruments organized for the performance of symphonies and other instrumental works, or to accompany an opera or other staged presentation.

orchestration   (1) The process of deciding which instruments or voices to use for a musical work. (2) A piece of music that has been assigned specific instruments.

orchestrator   A person who orchestrates pieces of music.

ornamentation   Notes that embellish and decorate a melody.

ostinato   A repeated melodic or rhythmic pattern.

out chorus   In popular recordings, the repetition of the final chorus that plays as the song fades out.

parallel harmony   A harmony line that mirrors the existing melody line, at a fixed interval.

parallel motion   Two or more voices moving in the same direction by the same interval.

passaggio   That point where the vocal quality switches from one register to another.

passing tone   A pitch located (scale-wise) directly between two main pitches; passing tones are typically used to connect notes in a melody.

pedal point   A note sustained below changing harmonies.

pentatonic scale   A five-note scale; in relation to a major scale, the scale degrees (not counting the octave) are 1-2-3-5-6.

percussion   The family of instruments that produce sound when you hit, beat, crash, shake, roll, scratch, rub, twist, or rattle them. Included in this family are various types of drums and cymbals, as well as mallet instruments (marimba, xylophone, and so forth) and timpani.

permutation   A type of melodic variation that completely rearranges the pitches of the original melody.

phrase   Within a piece of music, a segment that is unified by rhythms, melodies, or harmonies, and that comes to some sort of closure; often composed in groups of 2, 4, 8, 16, or 32 measures.

pit   A stationary percussion section used in drum and bugle corps and some marching show bands, consisting of nonmarching instruments such as timpani and marimba.

pizzicato   The technique of plucking the strings on a bowed instrument.

position   The specific placement of a trombone slide, used to produce different notes. Trombones have seven positions.

power chord   A rock guitar technique that sounds only the root and the fifth of a chord, with no third.

register   The specific area in the range of a voice or an instrument.

retrograde   A type of melodic variation that plays the pitches of the original theme exactly backward.

rhythm section   A small ensemble, either standalone or contained within a larger ensemble, typically consisting of one or more guitars, keyboards, bass, and drums.

rhythmic displacement   A type of variation that repeats the original phrase, but at a different place in the measure

roll   A technique used by percussionists to sustain a note on a nonsustaining instrument; accomplished by playing rapid multiple strokes between alternating hands.

rondo   A musical form that alternates a recurring theme with other themes, in ABACA, ABACADA, and similar constructions.

rudiment   One of forty official rhythms that comprise a drummer's repertoire.

sample   A digital reproduction of an actual instrument.

sample library   A collection of digitally sampled instrument sounds.

sampler   An electronic instrument or computer software program that plays back instrument samples and sample libraries.

SATB   Shorthand for soprano, alto, tenor, and bass. (Choral scores are sometimes called *SATB scores*.)

score   (1) The written depiction of all the individual parts played of each of the instruments in an ensemble. (2) To orchestrate a composition.

score order   The order in which individual instruments are written on a score.

sequencer   See *sampler*

shout chorus   In big band jazz, a section near the end of the piece that provides a climax to the arrangement.

shuffle   A groove where notated straight eighth and dotted eighth notes are played with a triplet feel.

similar motion   Two or more voices moving in the same direction, but by different intervals.

slash chord   See *altered bass chord*

slash notation   A form of notation for the rhythm section where individual beats or rhythms are represented by slashes.

sonata form   A four-movement form used in traditional symphonies, consisting of a fast first movement, a slower second movement, a faster third movement, and an even faster finale.

sonata-allegro form   A specific musical form, established during the Classical period, typically applied within a single movement of a longer piece, such as a symphony. The sonata form consists of three main sections (exposition, development, and recapitulation), with an optional coda.

song form   The structure of a short piece of music; usually diagramed as A-A-B-A.

soprano voice   The highest female voice.

stacked voicing   A type of voicing for big band where the trumpets are on top with close voicing, the trombones are directly below with either close or open voicing, and the saxes have open voicing.

string   The family of instruments that produce sound when a string is bowed or plucked. The bowed string family includes the violin, viola, cello, and double bass; plucked string instruments include the guitar, mandolin, electric bass, and similar instruments.

string orchestra   A large ensemble containing the five instruments of the orchestra's string section (first violin, second violin, viola, cello, and double bass), sometimes accompanied by a piano.

string quartet   A form of chamber music for two violins, viola, and cello.

structural tones   The most important notes in a melody; the notes that remain when you strip a melody of all embellishments. The structural tones of a melody create the *melodic outline*.

subdominant   The fourth degree of the scale, or the chord built on the fourth degree (IV).

subject   (1) A motif, phrase, or melody that is a basic element in a musical composition. (2) The initial melody or phrase in a fugue.

swing   (1) A style of playing where notated straight eighth or dotted eighth notes are sounded with a triplet feel. (2) A type of jazz common to big bands of the 1930s, 1940s, and 1950s.

symphonic orchestra   See *orchestra*

symphony   A large-scale instrumental composition, usually in four movements.

syncopation   An accent on an unexpected beat—or the lack of an accent on an expected beat.

tablature   A special type of guitar notation that represents the six strings of the instrument.

tenor voice   The highest male voice.

texture   The rhythmic and harmonic styles employed in an arrangement.

theme   A recurring melodic or rhythmic pattern or idea; the main melodic phrase in a composition.

theme and variations   Musical technique involving the statement of a theme and then the varying of that theme. See *variation*.

timbre   The distinctive character or tone quality of a voice or instrument.

tonality   The organization of musical notes around a tonic, or home pitch, based on a major or minor scale or mode.

tonic   The primary note in a scale or key; the first degree of a scale or a chord built on that degree (I).

transition   (1) Modulation from one key to another. (2) Short musical passage that acts as a link between two more substantial passages.

transpose   See *transposition*.

transposing instruments   Those instruments that are not notated at their sounding pitch.

transposition   Translating pitch.

tremolo   In bowed string instruments, the technique of moving the bow rapidly back and forth on the string while playing a single pitch.

trill   The technique of rapidly alternating between higher and lower tones.

truncation   A type of variation in which one or more notes from the beginning or end of the original phrase are deleted. Also known as *segmentation*.

two to a bar   See *two-beat*

two-beat   A musical style where the bass plays only on beats one and three.

unison   (1) Two simultaneous notes of the same pitch. (2) Voices or instruments all singing or playing the same pitch.

variation   A technique in which some aspects of the music are altered but the original is still recognizable. Typically used in conjunction with repetition. See also *theme and variations*.

verse   In popular music, the first or A section of a song, preceding the chorus.

vibrato   A wavering of the primary tone.

vocal tenor clef   In vocal music, a clef sometimes used for the tenor voice, that sounds an octave lower than written.

voice   (1) A melodic or harmonic line. (2) A specific note within an arranged chord.

voice crossing   Where two separate melodic lines, one ascending and the other descending, pass each other in pitch.

voice leading   The motion of a single voice in a musical composition or arrangement.

voice removal   The selected removal of notes from a chord to fit within a smaller voicing.

voicing   The way the notes of a chord are arranged.

walking bass   A style of bass playing, common in jazz, where the bass line moves up and down the scale in a step-wise fashion, typically in straight quarter notes.

woodwind   The family of instruments that produce sound when air vibrates a wooden reed. The woodwind family includes the clarinet, saxophone, oboe, and bassoon. Also included are the flute and the piccolo, which do not use reeds.

Arrangements

This appendix contains all the arrangements used in Part 3, "Real-World Arranging." In order, here's what you'll find:

- "Love Waits" lead sheet
- "Love Waits" chord chart, as played on CD track 1
- "Love Waits" big band arrangement, as played on CD track 2
- "Love Waits" marching band arrangement, as played on CD track 3
- "Love Waits" orchestra arrangement, as played on CD track 4
- "Love Waits" choir arrangement, as played on CD track 5
- "Love Waits" pop recording arrangement, as played on CD track 6

Note

I'm interested in hearing your own arrangements of "Love Waits," in any genre and for any type of ensemble. Feel free to e-mail me MP3 files of your recordings or PDF files of your charts; send them to arranging@molehillgroup.com. I can't guarantee I'll respond to all e-mails, but I promise I'll look at or listen to every submission.

Love Waits

Lead Sheet

Michael Miller

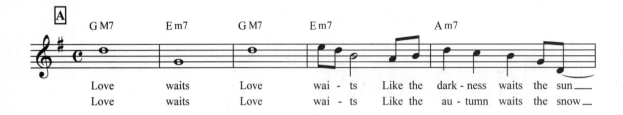

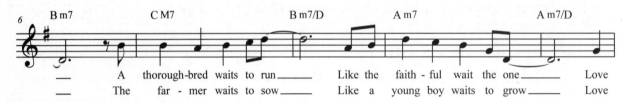

Love Waits

Chord Chart

Michael Miller

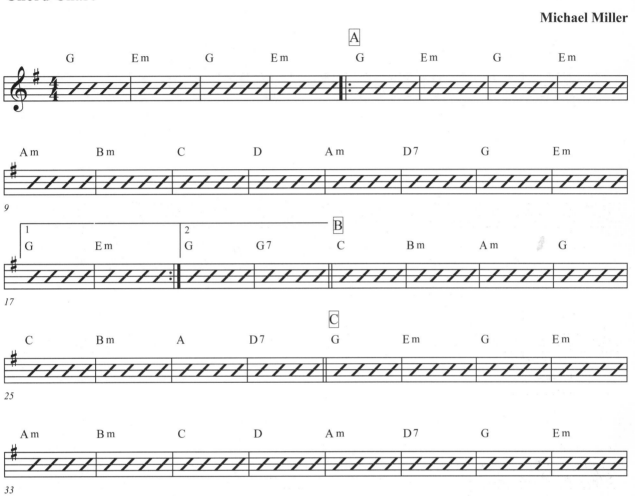

Love Waits

Big Band Score

Michael Miller

©2006

Love Waits

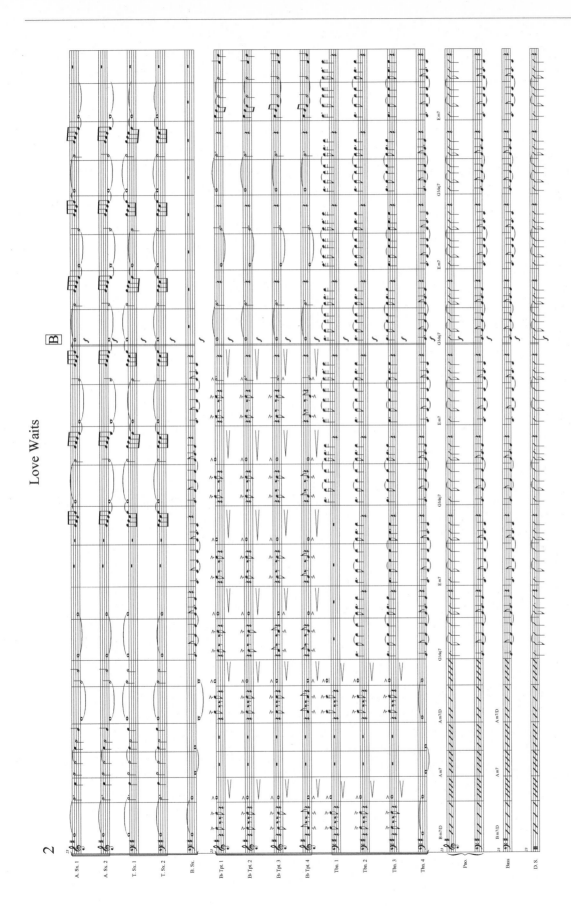

Love Waits

3

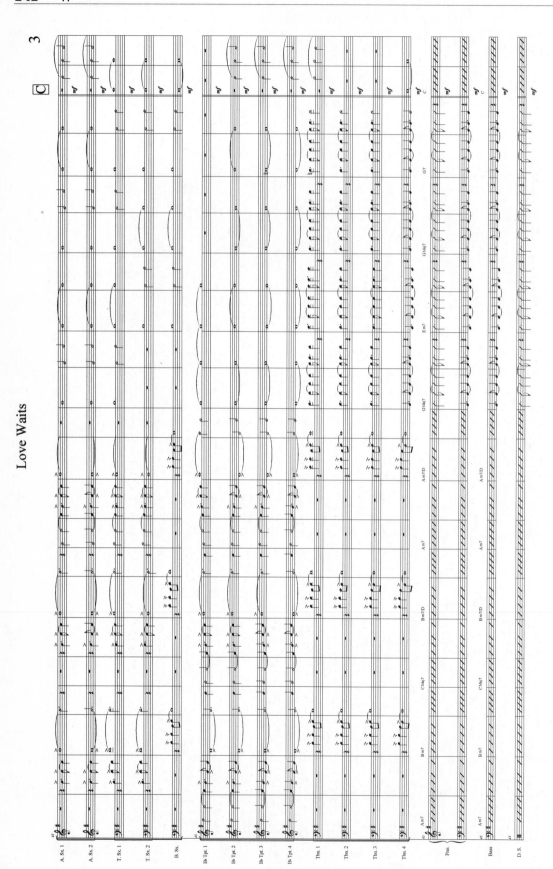

Love Waits

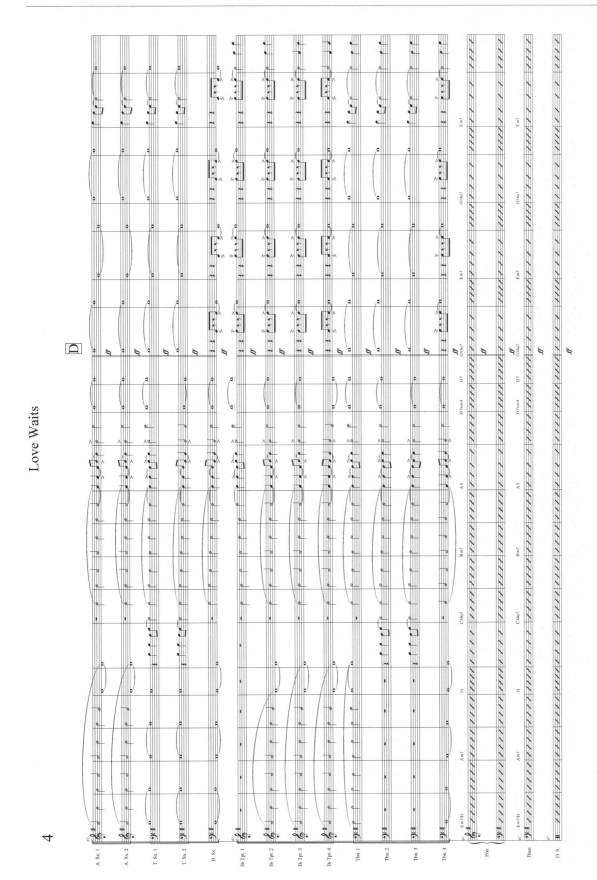

Love Waits

Marching Band Score

Love Waits

Michael Miller

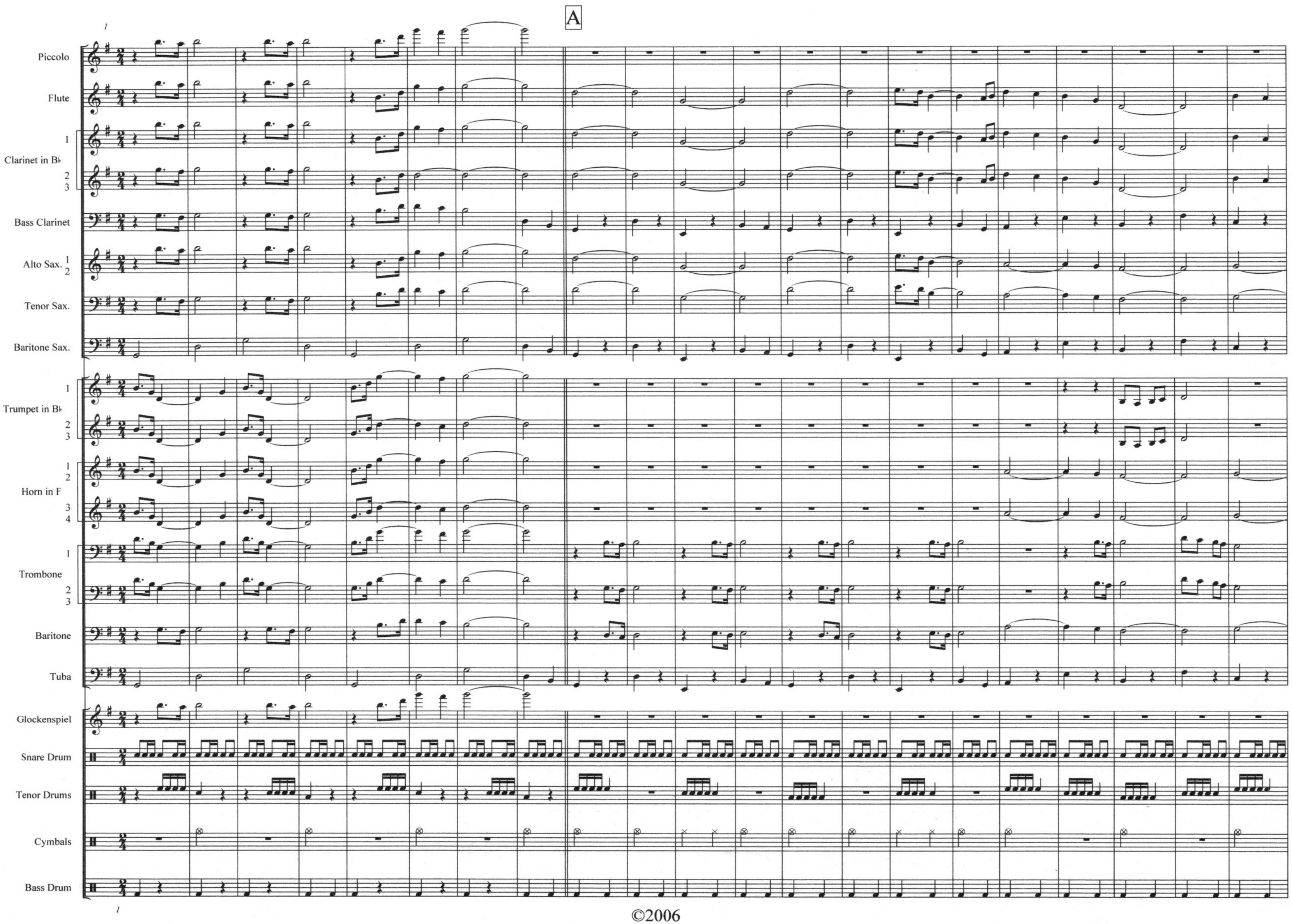

Love Waits

Love Waits

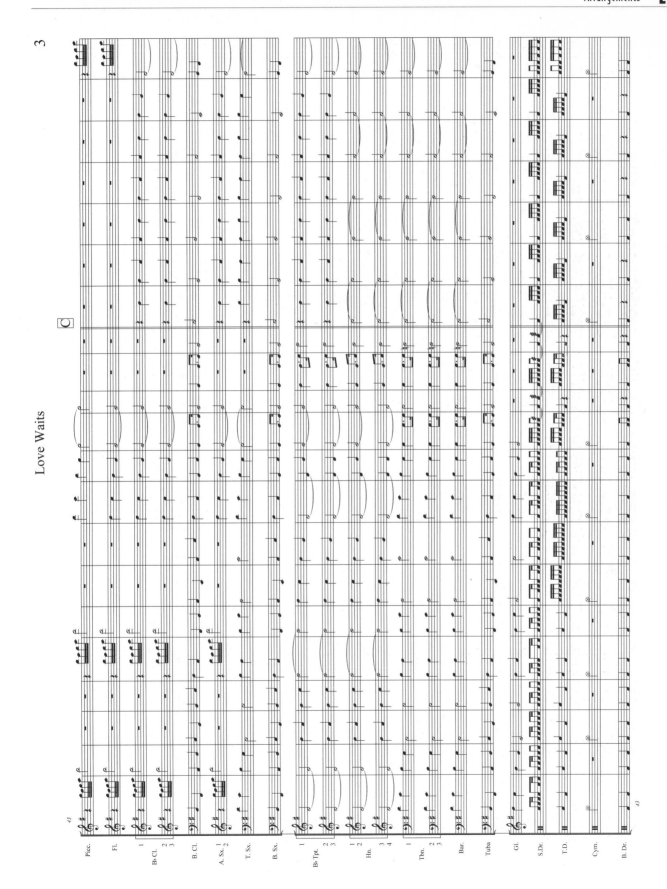

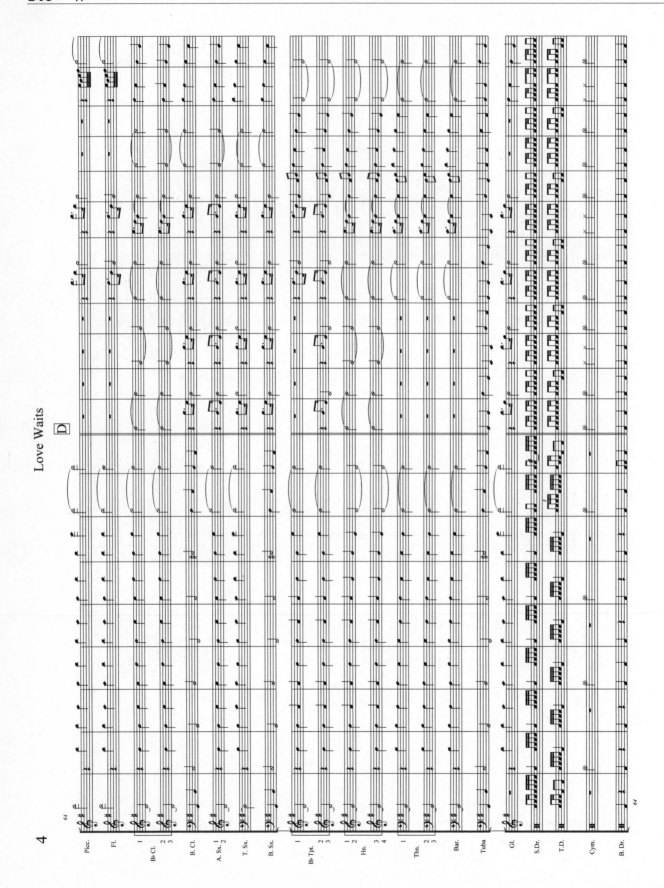

Love Waits

Love Waits

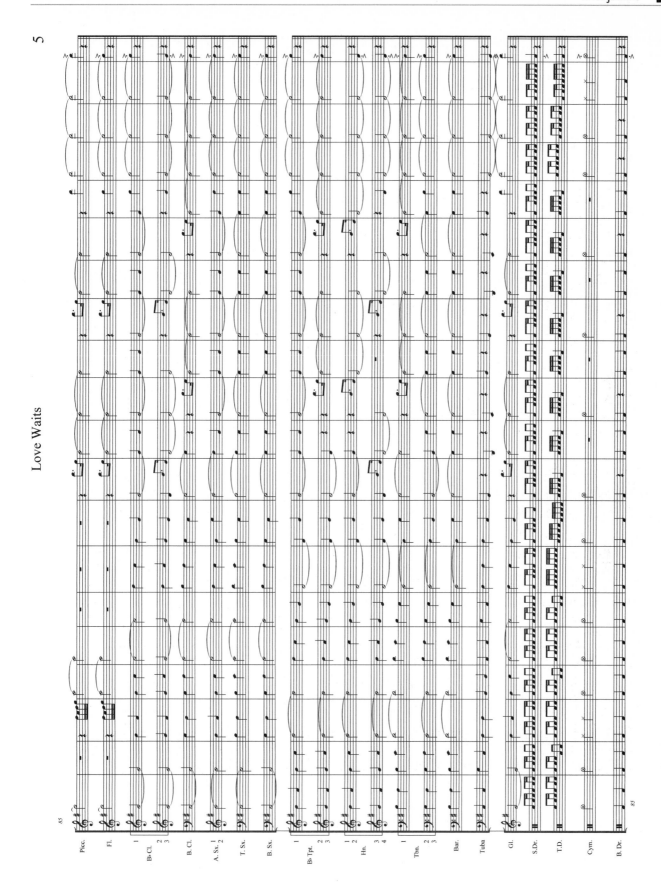

Love Waits

Orchestral Score

Michael Miller

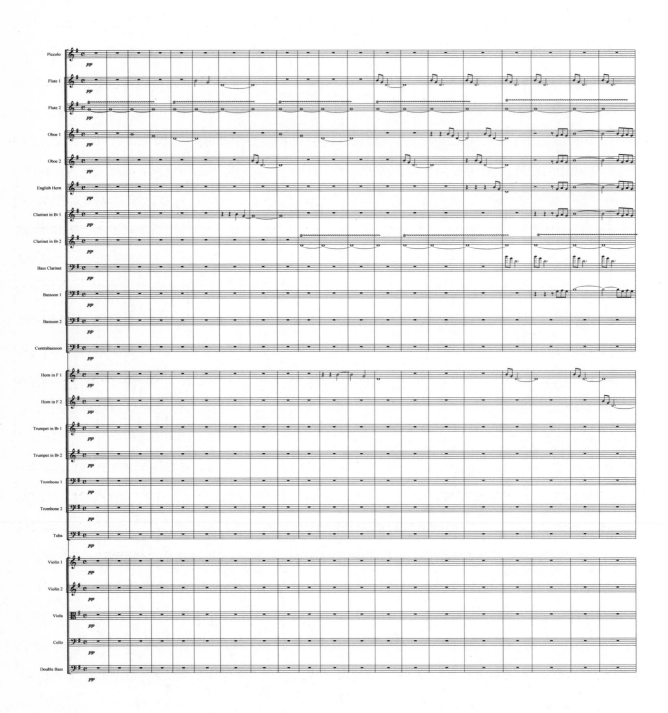

Love Waits

2

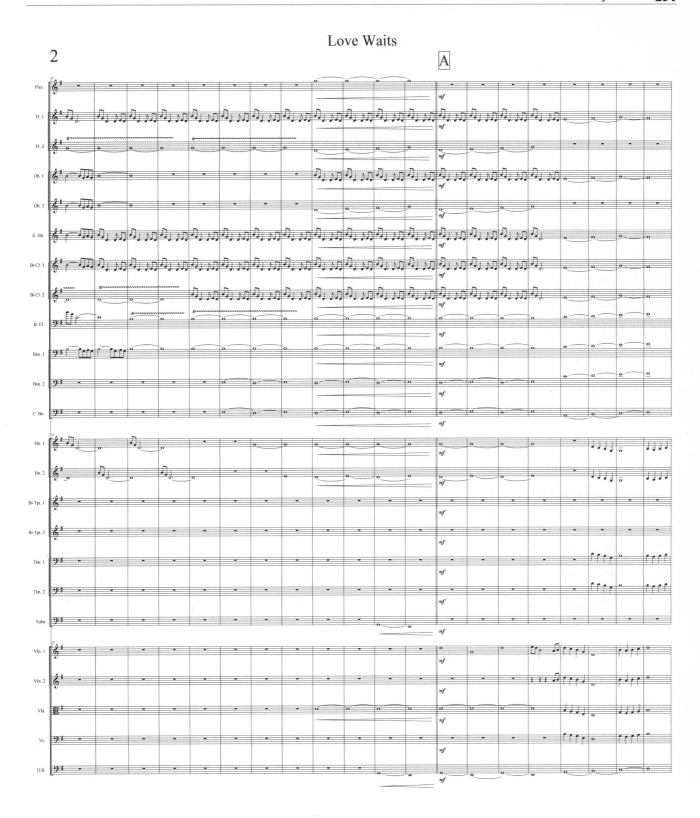

Love Waits

3

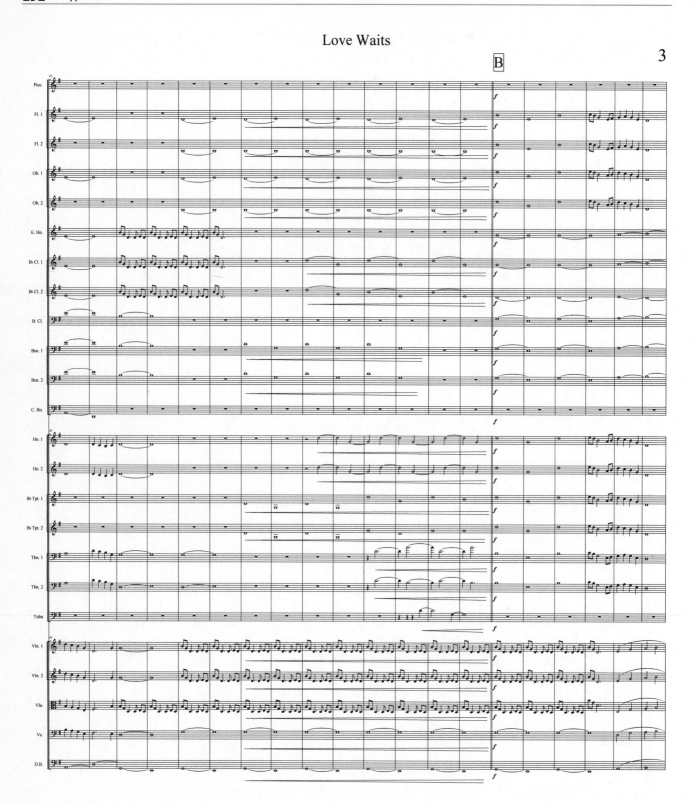

Love Waits

4

C
D
Picc.
Fl. 1
Fl. 2
Ob. 1
Ob. 2
E. Hn.
B♭ Cl. 1
B♭ Cl. 2
B. Cl.
Bsn. 1
Bsn. 2
C. Bn.
Hn. 1
Hn. 2
B♭ Tpt. 1
B♭ Tpt. 2
Tbn. 1
Tbn. 2
Tuba
Vln. 1
Vln. 2
Vla.
Vc.
D.B.
mf
ff

Love Waits

Love Waits

Choral Score

Michael Miller

Love Waits

Love Waits

3

Love Waits

Pop Arrangement
Recording Score

Michael Miller

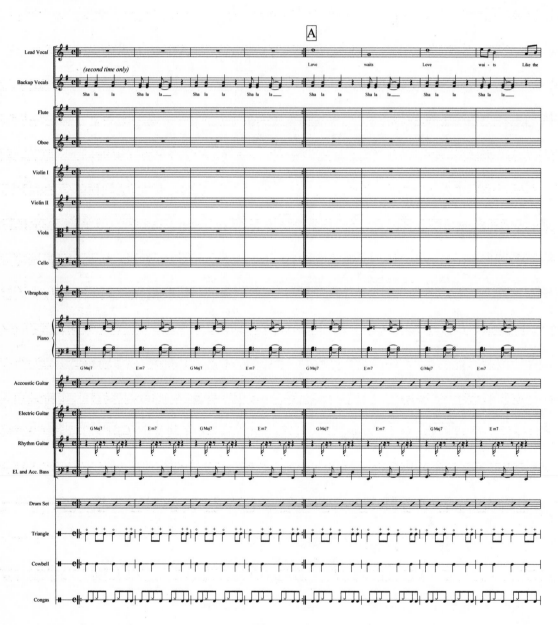

2

Love Waits

Love Waits

4

Love Waits

Love Waits

5

6

Love Waits

Love Waits

CD Contents

Full Arrangements

Track 1: "Love Waits," rock band arrangement

Track 2: "Love Waits," big band arrangement

Track 3: "Love Waits," marching band arrangement

Track 4: "Love Waits," orchestra arrangement

Track 5: "Love Waits," choir arrangement

Track 6: "Love Waits," arrangement for commercial pop recording

Rhythm Sections

Track 7: Rock beat

Track 8: Country beat

Track 9: Dance beat

Track 10: Latin beat (clave)

Track 11: Shuffle beat

Track 12: Swing beat (jazz combo)

Musical Examples: Chord Progressions

Track 13: Extended chords

Track 14: Altered bass chords

Track 15: Pedal point

Track 16: Pedal point

Track 17: Diatonic substitutions

Musical Examples: Voicings

Track 18: Basic triad voicings

Track 19: Major seventh voicings

Track 20: Open voicing (major 7 chord)

Track 21: Closed voicing (major 7 chord)

Track 22: Closed voicing (major 9 chord)

Track 23: Note removal (dominant 7 chord in three voices)

Track 24: Root doubling (major triad in four voices)

Track 25: Sparse voicing (one chord tone per section)

Track 26: Sparse voicing (different note assignments)

Track 27: Dense voicing (all chord tones in each section)

Track 28: Note cluster (close voicing)

Track 29: Note cluster (open voicing)

Track 30: Chord progression with static voicing (excessive parallel movement)

Track 31: Chord progression with varied voicing

Track 32: Skip-wise movement

Track 33: Step-wise movement

Track 34: Extended parallel movement

Track 35: Contrary movement

Track 36: Common tone emphasized in a progression

Track 37: Leading tone-to-tonic voice leading

Track 38: Bass line playing chord roots

Track 39: Bass line playing other than chord roots

Track 40: Quarter-note pulse

Track 41: Syncopated harmonies

Musical Examples: Countermelodies

Track 42: Original eight-measure melody

Track 43: Augmented melody (final two bars lengthened)

Track 44: Additional two-bar cadence added

Track 45: Space added between melodic phrases

Track 46: Melodic phrases repeated

Track 47: Additional notes inserted

Track 48: Additional motifs inserted

Track 49: Melodic simplification (notes removed)

Track 50: Selected pitches altered

Track 51: Syncopated rhythms

Track 52: Diatonic third parallel harmony

Track 53: Chord-based parallel harmony

Track 54: Pentatonic parallel harmony

Track 55: Countermelodic harmony

Track 56: Call-and-response countermelody

Track 57: Independent countermelody

Track 58: Arrangement with multiple elements

Track 59: Example countermelody

Track 60: Example countermelody split between two groups of instruments

Musical Examples: Instrumentation

Track 61: Same pitch on different instruments

Track 62: Melody doubled between similar instruments

Track 63: Legato string melody against staccato brass accompaniment

Track 64: Melody swapping between similar instruments

Track 65: Acute dissonance between like instruments; less-acute dissonance between dissimilar instruments

Track 66: Three trumpets playing in unison

Track 67: Trumpet and trombone playing in unison

Track 68: Dissimilar instruments combining for a similar sound—oboe and flute, trumpet and alto sax, trumpet and clarinet, trombone and tenor sax, trombone and baritone sax, trombone and bass clarinet, vibraphone and piano, xylophone and piccolo

Track 69: Dissimilar instruments combining for new sounds—high-register trumpet and flute, flugelhorn and low-register flute, piccolo trumpet and oboe, low-register clarinet and high-register trombone, cello and low-register clarinet, viola and French horn, electric guitar and Hammond organ

Bonus Track

Track 70: Building the "Love Waits" backing tracks instrument-by-instrument

Credits

"Love Waits" by Michael Miller, ©2006

Track 1
Vocals: Joanna Jahn
Keyboards and drums: Michael Miller
Guitars: Steinberg Virtual Guitarist 2 sample library
Bass: Steinberg HALionOne sample library

Track 2
Keyboards and drums: Michael Miller
All other instruments: Garritan Jazz & Big Band sample library

Track 3
Snare drums: Michael Miller
All other percussion instruments: Tapspace Virtual Drumline 2 sample library
Wind instruments: Garritan Jazz & Big Band and Garritan Personal Orchestra
sample libraries

Track 4
All instruments: Garritan Personal Orchestra sample library

Track 5
Soprano: Paula Lammers
Alto: Sherry Elliott
Tenor: Kevin Barnard
Bass: Tom Witry

Track 6
Lead vocal: Sherry Elliott
Background vocals: Paula Lammers and Sherry Elliott
Keyboards and drums: Michael Miller
All other instruments: Garritan Personal Orchestra, Steinberg HALionOne,
and Steinberg Virtual Guitarist 2 sample libraries

Tracks 7-12
Keyboards and drums: Michael Miller
All other instruments: Steinberg HALionOne and Virtual Guitarist 2 sample
libraries

Tracks 13-69
All instruments: Garritan Jazz & Big Band and Garritan Personal Orchestra
sample libraries

All tracks
Recording software: Steinberg Cubase 4
Mastering software: Sony Sound Forge 8
CD mastering software: Sony CD Architect

Index

D

U

V

W

X–Y–Z